THE TRUE STORY FOR GOD'S GLORY: THE LIFE OF SIOHVAUGHN L. FUNCHES-WADE

Siohvaughn L. Funches-Wade

ISBN: 0692721460
ISBN 13: 9780692721469
Library of Congress Control Number: **XXXXX (If applicable)**
LCCN Imprint Name: **Siohvaughn Funches**

SPECIAL DEDICATION

To You, Lord Jesus, my beloved Savior, I give my life, this masterwork of Your hands, and all the Glory. For truly this is, Your story, and without You, Jesus, I can do nothing, but with You, I can indeed do all things. I love you, Jesus Christ, with all my heart, mind, soul and strength.

Yours eternally,

Siohvaughn L. Funches-Wade

DEDICATION

To you, WOW Women, God has given this masterwork of His hands, and God the Father loves you no matter what state you are currently in. When God see's you, He does not see your sin, or past mistakes, God see's His beloved Jesus Christ and what He has done for you and Jesus has made you the righteousness of God in Christ Jesus and as Jesus is, so are you Women of Worth in this world. This continual love is not based upon your works, but upon the finished work of Jesus Christ on the cross for you. I love you and God loves you so deeply. This work, God led me to dedicate to you women of worth. God bless you,

Your Abba Father eternally

TABLE OF CONTENTS

INTRODUCTION

When I initially set out to write my life story, I thought it would be fairly simple. Shortly after that, however, I realized that in order to share my life, I would have to be vulnerable and open my heart as well as revisit some very painful places in my past. I've had to walk back inside courtrooms of injustice, remember emergency-room visits and the violence that led me there, and do much more in order for you to journey with me through my life.

I discovered while writing this book that revisiting some of these times in my life was very scary for me, and for months I stopped writing altogether in an attempt to avoid even the possibility of reliving certain painful seasons in my life. This became a defining moment for me. I had to make up my mind that, no matter what, I would allow God to tell this powerful story through me, because the purpose of this book is not publishing; it's destiny—both mine and that of so many others.

God assured me that many people would be healed and restored after reading this book, especially women. My love for God, and my love for you—and my desire that you receive the hope, healing, and restoration that God has graciously given me—caused me to keep pouring out my pain on these pages.

Now that the work is complete, I know it is worth it, God is worth it, you are worth it, and I am worth it. It is an honor that

God would choose me to write His story through me, and I am humbled that you would go with me on this journey of love, pain, loss, hope, redemption, and restoration. The truth is that this journey has changed my life and my family's life forever and for the good. I believe that sharing it with you will change your life for the better as well.

If I ever see you in person, I can thank you personally for coming with me on this journey, but if our paths only cross on these pages, I personally thank you now, blessed reader.

—Siohvaughn L. Funches-Wade

HUMBLE BEGINNINGS

Before you were in your mother's womb I formed you.

—Jeremiah 1:5, New King James Version

Like most humble beginnings, mine began with, and because of, someone greater than myself. God, my Creator, gave me life and the purpose of it; Jesus, my Lord and Savior, makes my life worth living; and the Holy Spirit empowers me and enables me to live the life God predestined for me to live, and to fulfill my God-given destiny.

Born September 6, 1981, through the love of God in Frank and Darlene Funches, I was a seven-pound, nine-ounce, fairly healthy baby girl. This miracle of life through my birth, however, was not without life-risking challenges and severe opposition from hell itself, it seems.

My mother spent seven out of nine months of her pregnancy with me in the hospital. At the fifth month of my life, while in the womb of my mother, it was medically recommended that I be

1

aborted, because keeping me put my mother's life at risk. My mother at that time had never laid eyes on me, but she had enough love for me—love from God—to lay down her own life and risk it for the mere possibility of giving me life. She rejected the opportunity to abort me. This is good news for us all, not because of the sacrificial love of God in my mom, but because her love demonstrates what God says in His Word. Jesus said, "If parents being evil know how to give good gifts to their children, how much more will God give to those who ask Him" (Luke 11:13). It's really okay to shout with joy, "Hallelujah!" and "Thank you, God!" I surely just did! But my mother was not shouting for joy at that time. She was fearful she would lose her child, and my father was right there beside her, consumed with the same fear because, unfortunately, the tribulation had not ended yet.

Now, after the plan of hell to abort me was destroyed, my life was almost taken again, as they medically induced my mother. When my mother was initially in labor with me things went smoothly, until the time came to give birth. The umbilical cord was found wrapped around my chest and neck and I couldn't breathe. The doctor frantically reached inside my mother's womb to turn me around because the umbilical cord was suffocating me nearly to death. It is evident that God has a plan for my life, because death itself has come knocking at the door many times, sometimes getting all the way inside my life, just to be evicted by my loving and all-powerful God. Without question, God caused me to overcome all this adversity, and He gave me life instead of death and parents, a sister, and grandparents who loved me. The death God defeated on my behalf at the beginning of my life was a physical death; however, later on in my life, I would need God to save me from an even worse death, a spiritual one.

As I reflect back on the beginning of my life, I have learned something profound from God, about Himself. It is profound because, perhaps if God taught me something about myself, it would benefit me, but because of God's love for you, He taught me something about Himself that benefits us all. So this I say to the women who are naturally pregnant, and to the men and women, who are spiritually pregnant: when that which is in your natural womb, or your spiritual womb, has been planted by God, there is no adversity, threat, diagnosis, sickness, evil, demon, man, woman, or any created thing that can stop or abort the plan of God for that which is in your womb. For what has been placed inside your womb is not of your own doing, but it is the very hand and heart of God that planted it there. Thus, it cannot be thwarted, and if you are the plan of God, you likewise cannot be thwarted. For no plan of God's can be thwarted (Job 42:2).

"You are fearfully and wonderfully made" (Ps. 139:14).

INNOCENCE INTERRUPTED

In this world you will have trouble, but be of good cheer,
I have overcome this world.

—John 16:33

As I reflect on my childhood, I want to say that I had a pretty normal childhood, but when I meditate on the word "normal," I keep asking myself, "What exactly is normal?" I say this because, what is normal or common for one person, is completely abnormal and distinct for another. In fact, distinction and inevitable uniqueness are some of the things we as people truly have in common. This uniqueness sometimes causes us to experience things differently. So, from my unique perspective, I had an overall fairly normal childhood, despite the hardships I had to overcome. I learned on this journey called life that God didn't cause, but He did use those hardships to shape and mold me, making me more like Him, and teaching me how to love others like Him. God has also used my family and my experience with them to teach me, and to make me who He called me to be, and so I will share with you a bit about them, in order for you to understand how God used them and these earlier experiences to really lay an unshakeable foundation of the love of God in me.

My immediate family was small in number but large in love. All of us were raised as Christians, although we all strayed from God at one point or another in our lives. The good news is that God never strayed away from us. My immediate family consisted of my dad, my mom, and my big sister. My parents, Frank and Darlene Funches, both loved my big sister, Garrica, and me very deeply, and by the grace of God, they provided for us and protected us. My grandparents did the same. As we were growing up, Garrica, who I used to call "Gee-Gee," was my only sibling, and I loved her strongly. We grew up in Robbins, Illinois, a small village suburb about twenty-five minutes south of Chicago. The fact that it's called a village tells you just how small it was. What that small title doesn't tell you, however, is how big the crime was, and how much bigger the poverty. My parents did a pretty good job of shielding us from the violence in the neighborhood. However, when a community is infested with crime, murder, drugs, and poverty, there is only so much shielding even an excellent parent can do. After all, we are parents, not perfect.

Despite the harsh environment, I thank God, because, growing up, all of our needs were met, and we were very blessed to have some of the things we desired. I personally may have needed a little less of what I desired. I became a bit spoiled. Not because my parents gave me too much, but because I had the wrong attitude about receiving the abundance they gave me. Don't worry. like my granny, Mattie Griffin, always says, "God deals with us all." And believe Jesus in me, God dealt with the spoiled spirit in me by correcting me and delivering me completely from the foolishness that comes along with the "me, myself, and I" mentality. Perhaps some of the reason they spoiled me was because I was very sick growing up. I spent a lot of my childhood in hospitals and emergency rooms with tubes down my throat, IVs in my arm, and breathing through a ventilator machine for asthma. The devil was still trying hard to kill the purpose of God inside of me, by taking my life prematurely. He had tried this earlier on while I was in my mother's womb, by making my mother so sick during her pregnancy with me that she was faced with the decision to terminate her pregnancy with me or risk losing her own life. God gave me this understanding later on regarding these life-threatening illnesses, as well as being misdiagnosed and administered medicine, which was literally poisoning me as a child. The enemy attacking my literal life was only collateral damage for what he was actually attacking and trying to kill, which was the purpose of God on the inside of me. God reminded me of how, in the Bible, Herod, sent out a decree ordering the execution of every male child of a certain age when Jesus was born. God told me the devil in Herod didn't really want to become a serial killer. He was looking to kill one particular child—Jesus, the Christ—for one particular purpose: to stop the purpose and the plan of God that would come through Jesus. But the devil failed then with Jesus, just as he failed to kill me, because Jesus and you, as well as me are a part of God's plan. And, thankfully, no plan of God can be thwarted (Job 42:1).

Growing Up, Can Be Hard to Do

As we were growing up, my parents never divorced but were separated. Despite this physical separation, I remember my dad and mom having a very strong love and respect for one another. I remember them loving one another, speaking well of one another, and honoring and defending each other, long after their separation, and throughout my adult life. I can only recall a single time that they argued seriously. But I cannot count the number of times I saw them love one another and defend one another, even to their own immediate family members. I know this had a lot to do with the way my father loved Garrica and me. You see, my father, Papa Frank, was not Garrica's biological dad, but he was indeed her father. It takes much more than a night of passion and a donation of male specimen to be a father. Being a father takes God. It takes the love of God, time, commitment, honoring the woman you conceived the child with, and so much more. God calls fathers to lead even more by example than with their mouths. God calls fathers to provide for their children, protect them, and raise them in the Word of God, teaching them to live a righteous life, even when nobody else is watching. I learned a lot about being a good father because of my relationship with God, the Father, and what God has shown me through my natural father, Papa Frank.

Everything Papa Frank did for me, he did for my sister, Garrica. There was no division among us. God truly blessed me with a loving father. He wasn't perfect, but his mind was perfectly made up to love us strongly and unconditionally. He provided for us both, and he protected us both. He also tried giving us both whatever we wanted. I remember that every Christmas, Papa Frank gave us both gifts, and for every birthday, he brought each of us presents. And for our good grades and behavior, he gave us both allowances. What I admired even more about my father is that he expected and required the same treatment for us from everyone else, no matter who it was. Once, when I was a little girl, I remember how one of my dad's family members came over with my dad and wanted to give me some money without giving any to Garrica. Papa Frank let him know that if he didn't have a gift for the both of us, he wasn't giving anything to one of us. That mandate spread pretty quickly throughout my extended family, and nobody ever tried it again. I thank my Heavenly Father for being a loving father through my Papa Frank to both Garrica and me. Papa Frank loved us both deeply indeed, and my mother to this day has not stopped saying how she will always love Frank Funches for the love he showed to Garrica and me. In fact, with so much love and honor between them, I couldn't understand for the life of me growing up why they were ever separated at all. My dad, until the time he passed, was still flirting with my mom, and I saw her flirting back. (Mama, you know it's true) My Mama is certainly laughing out loud right now and blushing as she reads this. She is also likely saying, "Siohvaughn LaRea!" And now, you know when your parents call you by your first and middle name, your goose is cooked!

I don't blame my mom for still loving my dad. My dad was a provider, a protector, and in my opinion, one of the world's best undiscovered comedians. It's true that his feet never hit the stage at a comedy show, but he elicited just as many laughs out of people, especially us. He could make me laugh until my stomach ached and tears rolled down my face from joy. His name was Frank, and he was just that: frank! My dad would tell someone exactly what he was thinking—and to their face. He held no punches, and he held no punch lines either. But he had a really big heart. I know why my mother loves him so. However, with that big heart came big strength to defend and protect. I am glad that God made my father the way that he was, though. We needed a strong and loving father, especially where we grew up. My daddy, and my mom, protected me, and I needed that. They protected me from whatever they could, mostly from outside forces. And this meant as much to them, if not more, than it did to me. I realized that truth when I went through a very trying time in my life, and I saw when my mom and dad realized that with all their love for me, they couldn't protect me from the deep pain it caused me. I watched my daddy's heart break, and my mom's, along with my granny's and mine, and all for the same reason. We all wanted to protect our children from pain, and we couldn't. The good news is that we all learned, God would protect us all. We entrusted God with our babies, and none of us regretted it. We had greater peace and no more burdens! Thanks be to Jesus Christ for bearing these burdens for us. We all learned an extremely valuable lesson: who we thought were *our*

children really are *God's* children, and God just graciously shares
them with us for a time, but they truly belong to God. This truth is
good news, because God will fight for what is His!

But as a growing little girl, I knew that whatever was in my Papa
Frank's power to protect me from, he would. Ironically, my first
black eye helped me see this truth more clearly. I remember it
like it was yesterday. Some bully-boy, older than me, took it upon
himself to punch me in the eye while I was waiting to catch the
school bus one cold winter morning. I don't know what made me
angrier—the fact that he hit me, or the fact that it caused me to
fall and land flat on my face in ice-cold snow. Anybody from the
Midwest, especially Chicago, knows that it is a miracle that I didn't
hit that snow and ice and get instantaneous frostbite! Oh, Jesus, I
forgive that little chocolate bully-boy, and I pray that his temper
and violence have left him, in Jesus name I pray. After school that
day, I ran straight to my father's house to tell him what happened.
I figured this was the right thing to do, but when I saw how my
dad reacted, it even frightened me. I watched my father turn into
his very own version of the Hulk—except that he wasn't green, he
was red! I knew my dad wasn't going to do anything to hurt me.
Growing up, he never so much as gave me a single spanking—or
even a "time-out," for that matter. So, I had no fear at all for my
own life. However, I just knew that the bully was going to die that
day! I know its been said, "an eye for an eye," but my dad was trying to go beyond even this level of wrath, saying, "an eye for a *die!*"
I remember thinking, I don't want my dad to go to jail for hurting
someone who hurt me. I tried to calm him down, but the fire that
kindled his fury was roaring way beyond my control.

My dad asked me where the boy lived, who had blackened my
eye, and reluctantly I gave the location. We got in my father's car,
and in what seemed like all of thirty seconds, and we were in front
of the bully's house. My dad knocked on the door of that house
so hard, the door could have fallen in. The bully's mom answered

the door, and as soon as she opened it, my father told her what happened and demanded that he speak to the black-eye bandit. When my father finished releasing pure wrath through his mouth, he let everyone in their house know that he had been to jail before for something stupid, and he would gladly spend the rest of his life there to protect his daughter. That said it all. I never again had any problems with that bully. He actually kept a pretty healthy distance from me from that day forward. After this experience, however, I kept in mind how my dad's protection of me was with merit but without measure or restraint. I knew my dad was serious about protecting us at whatever costs, even at the cost of his own life and freedom. I decided that, from that day forward, I would protect my dad from any negative consequences of protecting me. I decided that I would selectively tell my father about hardships I suffered.

My dad, was my hero that day, but like everyone else, he struggled with something. The kryptonite for this Superman earlier on in life was alcohol. I watched as my dad struggled with that addiction for years, and every time he told me, "Honey, this time I'm done" or "I am going to quit," I got elated with him, anticipating the day he would be free. And when he came and told me, "Honey, I'm sorry. I drank again," I felt hurt with him. The day God took us both off that emotional roller coaster and Jesus set my daddy free, oh, how both our souls were healed and thrilled! God showed me how I went with my dad on his road to recovery and felt the pain of disappointment when my dad attempted sobriety in his own strength and fell short. But God also showed me how my faithfulness to see my father get the healing he needed allowed me to be there when God delivered him from that addiction and allowed me to share with him the joy that came with that deliverance! I had not been addicted to alcohol, but when God set my father free from it, I was somehow set free too. Long before my dad left this earth, he left sober and with the mind of Jesus Christ.

Oh, how I thank God for His love and mercy that have endured all our shortcomings and failures. My father gave his life to Jesus Christ and renewed his vows to God that he had made as a child. My father repented for his sins, was saved, and was completely forgiven by God because of Jesus. I witnessed the power of God to deliver my dad from an alcohol addiction without the use of a medicinal drug, alcohol recovery facility, or any doctor's intervention. Jesus did it! So, if someone is reading this and is struggling with addiction, know this: the power of God is more than enough to deliver you, no matter what addiction that has come against you. The power of God can deliver you from any addiction. It doesn't matter if the addiction is alcohol, drugs, pornography, lust, lies, gossip, or the cancer-breathing cigarette. If God delivers you, you won't need a patch or a penny! Just Jesus! And rejoice, because whoever the Son of God (Jesus) sets free is free indeed (John 8:36). He did it for us, and God can do it for you and your family. God is no respecter of persons (Rom. 2:11; Acts 10:34).

This was a huge miracle indeed from God, but it wouldn't be the only miracle of healing and deliverance that God would do for this family.

After my parents separated, I lived with my mom, but I saw my father basically every day. My mother was incredible as we were growing up, and without any doubt, she loved my sister and me deeply as well. My mother was also someone through whom God provided for us. She worked diligently to do so. I had a mother who put my sister's and my needs above her own. I watched my mother be extremely giving to us, and what was even more honorable was that my mother would often give to others outside our family. She would give to them from her substance, like she would to us, whenever she saw someone with a need, especially a child. She instilled this virtue in both my sister and me. And although I tried to oppose it, when I was a young child, lacking maturity but filled with selfishness, this virtue is still bearing much fruit in me to this very day. God surely says it: "Train up a child in the way that he should go, and when he is old he won't depart from it" (Prov. 22:6). Those words are for every parent who instilled in their children Godly virtues. Because, notably, God didn't say, "Train up the child in 'a way' or in 'any way.'" God said, "Train up the child in *the way*." This is not a loose use of words. God is an intentional God, whose words are very well thought out and most excellent. He is filled with wisdom, and completely empty of mistakes. The Bible says, Jesus is "the way, and the truth, and the life," and that no one comes to the Father (God) except through the Son (Jesus) (John 14:6). So in other words, parents and guardians, God is saying, if you train up a child in the ways of Jesus, when that child is older, he or she will not depart from it! That's good news, folks. If you want to know what the ways of Jesus are, read the Bible, especially the books, Matthew, Mark, Luke, and John. These four books will tell you a lot about Jesus, and when you study about Jesus, you will learn His loving ways. Don't stop there, though. Read the entire Bible from the beginning, because in the beginning was the Word, and Jesus is the Word (John 1:1). One thing Jesus was, and still is, is a giver. Jesus gave up His glory to become a carpenter here on earth for our sake. Jesus gave up being rich so that we don't have to be poor. Jesus gave up His health so that we no longer have to be sick. Jesus gave up freedom so that we no longer would be bound. Jesus gave up being the King of all kings so that we can reign as sons and daughters of the Most High God! Jesus gave up being a heavenly being to become a human being so that he would sympathize with us and have compassion on our weaknesses. Jesus gave up being seated next to God so that we can be seated in heavenly places. Jesus gave up being close to God so that we can be one with God (Matt. 27:46). (And most importantly, but certainly not all He gave, Jesus gave up His life so that we would be saved and forgiven for our sins. None of this was taken from Jesus. He freely gave it. Jesus is a giver. So when my mom taught us to give, she was instilling in us the ways of Jesus, and to this day, giving has not departed from me. Unfortunately, some people took advantage of this kindness and wounded my mom deeply. Despite those difficulties, however, she was and still is a great mom and cheerful giver. She did the best she could, and her best was and is honorable.

As we were growing up, in my mom's house, education, structure, and discipline were all very important too. Education, though, was a top priority. This may be because God gave my mother a brilliant mind. God bestowed upon her the gift of wisdom and intelligence. And I believe that God gave those gifts to my sister and me, and He used my mother to cultivate those gifts and motivate us. I remember throughout my life working hard in school and being blessed by God to have good grades. There was a single time in my life that made for an exception to this norm. But other than that, I was very motivated to do well in school, because as I was growing up, my mom literally gave us money for each good grade we achieved. This gave "positive reinforcement" a whole new meaning, especially growing up where we did. God used my mom to lay a foundation of the importance of education, and every seed God sowed in me is still bearing much fruit to this day for the Glory of Jesus!

Along with my mom being a provider for us, she also, like my dad, was a very serious protector. I knew this truth for myself after a man tried to kidnap, to likely try to rape, Garrica. This guy, who lived only blocks away from our home, tried to lure Garrica into his car. What did he do that for? As soon as my sister came home to tell my mom what this *doomed man* had done, my mother became the first Transformer I ever saw. The Bumblebee had nothing on my mother that day! She went from sweet mama, cooking dinner for her babies, to a rampage against this man for even trying to harm one of us. As tears poured from my sister's eyes as she told my mother what happened, I watched as rage, and likely fear, filled my mother's heart. That's right—being filled with fear can cause someone to behave in ways that scare others. It's the cat-backed-into-a-corner theory but on steroids when it's a human being. I believe that is what I watched happen that day.

In about fifteen minutes, my mom found out the name of this man, where he lived, who he was married to, and how many children he had. Passion can be a powerful thing! Even though she was angry and probably very scared, I remember she tried doing the right thing first. She called the police, but this didn't go well at all. While conducting the investigation, one of the police unwisely told the man where we lived, and my mother found out. What can I tell you? I watched my mother transform again. This time, though, she went from a law-abiding citizen to a vigilante in seconds. I'm going to blame the officer in part for what transpired next. My mother got us in the car and went to the doomed man's house. She knocked on his door, and what my mom told this man and his wife, would make even the devil reconsider doing evil! She promised him she would lay down her life for us, and this man, who was later accused of molesting his own children, never even so much as came near my sister, or me ever again. He obviously believed what my mother told him that day. I certainly knew she was telling the truth.

My mother, like my father, had a love for my sister and me that ran very deep. They both would later on in life allow God to perfect that love in them, taking away fear, and putting in His perfect love that casts out fear (1 John 4:18).

My mom did a wonderful job of raising Garrica and me. This was no easy task for her, though. Garrica's biological dad was not around at all, my mom was separated from my father, even though he helped out, and Garrica and I presented my mother with our own unique challenges. This stemmed a lot from our experience and even more from our personalities and character. Garrica and I were like night and day. My sister was meek, quiet, and so loving that people often took her for granted. I, however, was outspoken, loud, and willing to fight, even if it was with someone twice my age. (I do mean that literally.) I remember my mother saying while I was growing up, "I wish I could put some of you, Garrica, in Siohvaughn, and some of you, Vaughn, in Garrica." What she was trying to say was that she wished for more of a balance in us. Garrica was meek, but that did not mean she had to be weak. I was outspoken, but that did not mean I needed to say everything I was thinking—because that is truly an unwise thing to do! That's a lesson I would learn the hard way and over the course of several years of my life. You would have thought that I would have learned it early on in life, since that is when experience began to teach me, and I began seeing the consequences of my decisions.

I told this girl who was twice my age and three times my size that I dared her to hit my sister. I said I would knock her teeth down her throat if she did. Secretly, I was praying that she wouldn't hit my sister, because I was terrified that she would hurt her. And furthermore, at my height, I couldn't reach this giant-sized teenager's teeth to knock them down her throat. I was scared to fight, but at the same time, I was willing and ready to fight for my sister. Even though Garrica was older than me, her quiet and meek personality made me feel like I needed to protect her. Well, this Attila-the-Hun-sized bully hit my sister, pulled her to the ground, and began tussling with her. Garrica was defending herself, but I felt compelled to help her. I took a nearby spectator's umbrella and hit the back of this bully until the umbrella was broken in pieces and the fight was officially broken up. This fight might not have been the best experience my sister and I had together, but it showed my sister, and even myself, just how much I loved and cared for her. This love wasn't always so evident, however, between us.

Too often, we argued over almost everything, it seemed! The truth is, I knew what got on her nerves, and I would push her buttons to aggravate her. Garrica pushed my buttons too. But as aggravated as I acted with her, I loved her. I remember thinking, one

15

year when she went to an out-of-state summer camp, "I am so glad. I will have the entire upstairs (where we slept in our bedrooms at home) all to myself." This celebration of selfishness that I had ended quicker than it began. As I stood with my mother on the top of a grassy hill, waving at my sister who sat on a bus packed with children ready for camp, I literally fainted when the bus pulled off, taking my sister away. I don't know what came over me, or what was already in me that manifested at that moment. All I knew was that I didn't want my sister to go, not even for a week-long summer camp. When I fainted, I rolled down that grassy hill, and when I finally came to, I saw my mother standing over me, smiling sarcastically, because she could hardly wait to ask me, "What happened to wanting the upstairs to yourself?" Alongside my mother was Garrica, looking very concerned. And as much as she wanted to go to summer camp, my mom told me she made the bus driver stop and go back when she saw me rolling down that hill of shame! Again, my sister and I bonded from this experience, but the serious bickering picked up again, however, this time would be the last time.

My mother had severe migraine headaches when we were growing up, and sometimes our fighting would wreck her brain—literally! One day, I knew we went too far with the bickering. But no worries, God equipped my mother with the cure! My mother handcuffed my sister and me together and told us that wherever one of us went, the other would go, and that we would stay stuck together until we learned how to get along. We thought she was joking until we would found ourselves eating together, watching television together, and going to the bathroom together that afternoon. Within one hour, the two of us were no longer angry at each other, but we were piping mad at our mother for this unique but effective method of correction. We went from foes to allies in sixty minutes flat. My sister and I got along better from that day forward, despite any differences.

Don't get me wrong. Garrica and I were not totally different and did have some things in common. For example, we both believed in God, we both did well in school, and we both agreed that Red Fox was one of the funniest men to ever live. Some of our internal character was alike as well.

I wasn't just a tough child, saying the first thing that came to mind and fighting for the ones I love. There was more to me than what was on the surface or what I allowed people to see, even family. I was a fun-loving child. I enjoyed long walks and late nights up with my sister and grandparents watching television and eating what my granny Griffin called "midnight snacks." This was a child's dream come true. Once in a while my Granny let us stay up late and eat strawberries and ice cream and all sorts of goodies. I spent my days at school excelling for the glory of God, and I spent my evenings with the family God gave me, or alone, where I would play for hours, my hair full of barrettes and my hands filled with dolls. Movies were another one of my favorite pastimes. I watched *Nightmare on Elm Street* until I had my own nightmare, right on 140th Street, where I grew up. It wasn't long before I learned that watching that hadn't been the wisest decision.

I watched normal shows as well, like *Bugs Bunny*—and *Tom and Jerry*, a classic and my all-time favorite! At least it was until my older sister told me that Tom and Jerry don't talk. I adamantly denied her statement, because of course I had been watching Tom and Jerry for so long, there was no way I wouldn't notice something as obvious as completely silent characters! Well, the next time I watched the show, I realized they *didn't* talk. It ruined the whole thing for me! I still can't believe that show was so entertaining without saying anything! As much as I enjoyed playing, I may have enjoyed reading even more. I had more books than I did toys. I would read children's books for hours on end, sometimes until I fell asleep. I'd wake up the next morning in my mauve-pink room and find one of my *Baby-Sitters Club* books or R.L. Stine books in bed with me. And as much as I tell my boys, "That's enough of those video games," I have to admit, I certainly had my favorites growing up too. I played enough *Duck Hunt* to land a leading role on *Duck Dynasty*, and so much *Mario Bros.* that my hands would literally cramp up. Well, I still play *Mario Bros.* with Zion and Zaire to this day! What can I say? This adult still likes to get a good game in with the children now and then. And when we do get a chance to play together, on the outside I'm like, "Zion and Zaire, I will play with you this time, but not too much of these video games." But on the inside I'm like, "Oh, God, I hope nobody picks Mario, so I can!"

It's things like this that reminds me of my childhood, while it was still innocent. I was loving my life then, and up until that point, nothing had seriously affected me. But life would get very serious to me at the age of seven. At the time I knew what death was, but nobody close to me had ever died. Before. Then my grandfather died. I was devastated. I don't remember what anyone else in my family was feeling at that time, because I went into a shell of solitude. I was enraged at God. I blamed God for my grandfather's death. I was extremely close to my grandfather, and I knew he loved me very much, and now he was dead and the only one I thought was responsible was God. Later on in life, I learned how dangerous it is to a person, to stay angry with God, or anyone. Getting angry may not be a sin at all, but staying there certainly is one (Eph. 4:26). But at the time, I was young in age and even younger in Christ. I was deeply hurt and feeling fury. It was what I like to call "piping-hot pain." That indeed is the dangerous kind, because it can turn into violence against someone else or depression within. God told me later on in life, often times depressed people are really angry or fearful people. God told me it's like the material suede and leather. It's something flipped inside out. Depression may very well be the fruit they bear, but anger and fear is the root, and if you can kill the root, you can change the fruit you produce (i.e. no more depression). That revelation was God having mercy on me as an adult, but even at that point in my childhood, I recognized that God was having mercy on me. Even with the misplaced anger I felt toward God and all the blaming I did of God, He still healed me, and most of the anger and blame I felt had subsided. Life had changed, but I was still able to be a child and enjoy a fairly normal life.

But my life was about to drastically change, and consequently, it would drastically change me. As I mentioned earlier, God gave my mother a very loving and giving heart. She seemed to always be giving love from her heart, clothes from her closet, and food from her fridge to whoever was in need—especially children. Most people appreciated her love, but sadly, some repaid her good with evil. About a year or so after my grandfather passed, my mom helped a wayward male teenager and opened the doors to our home to him. At first everything seemed fine. He was like the big brother I never had. He hung out with my sister and me. We ate together, laughed together, and for some time lived together. I remember thinking, "He doesn't seem at all bad like those who sent him away said." But eventually, this troubled teen troubled me greatly, when he raped me. My innocence had been interrupted, and everything changed because of it. The once bold and courageous girl I had grown to be became insecure, fearful, and distrustful, especially of men. I discovered quickly that the effects of the rape were far worse than the rape itself.

For many years, I believed what this boy who raped me had told me—that being raped was my fault, and that I liked it, and nobody would believe me anyway if I told them. Instead of going to God or my parents for help, I tried to deal with this devastation on my own. I held the shameful matter in and didn't tell anyone what had happened to me until many years later. I was filled with shame, hurt, guilt, and self-condemnation. Instead of turning to God for help, and to the family God gave me, I dealt with it the best way I thought how: I hid and I covered it. Naturally speaking,

I kept the horror to myself and kept the truth bottled up inside. Spiritually speaking, I ended up dressed with outer garments of toughness, pride, and defensiveness in an attempt to hide who I really was underneath. I wore these garments like a shield for a long time, because they provided a false sense of security, and I kept secretly hoping that no one would be able to detect and see the hurt, vulnerable, and fearful "woman" I had become, while still a child. As it turned out, the garments were not a shield at all but rather a magnet for bad things and bad people, and as you will see, they failed to protect me from pain.

"These things I have spoken to you, that you will have peace. In the world you will have tribulation; but be of good cheer, I have overcome the world." (John 16:33).

BROKEN BUT NOT DESTROYED

The Lord is close to the broken-hearted;
He rescues those whose spirits are crushed.

—Psalm 34:18

Despite what I had just suffered, I know now that God was still with me. And despite those garments I had dressed myself in, as a result of what I had suffered, I know that God was still having mercy on me. This horrific ordeal may have temporarily changed who I was, but it lacked the power to change *whose* I was. I was, and always will, be God's child, and I have learned something extremely important about this fact: God always saves those who are His (Rom. 8:38–39). This is the mercy, grace, and love of God manifested.

If anyone reading this is at all wanting to know how I can say that God had mercy on me after suffering something as horrific as rape, God wants you to understand and see the miracle in that madness. God shared this truth with me, and the answer is best given with a question. Ask the family members of victims of rape who were also killed during the rape, "Is it mercy from God that survivors of rape overcome the horrific event, live, and have the opportunity to be healed and restored by God while still here on earth?" Ask the mothers and fathers who have stood weeping over the caskets of their deceased daughters, having had countless tears pour from their eyes, while pain and grief pour into their hearts and questions flood their minds like: "Why wasn't raping her enough? Why did he have to kill her too?" Ask them, "Is surviving rape, instead of being raped and murdered, mercy from God?" I have no doubt that each of those victims' loving parents, family members, and friends would tell us, "Yes, it is the mercy of God to survive even something as egregious as rape." These loves ones understand, as do I, that God did in fact have mercy on me and my loved ones. The truth is that you can still live a full and completely healed and restored life, even after a hellish event like rape. I know that because God has done it for me. And if God did it for me, God certainly can do it for you if you too have suffered this. After all, God is no respecter of persons (Rom. 2:11). And while I know now that this complete healing and restoration is possible for God, I didn't know it back then.

At that point in my life, the monster had left our house, but he still took up residence in my mind. I still hadn't talked to God about being raped or told a single soul what had happened, largely because I still believed the lie I was told after being raped: that it was my fault. The lie he told was evil, but the effect it caused was worse. By then, condemnation had set in, and a guilty conscience had taken over, and like most condemned hearts, mine moved me away from God, rather than closer to Him where I needed to be. I have learned from this experience as well as others in my adulthood that it is extremely important not to condemn yourself or allow anyone else to. I must take a brief moment and expound on this because it has affected too many people for far too long. It's time to be free by the truth.

We will continue on with my life in just a moment, after we bless yours, because my life isn't the only one that matters; your life matters to God too.

Freedom from Condemnation

Condemnation is one of the worst things a person can be bound by. And because of that, I believe that Romans 8:1 reveals one of the most vital truths you can know about God. It says, "There is therefore now no condemnation for those who are in Christ Jesus, who don't walk according to the flesh, but according to the Spirit." I stress the importance of Romans 8:1 because God taught me this: when people are condemned, they don't even approach God. That is exactly what I did as a little girl after believing that I somehow caused myself to be raped, and it was exactly what I did as an adult, when I believed the lie that I had "out-sinned" God's grace. A condemned person believes there is no point in praying to God, because they don't believe God will ever forgive them anyway. This is the farthest thing from the truth. God doesn't forgive any of us because we get it right (Rom. 3:20). God forgives us because God loves us. Furthermore, having died for our sins, Jesus Christ is righteous, and when we go through Jesus to get to the Father, we take on Jesus Christ's righteousness as our very own. This is simply done by faith in God, which is sufficient. That's it! Jesus settled all claims of spiritual debts against us, so that means whether we are innocent or guilty, the verdict is the same as far as God is concerned: "not guilty" for those who are in Christ Jesus. Remember this truth the next time the devil or anyone else tries to convince you that you cannot be forgiven by God for what you've done wrong or what you haven't done right. Jesus didn't come to save the saint; He came to save the sinner! So if you are a sinner, and we all are, you are perfect for Jesus, and you are the reason His death and resurrection were not in vain. What a purpose even your sins have served! Don't ever be confused or misled about this priceless truth either. Yes, while we all have sinned (Rom. 3:23), and we've all likely committed different wrongdoings, no one sin is worse than another. They are all evil. So don't be condemned, either, because of the specific sins you've committed. God says that when someone sins against God's law in one area, they sin against the whole law (James 2:10). This may sound strong at first, but I assure you, this is good news. It isn't the best news for the people who believe they always get it right anyway, but it is a lifesaving truth for those of us who have believed that we have sinned much. I know this because God promised us that where sin abounds, grace abounds much more (Rom. 5:20). This means that whenever there is an abundance of sin, there is even more of an abundance of the grace of God in order for God to forgive us and restore us. I'm telling you, this is good news! And just as God is no respecter of persons, He is no respecter of sins, either. This, likewise, is good news! This means the gambler is no better than the prostitute, and the prostitute is no better than the cheater, the cheater is no better than the liar, the liar is no better than the thief, the thief is no better than the judgmental person, and the judgmental person is no better than the adulterer, the adulterer is no better than the gossiper...and the list goes on. But you understand what God is saying. So, to the condemned heart, God ministers this truth and hope to you that God gave to me: "Even if our hearts condemn us, God is greater than our hearts" (1 John 3:20), and God's love covers a multitude of sins (1 Pet. 4:8).

God told me once after I sinned against Him, "Siohvaughn, I don't want to lose fellowship with you for anything—not even your sin." I want you to know that the day I wrote that particular line in this book was the same day God spoke those liberating words to me. And as I shared them with you as I typed, tears poured from my eyes because gratitude and peace filled my heart. I thank God for just being who He is. I just needed to be loved, and the one thing God always does is love us.

Now, I must also say that I've learned in my relationship with God, and from life-changing experiences God allowed me to have later on in my adult life, that God will forgive your sins, even the most grave ones. Even those sins that others won't forgive you for—or you haven't forgiven yourself for. But I love you all too much to end it there. The whole truth is, God does resist the prideful person (James 4:6). Prideful people won't even acknowledge to God that they have done anything wrong, let alone repent for it. If they do admit they have done wrong, they likely will have some excuse for the evil they have done. Likewise, people who are so condemned often won't repent either and will instead just continue in sin. However, they usually do so because of erroneously believing they won't be forgiven. Both prideful people and condemned ones have this in common: they don't confess and repent for their sin, and therefore they miss out on the sufficient grace of God (Prov. 28:13). Repenting, is changing our mind about the sin we committed, God's attitude towards that sin and our belief about God toward us. It's really not complicated.

I feel led by God right now to tell you pray with me by renouncing all forms of pride and admitting the truth to God. We all have made mistakes, and therefore we all need the mercy of God. Together, let's renounce to condemnation, no matter what we have done or said wrong, and regardless of how many times we have failed, and let's believe what God is saying to us: God loves us enough to forgive us right now! The prayer may seem simple, but it's absolutely powerful. Pray with me:

"Heavenly Father, forgive me for the sins I have committed against You, heal and restore me back to You, and restore what's been lost because of sin, according to Your perfect will. Cleanse me with Jesus's blood, and fill me and my whole house now with Your Holy Spirit, presence, love, grace, strength, wisdom, peace, and joy and You cause me to be holy, as You are holy in Jesus's name."

God has forgiven you and me. Just like that! This truth is evident because God sent Jesus to die for our sins, before we even repented for them (Rom. 5:8). That's perfect love. So let it cast out any fear you may have that maybe God is mad at you or hasn't forgiven you, because indeed God loves you and has forgiven every sin you have repented for. That's deep love! That's everlasting love! That's God's love—God's love for us.

(By the way; thank you for praying with me, and know that I love you much!) Now, back to where we were in my life at that time:

I continued suffering silently from condemnation and began struggling with feelings of insecurity, which were a sure consequence of my having been raped. Despite the odds against me, God continued to have mercy on me and bless my life. I was able to excel in education. I made the honor roll and won several math competitions against some of the most intelligent children in Illinois and beyond. I had some friends and was very social. Teachers would often remind me just how social I was as they reprimanded me in class. (Since I'm an adult now, it's safe to say my mom won't be spanking me for that confession!) I was friendly, and I found humor in just about anything. The only thing I enjoyed more than laughing was making someone else laugh. I could also be very serious. It was God who made me like this. From the time I was an even younger girl, I was a very zealous advocate for people's rights. I realize now that even back then I hated injustice. And although this hatred for injustice would later grow for good reason, back then I had zero tolerance for it also. I went to Kolmar School, in Midlothian, Illinois, which at the time was an area where predominantly Caucasian people lived. Remember, I lived in Robbins, Illinois, where predominantly African-Americans resided. No school buses would come to Robbins, Illinois, to pick us for school, so this meant we had to walk to school, no matter what the weather conditions were near the Windy City. Now, because my older sister, Garrica, had her first car by then, I really didn't have to walk all the time, but if you saw her car you would know exactly why I chose to risk it with the weather rather than ruin my reputation. She drove an old lime-green Nova with a hole in the floor. But we weren't the Flintstones; we were the Funches family, but with that hole in the floor it was difficult to tell the difference! This car wasn't a nightmare either, because every morning when I woke up, that green boat with four wheels would be parked outside in our driveway. And it wasn't even so bad that the color of this large ship-like car was neon-green, so that all my friends would see it coming—color and size—from at least a mile and a half away. It also made a loud noise when she drove it sometimes. It would announce to whoever could hear that it was coming or had arrived. When it got below zero degrees, however, that green Nova was a safe haven, and I was a grateful little girl with nothing to say but, "Thanks for the ride, Garrica." But for the most part, I took my chances with gusting winds or gathered snow, and I walked with my friends to school. We learned pretty quickly as African-American children, however, that we faced much more than harsh weather conditions. We faced blatant racial discrimination, violence, and hate, all because of our race.

Many mornings and afternoons as we walked home from school, racists adults would open the doors of their homes and tell us, "Hurry up past my house, niggas," and "Get off my sidewalk, monkeys." Some would open their doors and throw rocks at us. Some of my friends wouldn't say anything back to them, and they clearly needed someone to fight for them, or at least that's what I figured. I often yelled back in our defense. It wasn't much of a defense, but it was something. I shouted a couple of "Old farts" and "Yo' mama's a monkey" back at them. To everyone around me, I seemed very tough, the toughest of them all, but inside I was afraid of being hurt and abused again, hoping that this outer shell of toughness would hide the truth. I was scared. By this time, I had learned a very self-destructive behavior, one that would haunt me by repeating itself in my adult life, nearly destroying it. I learned how to hide abuse, and consequently, I hurt myself while protecting the abuser. Regardless of this purported skill I had developed, I would soon learn something similar to the concept of gravity, what goes up must come down, but even more important some things inside must come out. Very often, God uses physical manifestations of things in us and in our lives to teach us spiritual truths, because these physical aspects are reflections of what happens spiritually. The example God gave me was our digestive systems. God showed me how whatever food we put inside our bodies when we eat, it must be digested and come out. God let me know that whether the food is good for your body or not, it isn't meant to stay in there. It is meant to be released. There are things that get inside of us emotionally or spiritually that must come out, whether good or bad. And when they don't come out, like food, the result is the same. It's deadly but in an emotional or spiritual sense. God also showed me how some things are harder to digest and get out than others, like pork or steak. Pork and steak are harder to digest than foods such as chicken and fish, but nevertheless, they must still come out, or they will kill the body they're in.

Likewise, emotionally and spiritually, some things are more difficult to get out of us, but they must come out, and abuse is one of those things. If you are being abused in any way, I would encourage you to get out safely from the abusive environment you are in and also get the abusive environment out of you. Not doing either could be deadly. God also showed me how things that go inside that are meant to come out will sometimes do it without the consent of the person whose body it is. You know this if you have ever tried to stop yourself from vomiting. (I don't want to be gross, but if we have to go there for someone to be free, we are going there!) Trying to hold in vomit is almost 100 percent of the time a useless effort, because it's coming out. You might be able to delay it, but you cannot deny it! It's coming out, with or without your consent.

The same thing happens to us emotionally and spiritually. Some things will just come out and to the surface even when you try and bury them deep inside. And I know what God says is true, because it happened to me.

Saying Good-bye is Sometimes Hard to Do

I began acting out. The way I acted out was, and still is, bizarre to me. I used to wonder how someone could choose such bad relationship partners, sometimes over and over again. When I was writing this chapter, God revealed to me the answer. He said, "Because they chose." You see, God has a plan for our life, and in the plan, God has already chosen the what, the when, and the who. The choosing is for God, and when anyone else chooses other than God, they have chosen disaster, because it is a choice outside the will of God. In fact, we don't even choose God. God chooses us. God said it: "For whom He foreknew, He also predestined to be conformed to the image of His Son, that he might be the firstborn among many brethren. Moreover whom He predestined, these He also called, and whom He called, these He also justified, and whom He justifies, He also glorifies" (Rom. 8:29–30).

Well, I didn't let God choose, and that, my friends, was a costly mistake. I chose with my eyes, not even my heart. I saw tall and handsome. If handsome had a brother, I am telling you, it was him. I won't mention his name, but we can call him, "handsome gets what handsome wants" (HGWHW) for now. Well, at least to me he was "HGWHW." Oh yeah. And a couple months later I would find out he was the same to a lot of other girls! Making that long nightmare short, this guy was charismatic and cute, and he told me what I thought I wanted to hear. The truth is that he was a distraction. I failed my first class in school because of being focused on him rather than studying for geometry class and focusing on my education. I paid for that—and in more than one way. I spent my first and only time in summer school, which was like a division of

Rikers Island Maximum Security Prison. I remember sitting inside the hot classroom while I watched my free, class-passing peers play their hearts out under the sun, which is even more valuable in the Chicago area because most of the year we spend in snow flurries with gray skies. Oh, I was paying—serving a literal sentence. I was inside a place against my own will, could not leave, and they served the worst food on that side of town. You see, it was like prison! (I'm laughing now, but I was crying then.) Parents, sometimes children will learn all the lessons they need to by the consequences of their own behavior. Sometimes there is no need to add anything to it, because the consequences alone are sufficient.

I knew I should have left this distraction long ago, and I even knew he was with other women, but of course, I thought I loved him, so I looked the other way and stayed with him. I paid for staying with him too. I caught him with a girl who was supposed to be my close friend at the time, and I do mean that I caught him, literally. That wounded me deeply. I ended up walking down the streets of Robbins, Illinois, in the middle of the night and could barely see what was in front of me, because my vision was blurred by my own tears. The image of what I had witnessed was in my head, and the scar was on my heart. Thankfully, after walking for what seemed like hours, I ran into a man I knew from the neighborhood for years. He was well-known for his drug-abuse problem. But that night God used him to help me, in spite of his addictions. God spoke clearly through this man to me. When I first began talking to him about why I was on the streets, wandering like that, he was obviously high and reeked of alcohol and marijuana. I thought to myself, "What is the use? This man is high." It was God that had me stay and continue to confess, because God was about to bless me through him with words of truth that made me free. He began speaking to me and telling me how I was worth more than that and should not allow anyone to treat me that way. His words were amazingly and liberating. And I couldn't help but notice and be amazed at the fact that he was completely sober and with a sound mind when he provided me with that truth and hope. That is how I knew God spoke through him. And although the words didn't stop the pain, they gave me the strength I needed to help me make up my mind to walk away from that horrific ordeal completely. This would prove easier said than done, but thankfully, with God it was not impossible.

It was very difficult because I had sex with "HGWHW" already. At that time, I didn't understand why this made leaving him so arduous, but I know now. My soul was tied to his from having sex with him, making it nearly impossible for me to just walk away. You see, God taught me that marriage takes place even when people don't exchange vows or have a marriage certificate issued by the state. Sexual intercourse will do this, spiritually and emotionally. It will do exactly what marriage does: take two people and join them as one flesh. Sex has consequences well beyond an unexpected pregnancy or sexually transmitted diseases. Some people wonder why they just can't get that ex out of their mind, or why they find themselves comparing them to their current spouse, or why they still even crave them sexually. This is because their souls are still tied to that former sexual partner, and they need God to set them free because it is a form of bondage.

I also remember regretting for a long time not waiting until I got married the way God ordains marriage in order to have sex. I felt like my virginity was a gift that I wanted to give the man I actually married but couldn't because I had already given it to someone else. My heart was heavy with that regret until God let me know that He has the power to take a man or woman who have had sex and purify them making them virgins again. God has the power to purify hearts and bodies. So it's never too late with God because with God all things are possible (Matt. 19:26). And God let me know also that, I got to do something even more powerful than being a virgin on that wedding night: I got to keep the vows I made. When God told me this truth it set me free.

31

It amazes me to think that at the time I was walking those streets that night, only months later I would begin dating my best friend at that time, whom I eventually married. There is a valuable lesson in that too. Saying good-bye is sometimes hard to do but very often worth doing. God taught me this important truth as I reflected back over my life. Sometimes while we are crying over who or what we have to let go of, we stand so close to receiving who and what was meant to be—what's worth letting go of the old for. At the time, though, this did not make saying good-bye any less difficult. I found myself singing in my heart, "One less bell to answer…one less man to pick up after…I should be happy, but all I do is cry." Some of you may know the lyrics to that song because you heard Gladys Knight and the Pips sing it. It was the tune my heart sang during that time, and I was all too familiar with it. I was having a difficult time letting go of what I knew was no good for me. But I was getting ready to receive some news that literally changed my life forever, and God used it to help me be free from the prison my soul was held captive in because of the awful decisions I had made during that time in my life.

Broken

I remember the day everything changed. I was sitting on a chair in front of the television, watching an episode of *Jerry Springer*, when I got the phone call. It was Aunt Ruth, my dad's sister, on the other line. I knew immediately that something was wrong, because she never called me before. She stumbled over her words, and I could tell by the way she was stuttering and struggling to form words and get them out that something was wrong. I instantly thought something bad had happened to my mother. My stomach was filled with anxiety at that moment as I tried hard to listen very carefully to what she was trying to tell me. Finally, she said it: "Garrica was in a car accident, and she is dead."

I couldn't believe what she had just said to me so I called my mom, but my she was already on her way over to the house where I was and told me Garrica was killed in a car accident with her best friend in Texas. That was it. For the first time in my life, I felt pain like no other. My mother was crying and hurting beyond what I am able to describe. Garrica was the only sister I had, the only sibling I had. I felt very alone, even with a bunch of people around me. I didn't know what to do. My whole family was suddenly broken, devastated, and in deep grief and mourning. When I went home I remember it being very dark. My mother lived in darkness for what seemed like forever to me. I tried to comfort her, but I could not. I tried to remind her that I was still there, but she could not be comforted by me. I know she didn't do this on purpose, but I felt such rejection. I felt like my mom died when Garrica did, and I wasn't reason enough for her to live again. We were a family hurting very badly. We didn't know what to do with the grief, with the pain of this loss. We all loved Garrica very much, and this death was too much to bear, it seemed to us all. I couldn't stand seeing my family in this pain—or endure it myself. It was heavy unbearable pain- a deep grief had come over me. I didn't see any light in that dark place...none. "My big sister is dead, but she was only twenty-two years old, God," I thought. "I don't understand. Why did you leave me here to deal with this? You should have killed me, and left Garrica here to help this family. Maybe she would have helped them better and dealt with this better." I felt such sadness, very afraid and even angry with God. "Why, God? Why?" These were my meditations. I was mostly scared and sad, though. I felt our family, our immediate family, was not that big to begin with, and with Garrica gone, there were just the four of us left. I do believe that was a part of the reason I wanted to start a family of my own, to extend the one I had, which seemed to be fading too fast.

The police informed my mom that my sister was traveling as a passenger with her best friend on a highway in Texas, when a young woman who was speeding hit them from behind so hard that the car Garrica was in went across the highway and hit a truck headed in the opposite direction, head-on. The EMT reported that she had died right then and there from internal trauma and bleeding. Her best friend died with her that day, instantly too. My sister was in Texas because she was stationed there in the military, and she was currently in Medical School, where she was excelling academically and wanted to become a Pediatrician. Garrica loved children, and although she didn't get the opportunity to have her own she did help raise me.

My mother went to Texas to identify my sister's body but I didn't go. I couldn't go. Afterward, my mom had Garrica's body shipped back to Illinois for her funeral. I remember I went with my mom and my granny to make the funeral arrangements and as I stood over Garrica's body, I felt as if I weren't in my own body. It felt as if I were looking at myself instead of experiencing this for myself. I remember just standing there and rubbing my sister's hair and thinking, "Garrica, your hair grew a lot." Then we had to pick out her casket and what she would wear. Partway through that conversation, I broke down, and I was not able to stay with them and help. My mom and my granny handled the funeral. I was in pain then, and it was hard for me to think about the pain my family was in too. I felt very scared to see us all broken like that. I didn't know what was going to happen next. I was scared that another one of us would die, and I feared being the last one left to mourn everyone else's death. I was overwhelmed with grief, anxiety, and fear. I was used to being funny and making jokes and causing others to laugh, but at that time, I had nothing to give. Nothing was funny anymore, and I had no reason as far as I could see to smile again. But I can see now that God literally made me strong. He made my family strong. That news would have likely killed someone else, but it didn't kill us. That was one of those times in life where if you survive it, that's the victory—a time where survival is the goal.

In those days, I thought a lot about the last time I spoke to Garrica, the last gift she ever gave me. She had told me that Mama was coming back home to Illinois from visiting with her in Texas earlier than what was previously scheduled, so if I had any company in the house that Mama didn't know about, I'd better get them out now. She was what I call "good looking out." I had company by the way. She also told me about getting my math grade up. (Remember, I had to go to summer school for the first time in my life for failing a math class, and Garrica and I were raised to do well and excel in school.) The last gift my sister gave me was a gold chain with a gold charm on it that said, "1 in a Million." I realized, after spending years trying to find a friend who would be like a sister to me, that Garrica was the one who was one in a million. She was irreplaceable. I thank God to this day that the last memories I have of Garrica were with her loving me, correcting me, encouraging me and her looking out for me.

This was hard to believe, and even harder to accept; Garrica, my only sibling was gone. It was even very hard to form the words, "my sister died." It was literally too painful to get those words out of my mouth, so I avoided saying it.

It was even more painful watching everyone I love so deeply all suddenly become broken at once, with pain running so deep that none of us could comfort each other. I remember, as I sat at my sister's funeral, looking at her body in a casket and feeling like everything inside me was broken. Pain, hurt, and sorrow just simply are not a good enough description of what I felt at that moment in time. My mother sat beside me weeping, and the sound of my grandmother wailing as she mourned with deep pain was killing me. I looked over at my father, and for the first time in my life, I watched my daddy cry. The feeling of helplessness cut deep within me. I watched the people I loved the most be completely broken, and there was nothing I could do or say to ease the deep pain they were in. I then realized, at that funeral, that this pain was not going away anytime soon, if it ever went away at all. At the same time, I realized I could not handle it. Mentally and emotionally,

I checked out of this painful reality. I believe that was one of the most selfish things I have ever done in my life. I made a conscious decision not to deal with Garrica's being killed in that car accident. I literally thought, "I am just going to act like she is away in the military again on active duty, and I can't talk to her because of it." The reality of her being gone just hurt too bad for me. I literally could not deal with it. I tried to act as if I were somewhere else while I was there at the funeral, as if I were not saying good-bye to my only sister.

I remember at that time a lady was singing the song, "His Eye Is on the Sparrow." Now, I have heard this song before in my life, and I know it's a fairly short song; however, the lady who sang at Garrica's funeral sang that song for what seemed like two days. Every time the song was supposed to end, she remixed it, making it drag on. I thought, "Garrica, if you can hear this, you are probably thinking who hired her to sing!" I thought, if the car accident would not have done it, that lady's singing would have. Later on, I told my mother what I was thinking at the funeral while the lady was singing, and for the first time in a long time, I saw my mother smile. It took us all a long time before we were able to just smile again. Just now, as I was writing and recalling what we all suffered and endured at that time, tears poured from my eyes, causing me to have to stop writing as I cried uncontrollably. I wept aloud and turned completely red as I remembered this pain. I believe this cry that just came from my heart and soul as I shared this testimony with you were the cry that I needed to release when I was sixteen years old and at that funeral. It was the cry that I chose to hold in for all those years, because of not wanting to face the painful truth that the only sister I had was gone from me. I loved my sister, and for the longest time, I tried to find a sister to replace her. Whenever I had a close female friend, I would call her my sister. My soul longed for that void to be filled. This longing is why when friends turned on me and betrayed me, it hurt me much deeper than usual.

I remember at that time in my life not wanting to be close with anyone again, especially my family that was left. I pulled away from my mother, father, and grandmother as much as I could. I was deeply afraid that if I remained close to them, I would love them as much as I loved Garrica, and when they died, assuming they did before me, I would be in as much pain or more. I figured if I pull away from them, then it wouldn't hurt so bad if they left me too. So I left them first, and it was when they needed me the most, and the guilt has been heavy on me for years. I remember crying in 2015 and asking God to forgive me for this. I wept alone in my home in the presence of God, and I prayed and asked God to help me, that if I were ever given another opportunity, no matter how much it hurt or what pain I was in, I would be there for my remaining family and not abandon them again because of grief and selfishness. The very next day, my mother called me and told me that my father had passed away. This time, I prayed to God for my family and myself. This time, God blessed me to keep my word, and I was there for my family. This time, I didn't abandon them, no matter how much pain I was in saying good-bye to my daddy. This time I did the right thing, and I honored my family. This time, I stood by their side the whole time, and I grieved for my dad and wept because I could not speak to him or hug and kiss him. This time I thanked God for the life he gave, rather than being angry with Him for that life ending here on earth, because I know surely my dad and sister live on! Jesus caused death to lose its grip on believers, and that truth my soul knows very well. It is because of the work of Jesus Christ on that cross that I have tremendous joy and peace even after death.

We, meaning my family and I, also learned some very valuable lessons because of this. We learned that God is indeed close to the broken-hearted and saves those with a contrite spirit (Ps 34:18). I personally learned the importance and necessity of letting healing take its course, because when people don't, and they choose, as I did, to pretend the pain wasn't there, or they attempt to distract themselves by keeping busy or using the infamous sweep-under-the-rug tactic, healing doesn't occur, but it remains inevitably necessary. Then the healing comes, and the necessary, facing-the-hurt phase of healing, at a time when you would have already been healed if you had allowed God to do so when you got wounded. I am not saying that it's the easiest thing to do in life, but I am saying that I know it is necessary. Healing is a part of life, because hurt is. It's not God's will for us to never be hurt, but it is surely God's will that we always be healed. I believe that Garrica's death was as much a part of the plan of God as Garrica's life. That's not the easiest thing to accept, especially when trust in God is lacking or not present at all. The word of God says, "God wounds, but His hands make whole" (Job 5:18). Trusting someone who has wounded to heal requires both faith and trust in God. But God showed me later on in my life that this happens all the time with people and their doctors, who are only human and certainly flawed. Nevertheless, we have trusted our doctors, even when they wound us. God showed me how doctors give patients shots with needles to heal them or to prevent them from being harmed worse. Needles hurt! The doctor takes this sharp metal object and penetrates the skin, surely causing bleeding, but the doctor's purpose is to heal, not to hurt. The doctor's purpose no matter how noble, however, doesn't stop the pain of the process of the healing it brings about. But if the doctor says the shot is necessary, you trust her or him to administer the shot to you, despite the pain. Likewise, and greater, we must trust God to heal our brokenness, even if we feel afraid that it will hurt. Eventually, I learned to trust God with my pain and allow Him to heal me whenever needed.

Not Destroyed

It amazes me how, after Garrica's death, I finally began to really live again. God told me one day, "Some must die so that others might live." This was a hard pill to swallow at first, but when I reflected on what God was showing me, it made sense and is so true. Many have laid down their lives or had their lives taken so that many more would live. Jesus is the ultimate example, having lain down His life and died in our place in order for us to obtain eternal life (2 Cor. 5:21). Others, like Dr. Martin Luther King Jr., died, and because of that many others were able to live, literally and figuratively. It was after his assassination that caused both legislative and case law reform in segregation. African-Americans are able to go to the schools and colleges of their own election now and are to no longer be denied admission on the basis of their race. He died, and we live!

Amber Hagerman is another of these countless examples. At the tender age of nine years old, Amber Hagerman was kidnapped and murdered. Subsequently, her parents fought, and prevailed, at having legislation passed that helps find kidnapped and missing children. The AMBER Alert system was created and developed in states across the country, and eventually, in 2003, it was enacted into law under the Protect Act. Many children have been rescued and lived, having their parents spared from the pain of losing a child, because of the death of Amber Hagerman. Likewise, God used my sister's death to cause me to live.

My life turned around for good after that. I walked away from that toxic relationship from the past. I focused on my education and was blessed by God to do well in school from there on out. In finishing high school, I tried out and was chosen to join the school's top choir, and I did what I truly love to do: I sang. Near graduation, I was awarded with one of the highest academic awards possible. I was given the High Honors with Distinction Award for having excelled academically beyond the many of my peers. I was also the only African-American female who received that recognition during that time. I was enrolled in honors classes, and I was able to obtain college credit for the advanced courses I took in school. I learned another language and joined the Spanish Club in order to push myself further toward the future I anticipated. I also began going to high school dances and hanging around my old friends again—friends who were actually my own age.

I was blessed to go on a college visit at Eastern Illinois University during this time also and to live on campus for a few days, touring both the campus and the college classrooms. God truly ordered my steps and arranged for me to go on this college visit. God used it to help turn my life around in a huge way. It ignited a passion in me to pursue my dreams of becoming a professional counselor. I left Eastern Illinois University's campus tour visit with a strong desire to go to college. My parents didn't need to talk me into it; I wanted to go. I did previously speak of going to college and had desired to attend, but nothing like after I went on that college visit. God used it to inspire me and ignite something in me. (I recommend that parents who are able to take their children on a college visit do so. But as always, pray and ask God for wisdom, guidance, and direction.)

I also began dating my then best friend, whom I eventually would marry. I went to two proms, as we were one year apart in high school, and I learned to drive my first stick-shift car. My sister left her new candy-red Dodge Neon behind, and for months I would not drive it at all. She didn't even get a chance to put any real miles on it. I felt incredibly guilty for even the thought of enjoying something only because she was not here to enjoy it herself. Thus, I refused to drive the car, and I just let it sit in my mother's driveway for months. I walked past the car to catch the bus to go to school instead of driving for quite some time. Eventually, my then best friend talked me into getting into the car and learning how to drive the stick shift. We were able to get to school without waiting for a bus in the Chicago cold, but learning how to drive this stick-shift car had its setbacks. I won't ever forget that we were in traffic one day, and I went to cross the intersection, and the car just cut off. The car wasn't broken, but my ability to drive a stick-shift was! A semi-truck was coming right at us, and the driver was in full-blown panic mode. Even though I was in as much danger as him, the look on his face, with his eyes basically coming out of his head from fear, was flat-out hilarious! I laughed so hard. That was, of course, after we got out of that intersection. I was having the time of my life with him. We spent almost every day together, and when we were not at each other's house, we were on the phone for hours together. We would literally fall asleep on the phone together. I remember lying on the living room floor at my mother's house with the love of my life and watching the classic movie *Love Jones* so many times that I lost count. It wasn't all romance with us, though. I was way too silly for that. We would watch *Liar, Liar,* starring Jim Carrey, and I would laugh until I cried. As my boyfriend's his home became increasingly unsafe due to violence, he ended up living with my mom and me. I was very protective over him then, and even well into our marriage. One thing I could not tolerate was somebody hurting him. I felt a sense of responsibility for him. I loved him deeply and had a strong desire to protect him, no matter who it was who tried to harm him. I had even told his own father a few choice words before when I felt he'd hurt him. I had this same protective spirit for a long time, and I ended up defending him at all cost, even from myself.

Now, I know that I was on the right path and supposed to be committed to doing the right thing, but I loved my boyfriend, and I thought the way to express that love was to have sex with him, and so we did. This seemed to be all fun and of no consequence until I ended up pregnant. "Somebody has to tell my mother" was basically the thought that took over in my mind, followed by fear. The sin of premarital sex led me right into another sin: we decided to abort the child. I still remember us going to the clinic in downtown Chicago and sitting in the waiting area listening to the screams of another adolescent girl who was getting an abortion. It was horrifying. As much fun as I thought I was having when having sex, the consequences of it took all the pleasure right out of it. I was forced to look at all these brochures and documents describing the details of what an abortion is and how the child's life is terminated. Guilt had set in, and condemnation was back to haunt me. Afterward, I became ill, and I was in terrible pain for some time. I was diagnosed with having precancerous cells. I know God did not punish me with sickness, but I became ill because the wages of sin is death. Sin has consequences in and of itself. Sickness was the consequence of my sin then. But I thank God again for having mercy on me, when I clearly hadn't done anything to deserve it. Despite my faults, God healed me from every cancerous cell and blessed me to finish high school strong. God also blessed me to be accepted into the college I desired to attend, and to be awarded several academic scholarships. By this time in my young life, I had been through more than some adults twice my age, but God clearly had a plan for my life that He wouldn't allow anything or anyone, including me, to stop it.

I can truly say that God wrote this through me, and He has completely allowed me to pour into this book my heart, soul, and tears. I have truly experienced that saying good-bye is sometimes hard to do, and even extremely difficult at times, but God taught me, "Saying 'I will see you later' isn't as difficult." You see, in Christ, "We pass from death to life…" (1 John 3:14, in part). So I wasn't really saying *good-bye* to Garrica. I was saying, "I will see you later." I miss my sister still, and I love her as if she'd never left, but God has healed me. I've undoubtedly been broken, but thanks be to God, I am certainly not destroyed!

"We are hard pressed on every side, but not crushed…struck down, but not destroyed" (2 Co. 4:8, in part).

THE COLLEGE YEARS: OFF-CAMPUS LESSONS

Behold, I will do a new thing, now it shall spring forth...

—Isaiah 43:19

The college visit that God took me on really paid off, like all the many other blessings He provided me. I worked hard to get my grades up, and even though I was dating my best friend, the then-love of my life, I kept my grades up. I applied and was admitted into Eastern Illinois University (EIU), the very college I had visited while still in high school and the one I was become determined to attend. As excited, as I was to go off to college and leave home, I was equally sad and nervous because I was leaving behind my boyfriend and my parents, especially my mom. I was mostly nervous because I had not ever lived on my own before... ever. It's scary stuff for a fresh high-school graduate. (Parents, if your children act like they can't wait to leave home, or if they even voice that sentiment, have no worry about it. Soon, reality will beg to differ with their opinion, and whether they admit it or not, they will miss you and home. As the saying goes, "There's no place like home").

EIU was located in Charleston, Illinois, about four and a half hours from where I grew up and lived, so my mom drove me down to begin college, and she allowed my boyfriend to travel along with us. I was so excited the entire time in that car. It was an emotional high. But when I looked outside my dorm room and waved good-bye to my mom and boyfriend, I hit an emotional low. I learned many valuable lessons from this. I wouldn't recommend that anyone allow themselves to get really high emotionally. It is wise to remain emotionally stable and control your emotions, even when things are going exceptionally well for you, because emotions have something like a built-in gravity, and what goes up must come down. And of course, the higher the climb up, the harder the fall down. I do believe this is the pure wisdom of God. Even if God does a miracle for you, control your emotions. Getting too high emotionally is similar to getting high physically with drugs and can be damaging and lethal as well. Drugs, like the emotional high, feel good, and something inside desires to feel the *high* again, but when the high isn't obtained, normal feels low, and lower feels much lower than what it actually is. Likewise, the highs cause people desiring to obtain them again to take unwise and damaging measures to do so. Those seeking the physical high that drugs and sex bring often steal or even murder for drugs. Those seeking the sexual high tend to sleep with anything with a pulse. Others don't even require a pulse and have sex with dead bodies. Those seeking emotional highs get in new relationships to feel the high of meeting someone new—the "honeymoon phase," we can call it—but they never commit to anyone, damaging their own emotions and soul, and often those of others as well, because after just a few weeks into the relationship, the "high" that comes from the new isn't there because new inevitably becomes old. People are shopping and spending outrageous amounts of money on things because the shopping produces some kind of high. However, when the credit card bill is due, or the accounting is done and the reality of the damaging effects of getting high sets in, there comes the extreme low and the feelings of guilt that weigh heavily on a person. God told me this happens also with the so-called ladder of success.

The higher someone climbs it, the worse it hurts, or even kills, them when they hit the bottom. That would explain a lot of the suicides that took place in the 1930s when the stock market crashed, and very rich people killed themselves when they plummeted financially along with their stock investments. Hidden behind all these desires to get "high" is greed. Greed says, even after getting the high, to get it more, because enough is never enough with the spirit of greed. We have to be careful of this even when obtaining academic and work-related promotions and accolades. Be aware of greed trying to creep in disguised as achievement and the desire for it. When God calls someone to accomplish something, that's perfect; however, when people begin to set their own ambitious goals, greed is present, and good will never be, good enough. That's why a man with millions of dollars can forsake his wife and children on a regular basis, claiming to do so in order to make them more money. The millions aren't enough, because enough is never enough for greed. It is never satisfied, and where there is no satisfaction, there is a search for satisfaction, and so long as that search for satisfaction continues, there is no rest and peace for that soul who refuses to let God satisfy it with this truth; God is more than enough! I'm certain if God has me writing this, someone reading is being set free right now. God knows I didn't intend to write that, but the wisdom of God is pouring out because God is determined to deliver those reading and needing. In sum, God said to have a sober mind. And this means so much more than not getting drunk or abusing drugs (1 Pet. 5:8).

Life on Campus

It was true that I missed my family, friends, and boyfriend a lot at first. However, it wasn't long before I made new friends, got busy with class, and took a deep dive into the ocean of "way too much fun." Oh, I began to love college life, especially on campus! I was never the party type; however, I tried it when I went to college, and it took drastic measures before I would regret it. I learned the college system pretty fast and maintained my grades, by the grace of God. I found a church to attend on campus and became friends with another freshman I liked so much that I almost became roommates with her. *Almost* was as far as I got, however, because I liked having my dorm room all to myself. If I had to choose between feeling alone and a roommate getting on my last nerve, it was going to be me, myself, I, and God! Soon after, I began going to sorority and fraternity parties on campus.

I quickly took an interest in sororities because it was supposed to be a sisterhood, and ever since Garrica died in that car accident, I wanted to find a "sister" to fill the void I had. Specifically, I wanted to join the Delta Sigma Theta sorority. This decision would nearly cost me my freedom, entire college education, and reputation. God had warned me prior to my even getting on campus about the dangers of sororities. An old friend of mine who went to school first told me that her school completely forbade the Delta Sigma Theta sorority from being active or initiating any new members because their hazing killed a girl pledging their sorority. I didn't take heed of this life-and-death warning from God, and I continued to pursue a sister in that "sisterhood." My "almost roommate" and I both decided we wanted to join, so outside of our classes, we would attend any and every event that the Delta sorority had. I became associates with one of the older Deltas on campus, and I took a strong liking to her because she was older than me and reminded me of Garrica physically. Next thing you know, I was at parties and sorority houses where drugs and alcohol were as common a thing in the house, as paint on the walls and carpet on the floor. I tried marijuana, and I am glad God left me with asthma at that time, because I felt like I couldn't breathe. Good for me! I didn't want to smoke that ever again in my life. I tried to drink with the so-called "in crowd" and the sorority and fraternity members, but that didn't last long either. I hate to eat or drink anything that doesn't taste good, and alcohol tends to be very nasty. By the time I finished mixing the alcohol with juice so that I could actually swallow it and pretend to have a good time, I didn't ever get drunk, but I got plenty of exercise making trips to the restroom, pretending to drink a lot and "keep up" with the so-called cool kids, who were actually functioning alcoholics—some almost as old as their professors because they kept failing classes. They were often called "six-year seniors." Looking back, I don't think they were not bright at all. They had completed the majority of college, but they kept failing toward the end. I believe God has shown me that they failed their classes intentionally because they were afraid to go on.

College is a taste of the real world, minus all the responsibilities that are actually in the real world. The bird has left the nest, but he still has a key—and parent birds who are willing to let him use it to get back into their nest when needed. In the real world, which begins after college most of the time, you build your own nest and stop relying on your parents to permit you back into the nest they built. Fear of responsibility and fear of failure cause some to stay right at the edge of victory without ever embracing it—right at the edge of graduating, without ever receiving their diploma. God surely showed me correctly, because fear has tried to hold me back from taking the next step in life too. But I learned from God to "fear not" (Isa. 41:10).

Although at that time in my life, I wasn't afraid to finish college, I got involved with the Delta Sigma Theta sorority, which almost finished me. Everything was going well, and I can honestly say I didn't see the trouble that came next. The most difficult thing I had to deal with at that time in my life was trying to get enough money to get a bus ticket to go home and visit my family and boyfriend, getting tired of eating ramen noodles (the chicken is still my favorite flavor!), lack of cable television, and the length of financial-aid applications. In other words, I didn't have any real problems. Things were looking up. I made it through my first year of college pretty much consequence-free. My grades were pretty good, and I was awarded a few academic scholarships to help pay for school.

During Christmas break of 2001, my second year in college, one of my life dreams became a reality. My boyfriend proposed during Christmas break over a steak dinner at my mom's house in Robbins, and I accepted with joy. I was so happy. My love was growing stronger, and my desire to be with him was even stronger. After Christmas break that year, I left home again and headed back for college with a smile on my face and in my heart. That smile, however, was about to be turned upside down.

Sorority Life Gone Sour

Although things were going well, I still had pain in my heart over the loss of my only sibling, Garrica. I was constantly trying to fill that void. These efforts did way more harm than good. I kept faithfully attending events Delta sorority hosted and studied their history and finally I had the requirements to join, because I was officially a sophomore in college. I was headed in the pledging direction, but violent hazing turned me around.

One night, I was coming out of my dorm building with a friend and going to get into my car, which I had inherited from Garrica after she died. This car was Garrica's first, and it consequently became my first. The car was red. Delta's sorority colors are red and white. Even though I had not even applied to be in the sorority, several of the members had taken notice of my interest and decided to come to the parking lot where I parked my car and block me in with their car, preventing me from leaving the parking lot. One of the girls came up to the car with a sharp object in her hands and was yelling at me for having a red car. She was screaming, "So you think you're a Delta already? You think you are just going to get in and not go through anything, don't you? That's why you got this red car!" She went to the front of the car and began to scratch into the hood of the car a pyramid (the Delta Sigma Theta symbol). When I realized what she was doing, I began to cry and beg her to please not harm the car because it was my dead sister's car. She just kept yelling and cursing at me and scratched the pyramid into the hood of the car anyway. She, along with about eleven others, one of whom was a male student, rushed at me. I didn't see my friend in sight anymore, and she certainly wasn't helping me.

I then remembered my mom had given me a toolbox to keep in the trunk in case I had car trouble. My car had not broken down, but I was clearly in trouble. I managed to get to the trunk and I grabbed a tool quickly from the car, and I began swinging it at who-ever and whatever was close enough to me to be hit. The hammer hit the car window of one of the girls, and with all the yelling and cursing outside on campus, the inevitable happened: the campus police had been called. I willingly went down to the police station. I did this not because I am America's dumbest criminal but because I had common sense and knew I had not broken any laws. So I volun-tarily went to the police station to press charges, but to my surprise the police officers informed me that the eleven people who came after me that night were all saying that I, who weighed 130 pounds, attacked all eleven of them. Now, I didn't know everything, but I was far from dumb enough to attack eleven able-bodied people, in the middle of night in Charleston, Illinois on a college campus as an African-American. (Even though I enjoyed campus life, off-campus life seemed to be plagued with racism in Charleston, Illinois.)

As bad as it was going that night, the worst had yet to rear its ugly head. In fact, the only thing I found worse than eleven liars that night was a police officer buying the lies that were being sold. I just knew I was still home free, though. I remembered my friend who witnessed my being attacked. Surely she would tell the truth. She was my dear friend—and almost my roommate. We had become really close friends while away at school. But Judas surely surprised me, yelling, "Crucify her!" basically with the rest of the crowd. This lady lied. She later came to me privately and apologized and told me why she lied. She wanted to be a Delta too and didn't want to risk being denied access into the sorority. So I went to jail so that she could have only a *chance* of becoming a Delta! By the way, I don't even think she joined the sorority.

The police arrested me after my friend, not even my enemies, had given testimony to cause my arrest and imprisonment. I couldn't believe that was happening. The police did a cavity-like search and everything, as if I were a murderer or something. I don't ever have to see Charleston, Illinois, again, by the way. Afterward, I was placed inside a real jail, and was made to wear jail clothes and I had roommates who were in for serious crimes like stabbing people. I was a second-year college student on the honor roll, trapped behind metal bars with women who made Mr. T. look like a little girl! I'm laughing now, but I was crying then; however, I was crying inwardly because my natural instincts kicked in while in jail and told me, "You better not let Butch, disguised as Barbara, see you crying, or you may end up underneath the bottom bunk!"

I remember one of the jail guards sliding us sandwiches across the floor and into the jail cell. As disgusting as that was, I couldn't eat anyway, even if she had brought freshly cooked collard greens. (Somebody is hungry now.) The guard came back the next day and realized that I hadn't eaten the sand*witch*—that's not a typo—she had slid across the floor of a jail cell to me. I remember clearly that she told me I wasn't getting out of jail by trying to starve myself to death. I was a college student but this jail guard had me feeling more like a member of Death Row Records with each passing day.

I should have made a rap song afterward, because I felt like Tupac anyway when I got out! I had a jail story under my belt, and where I'm from, some people erroneously believed that going to jail gave you street credibility. This "street credibility" was considered a good thing and earned people's respect. The dean of my university didn't see it that way, though. I was notified after I was bailed out that I was in even more trouble than jail and the $10,000 debt I owed from the astronomical bond that had been set. I had spent days in jail because my mom didn't have $10,000 to get me out of that mess I was in. I was very scared. All I knew to do was pray, and say, "Jesus, help me, please." I didn't have any fancy prayers, but I knew to cry out to Jesus and pray in the name of Jesus. God heard me and performed a miracle! A football player, who I barely even knew, heard I was in jail and posted my bail—all $10,000 of it! He even said he didn't know why he was bailing me out, and that he had no idea if I would even pay him back, but he was doing it anyway. Neither of us understood why he would do something like this for me, and he barely even knew me.

This, my friends, is the definition of a miracle! God heard my prayers and answered me, even though He warned me not to try to join sororities, and I didn't listen. God is faithful, even when we are unfaithful (2 Tim. 2:13). God's faithfulness, however, didn't mean that my disobedience to Him was without consequence. It certainly had those, but His mercy saved me from what really could have happened to me. I promised the student who bailed me out that I would pay him back, even if I had to take out a student loan. I was very grateful. God had indeed answered my prayers through that man of God, that angel. He didn't even tell me I had to pay him back within a certain time. By the next semester, God had blessed me with another miracle, and I was able to pay him back in full. I had to go to court a few times, and I had hell scared out of me, if any was in me, but God's mercy saved me again. The prosecutors didn't pursue the case against me and dropped every charge against me. God had given me justice, mercy, and victory without the hardships and expenses of a trial. I was grateful to God with everything in me. There was still another battle, though, and it was equally important to win.

School Hearing: My College Future Was on the Line

Because the hazing had taken place on campus, the university decided to hold a hearing to determine whether I should be expelled from college. That was heartbreaking. God had caused me to do so well in school, and my parents were so glad with the progress I had made academically. I was scared. There were now twelve witnesses against me, and it was just me, silently praying and crying out to Jesus to save me and not allow me to be kicked out of school. I was praying, and even though I didn't realize it then, I certainly know it now: God gave me wisdom and a strategy on how to attend the hearing and prevail. God even showed me what to wear. God specifically told me to where a light-pink-colored top and a skirt on the bottom. This makes sense now. God said it: man judges the outward appearance, but God judges the heart (1 Sam. 16:7). God had judged my heart and found me not guilty when I repented to Jesus for my part in even trying to join the sorority, and God knew the panel of men I would sit in front of would judge my outward appearance, so God prepared me outwardly in detail. I had no pastor there to pray with me, my mom worked in the Chicago area and could not attend, and my boyfriend had gone off to college by then himself, and we lived even farther apart than before. God spoke to me and told me some of the things those who had testified against me were saying about me. God gave me wisdom and told me that without having to say they are lying, I would make sure I controlled myself and behaved calmly, no matter how difficult it was to hear the lies they told.

Sure enough, the panel of judges told me a lot of the lies they told, and they read from the statements they made. I did everything

God instructed me to do, even when God told me to control my tone so that the judgment of man wouldn't mistake it for anger and in turn say anger equals violence—which, by the way, is not true. God said, be angry but sin not (Eph. 4:26). Anger is not a sin. It can be a holy response to evil—especially injustice. Something is wrong with the ones who rejoice in evil, not those who cannot tolerate it, and who hate it. But nevertheless, I took heed to what God instructed me to do, because mankind judges the outward appearance. God did it again and got me out of trouble. After the hearing was finished, I was made aware that I was free to continue my education at EIU, and I was no longer on academic probation as the hearing decision was made in my favor.

I found this panel of judges wiser than the police. They wanted to know relevant questions, like "What would make someone try to physically attack eleven other people?" That is a good, common-sense question, but I learned after this experience what I heard the dean of a law school say later on in my life: "Common sense isn't that common."

Even though God delivered me from all the legal troubles that came against me, took me out of jail, removed and paid in full the $10,000 debt I owed, and permitted me without consequence to go back to class and finish my education at EIU, the hazing turned into intimidation and even stalking. Some sorority members would wait for me after class, and when I left the classroom to get to my dorm room, they would follow me and make statements, making it clear to me that the battle was far from over as far as they were concerned. I endured it for weeks until I simply could not take it anymore. I told my mother I did not want to be at EIU anymore, and I was coming home. The stress and intimidation were too much.

Transitioning

Good-bye, EIU, and hello...I didn't have a clue! I came back home with no idea of what school I would go to. I attended Chicago State

University, but nothing there felt like EIU. I missed the campus and campus life. Going to school from home was a wholly different experience. I felt like I was passing through the campus, rather than enjoying it. I was clearly transitioning out of the old into something new, which can be uncomfortable for some—and I was clearly one of the some.

By this time, a friend of mine had a daughter I would frequently babysit. The more time I spent with this baby, the more I wanted a child, and the more I believed I could handle it. I even did some financial calculations, which were a poor attempt to calculate the cost of raising a child on our purported income, which was more like *outcome*, because more went out every month than it went in. I still wanted a child, and I spoke to my fiancé about it, and soon after that, I was pregnant. I never told him this, but I used to pray that we had a boy. I had heard him say he really wanted a boy. I would try to tell him it could be a girl, and I didn't want him to feel disappointed. Then he, of course, told me he would be happy with a boy or a girl. Then not even ten seconds later he was saying, "But it would be nice to have a boy." I felt incredible pressure to give him a boy. I knew that was not up to me, biologically speaking, but I could pray. And so I prayed. We also decided I would attend college where my fiancé attended school and played basketball. We were clearly about to be a family all the more, and he wanted my help academically too, as we both found the college he attended to be more academically challenging than our prior educational experience. And even though we were still in college, the college years as I knew them had ended, and being a family had taken precedence and priority over my college education. Eventually, family life would even take priority over my own life entirely. I had gone a long way for love, but not as far as I would eventually go.

"I am the Lord your God, and I will be with you wherever you go" (Josh. 1:9).

A FAMILY AFFAIR

For this reason, a man shall leave his father and mother
and join his wife, and the two shall become one.

—Genesis 2:24

I learned very quickly that my hasty decision to have a child at the tender age of twenty-one was the biggest responsibility I had ever experienced. It was a lot more difficult than a few hours of babysitting. For one, babysitting usually meant I was given money. Having my own child usually meant I was giving away all the money I had. Up until getting pregnant, all my thoughts about having a child involved a baby who was born. I quickly found out that being a mother begins long before the child is ever born, and it includes an equally important time for the mother and the child. I also gave no thought to people judging me until I was asked the question numerous times, "Are you married?" It felt very shameful that my answer was "not yet." There I was, clearly pregnant, but without a husband. Doctors would ask, other mothers would ask, strangers would ask. And the more they asked, the more I felt humiliated and even angry. My fiancé did not have that same shameful experience, since his stomach did not stick out in front of him like mine.

My stomach was so big it seemed to make it into every room I entered long before I ever did. This, I must admit, had nothing much to do with being pregnant. I remember making a conscious decision to eat without regard, because to me pregnancy was one of the only times it was cute and excusable to be huge! Only a monster would call a pregnant woman overweight or insult her for it. I took advantage of being pregnant and ate everything but my fiancé. I regretted the greed, however. After delivery, I went from shopping the maternity section to the plus-size section, for a long time afterward. I should apologize to my ex for that—for saying in my heart, "Love me anyway, even if I am sitting on both sides the room at once."

Well, pregnant and all, I remained supportive of him. I would drive for ten or twelve hours to be at my fiancé's basketball games, only after my dad would give me the money to rent a car and go. I left most of these games hoarse, because I never agreed with the referee when he didn't agree with my fiancé. It was fun. I also drove for hours to get to the school he attended because he needed help with schoolwork. Universities require that people on sports teams maintain a certain grade-point average, or they are not allowed to play—or worse, they are removed from the team entirely. We didn't have much money then—sometimes we literally had none—but we had God, love, and one another. And I had joy. I thank God because my pregnancy was a healthy one, without medical complications of any sort. Delivery, however, would prove to be much different.

Laboring in Labor

It was February 4, 2002, and I was at Christ Hospital in Illinois, ready to give birth to Zaire. I was induced, because I wanted to make sure that my fiancé didn't miss the birth of his child, so I scheduled the birth of Zaire around my fiancé's basketball schedule. This sentiment was considerate but perhaps not well thought out. Let me explain. Being induced (forced to go into labor) hurts much more than normal childbirth pangs. The pain was excruciating! My mom and fiancé were inside the hospital room and in great joy. Of course—they were pain free! I, however, was in serious pain, and I looked up one moment during a strong contraction and noticed that my mom and fiancé were laughing and playing cards, UNO specifically.

Now, two things made me angry. Number one, these people knew that was one of my favorite games in the whole world, and they were playing and having a good time when they knew I couldn't get in the game and beat them good! And number two, I was thinking, why in the hell are they laughing if I am dying? Well, at least it *felt* like I was going to die! I was a bit upset, because nothing was funny to me in labor. They could have managed to put Red Foxx and Richard Pryor on the same stage, and it still would not have been funny! Okay, maybe just a little funny, after all we are talking about Red Foxx! (If any of you are thinking, "Who is Red Foxx?" he was the father from the television show *Sanford and Son*, the one who had about two fake heart attacks per episode).

Nevertheless, we all made it through that labor. I want to take this time and thank God for the person to whom He gave the epidural idea to, which has indeed blessed many women in labor and saved the man's life who helped get them in labor! All the mothers and fathers in the world should thank God for the epidural. As soon as I got my epidural, I went from pain and suffering to a tad bit happier than normal. (Oh, by the way, I got in on an UNO game before Zaire was born, and I won!)

"It's a boy!" These moments aren't like many others in life. God can give people many things, but when God blesses you with a God-given family, whether it includes children or not, it is a blessing.

God calls Himself our Father; we are His children, and Jesus is our brother. That's a family affair, and we were too. Now, I know what it is like to have real joy. The reflection of who God is to us, on earth as it is in Heaven! This was a joyful time indeed. And God wasn't done yet. He was literally answering all of our prayers.

After Birth

I was elated to have a baby. Oh, what a joy God brought into my life through this little boy. I stayed at home with my mom for the first few months, because, God bless my mother's soul, she took off work for months to help me with my firstborn child. (What a mother!) She didn't beat me up; she was there for me completely, and she was experiencing joy as well, because "her baby" was born. My fiancé had to go back to school. That was hard on me, because I was left without his help with a newborn baby, and I was in a lot of respects still a baby myself. For some reason, however, I felt really down—very low, and I could not explain it. I noticed back then that, when I would feel down, I would next feel an overwhelming amount of guilt about feeling down. I would think, "How can you have these feelings of sadness when you just had your first child? And, how can you be thinking thoughts like maybe you are too young to have a baby and are you really ready to have this child? What kind of mother would be sad and think these thoughts? You should not have become a mother, then." This baby is innocent and needs you; don't be selfish. The thoughts were numerous and over-whelming me with guilt. It was those thoughts that weighed most heavily on my mind whenever I felt like being a mother was hard and that having a child was a lot more difficult than I thought. I tried to deal with this vicious cycle inwardly, but it got so bad that I was diagnosed with postpartum depression. After I heard on the news that a medical doctor's wife had committed suicide after having their baby, and that she had postpartum depression, I finally stopped pretending to be happy and confessed that something was wrong with me. I didn't want to end life the way she had, so I spoke up. I realized that I spent a lot of time not saying anything because, where I grew up, in a predominantly black community, depression was viewed and voiced as a sign of weakness and not something black people *get*. But depression is a demon that does not discriminate. It is not a disease; it is a devil dressed in disease. And so long as people misdiagnose this devil, he tries all the more to stick around. But I thank God for having mercy on me and delivering me from it.

God used the testimony of a doctor's wife who had postpartum depression and jumped off a building in Chicago, killing herself, in order to cause me to start getting the help I needed. I obtained pastoral counseling and went to see my labor-and-delivery doctor. I still believed in the power of God to heal. I took the doctor's advice, but I declined to take that particular medicine. I prayed. I was suddenly healed from depression, and there was no symptom in sight! I began having joy again. I still was not getting much sleep, though, because every time my mother said, "I will watch Zaire while you sleep," I would shut my eyes until the minute I heard him even breathe, or cry and I jumped out of the bed and went running in Zaire's direction. I was a sleepless wreck. Amazing how things changed. When I had Zion, our second child, I slept through the night when my mom volunteered to help. Maybe it was what doctors have yet to give a title to, for parents who have had their first child: first-time-parent paranoia.

A Dream Come True

My dreams had come true. There were a few true desires that I had in my life and getting hitched was on of them. I'm thinking, "Yeah! I'm getting married!" Funny that I wanted to get married more than anything else in the world at that time, and I was late for the wedding. Oops! I was a bride, but also human. Eventually, I made it to the church and to the altar. We got married in Chicago, in the same neighborhood where my fiancé grew up, across the street from the church we frequently attended together then. The wedding and reception were small in size but large in love. I wouldn't have changed a thing, even with the money to do so. The honeymoon was sweet like honey. It was also funny. I told you I could find a joke in just about anything. There we were at the hotel, ready to celebrate our becoming one the right way before God, and the jokes were setting it. Let's just say the hotel we stayed in was not the Ritz Carlton. It wasn't even Motel Six. It was more like the honeymoon suite of the Bates Motel. But truthfully, I was loving every scary moment of it. I remember wondering, "Is it safe to get in that Jacuzzi?" But none of that mattered. After all, God had answered my prayers about having a family, and I had married the love of my life. There we were, the family I had prayed earnestly for.

By the summer of 2002, we had found and moved into our first apartment and were getting ready to live together alone for the first time as a family. I felt so grown up. I remember my husband laughing because I started drinking coffee. I figured *real adults* drink coffee. (The true thoughts of a child!) We were quickly faced with a very adult decision, however.

We were told that my husband could enter the NBA draft that year.

Love over Money: The Choice Is Clear

I felt knots in my stomach. All I kept thinking was, "We just became a complete family." I spoke my mind when he asked me, "Vaughn, what do you think I should do?" I very clearly told him, "I don't think the foundation of the marriage is strong enough this early on to survive something like the NBA life." He reminded me that we barely had enough to pay our bills and were broke. I reminded him that being broke financially was better than being broken as a family. My choice was clear. I knew this was his dream, and it had become my own, but I did not believe that we had to forfeit our family for finances. The devil is a liar! So I turned down the million-dollar lifestyle, and we went on as a family in our tiny two-bedroom apartment. We were safe—safe from the snakes that are tailor-made to suck the life out of the rich and famous. But we weren't completely safe. The college campus was filled with "groupies" (aka gold diggers). Oh, I'm keeping it real. A prostitute is someone who has sex with a man in exchange for money (general definition). Groupies also have sex with men for money, or for the possibility to get some future earnings out of it. They invest. It's a risk. The guy may never go to the NBA, but it's a risk many took because of the chance that the guy *would* go to the NBA. As bad as this was, it was way worse once money actually came, and the news imprudently announced the wages an NBA player made. For the most part, however, family life up north was good. We were all settled in, basketball season had begun, and I had been accepted into Marquette, and things were pretty nice.

I had a pretty routine life. A schedule was a huge part of survival. I would rise early in the morning and make breakfast for my husband and prepare breast-pumped milk for the baby. Then I'd get ready for class and prepare the baby for daycare. Once on our way out to class, we would often walk together in the Milwaukee weather, overcoming snow and ice with a stroller and heavy book bags. I would then kiss the hubby good-bye, take Zaire to daycare, and often barely make it to class on time. Once classes were done, I would head to daycare, get Zaire, and head back to the apartment quickly to cook and clean before my spouse arrived home. I loved cooking every day for my husband. Those were the real joys of that marriage to me- a clean house, a hot-cooked meal, and a family to enjoy it. To some these family things are regarded as small, but for me these blessings were far from small. They were some of the things that mattered most in life.

On game days, things got really exciting. One of the ladies who worked at Zaire's daycare lived in our same apartment building.

That was good news, because I wasn't afraid to have Zaire out of my sight for more than thirty seconds anymore (good-bye, paranoid parenting; hello sleep!). Game days were some of my favorite days. I was the definition of *supportive*. It didn't matter if the games were in Ohio, Indiana, Louisiana, or any other state, I went! I was there, face painted, voice ready to yell at a ref until I ran the risk of getting put out. I would drive for ten or twelve hours sometimes to be at my husband's basketball games and leave most of these games hoarse. It was fun. We didn't have much money then, sometimes we literally had none, but we had God, love, and one another. I had such joy. As busy as I was, I must not have been too busy, because I found room for an unbelievable act.

I foolishly took notice that the Delta Sigma Theta sorority was on campus. Yes, I did it. Don't yell, please. Being "on line" (going through the process of becoming a member of the sorority, including being hazed) taught me enough of a lesson, and becoming a member taught me all the more. But I pledged anyway. I joined the very sorority God warned me not to, the same one He had to deliver me from a jail cell and school expulsion after failing to listen to Him the last time about it. I thank God for being faithful to forgive, because that decision I made was blatantly asking for trouble.

It was terrible being on line. I would be up late most nights with a toddler, and then rising early to run errands for "Big Sisters" of this sorority, which were always the runaround, because some of the hazers thought it, was a good idea to make life miserable. I was sleep-deprived and often forced to do the most humiliating things. I don't know how someone can tell the lie that God is for something that beats, humiliates, intimidates, and even kills people just for trying to become a member of an organization. You cannot reconcile such evil with Jesus. There are wiser Godly ways to cause people to bond like sisters, ways other than physical, emotional, and mental abuse and humiliation! I later in life began calling sororities educated gangs. Think about it—they're very similar.

When my former spouse noticed pledging was keeping me up late, which meant breakfast was late, he began to dislike my decision to join all the more. We both did. Well, I was born a fighter, and one night I watched a member who was initiating us hit one of the girls I was on line with in her chest and this was during a time she was dealing with a serious medical issue. I loved this girl—and not because she wanted to be a Delta, but because she was loving. When they hit her, I went off. That night, enough was enough. They had crossed the line with me by hitting my friend in her chest. That was, as the cliché goes, "all she wrote!" I had a "go to hell" attitude toward many of them after, and most didn't like me, but some respected and loved me. Later on that semester, I passed the Delta test, avoided going to jail this time, and became a member after swearing and pledging an oath to this organization.

After this it became my turn to bring in new pledgees. I am sure some members didn't like me even more—oh well! I refused to abuse others the way I was abused. I had foolishly allowed myself to be abused, but I would not hatefully abuse others. I refused to be evil toward them...having taken a pledge or not.

Later, God told me to renounce that entire pledge I made. The oath to put Delta first was a pledge to the organization in the place of God. God reminded me that words have the power of life and death (Prov. 18:21). God also told me many marriages were suffering and ending because the spouse had pledged themselves to the sorority, putting it in their husband's place. Afterward, real-life lessons sank in for me and took out any fun in being a member for quite some time.

One of the women who had brought me in when I was a pledgee was strong, but she was also loving. She had gone through a lot personally, even experiencing the death of someone close to her. I was at her house, for the glory of God, mourning with her, crying with her, praying for her, and encouraging her to please not give up. When I noticed that I was there with her alone those days, I realized that this sisterhood was not the sister I wanted. I remained close with one of the girls I was on line with, that one "big sister" who brought me in, and one girl who came in after me. I let go of Delta in my heart. I had a sister and lost one, and when I witnessed what I did as both a person pledging and as a big sister bringing someone else into the organization, I was done. I stopped paying dues and was done. I wore the jacket but it didn't wear me. I realized too, that Delta did not give me the friends I gained while at Marquette, and Delta couldn't take them away. They were from God, for His purpose.

My college years had truly transitioned into a family affair. When I wasn't cooking, cleaning, and caring for our son, I was attending basketball games to support my spouse. Other times when there was no school or game to attend, I would drive back to Illinois with Zaire to visit with family. I would be in the car praying, for the entire two hours it took to get back to Illinois, that Zaire would sleep the whole drive. Sometimes he did. Other times he didn't, and I found myself having to stop, pull over and feed him. I learned those highways like the back of my hand, so to speak, because I drove them so much. Well, at least when our car was working. We had two of them, but one of them was absolutely by definition a lemon, and the other was the Dodge Neon I had inherited from Garrica. Although that Neon held up a lot more, it too caused us some trouble, and we walked around Milwaukee many times in freezing-cold weather because our transportation refused to transport us.

I spent a lot of my nights inside the basketball gym with my husband while he practiced. I would rebound the ball for him or act like an opponent, putting my hands in his face and yelling while he took a shot so that he could get used to opposition and distractions on the court but still make the shot. We would go at it for hours, even exercising together using the basketball team's exercise techniques to help him improve. I think I sweated more than him with all that rebounding and practicing on the court with him for hours. That, and it was always hot in that gym. I can only hope by now that they have their new basketball players there in air conditioning. After late nights like this, I still had homework to do—often mine and his. I would then rise early just to do it all over again. Family life was not easy; it was work, but to me, it was well worth it.

One night was more remarkable than most. We had disagreements like anyone else, but this would be the second time it went from disagreement to disaster. The disagreement turned physical, and the violence was present. Before it was over, I had locked myself in the bedroom, and he had punched a hole in the door. Eventually the police were called, and I left. I stayed out, just driving around for about four hours, crying. I was hurt and confused. In my mind I found excuses for the violence, and I forgave it and moved on.

Then things were going well again, especially in basketball. The team, which I clearly believed was my team, had gone very far in March Madness, and I was extremely proud of my husband. As excited as I was that we had made it to March Madness final four, I was more excited to see Ashley Judd at the game. If you ever saw *Double Jeopardy*, you know what I am talking about. We didn't win the game like we hoped, but I felt victorious regardless. It was an accomplishment to make it that far—and we had worked so hard together that his accomplishments felt just like my own, and his dreams were becoming mine too. As endearing as this may seem, it was something I would later regret more than most other mistakes I made in my life, because when I became a fan of his dreams, I forfeited my own. That was simply not something God wanted me to do, whether married or not! When God created me, He did so as an individual, and God gave me an individual purpose too. But at that time, of course, and for a long time afterward, I didn't know anything was wrong with it, so I just kept encouraging him to fulfill his dreams. Just when the college goals seemed to be getting met, another offer came for my husband to enter the NBA draft and play professional basketball in the NBA. I don't think I will ever forget having this talk the second time around. It marked our lives and our marriage forever.

We were sitting on the edge of the bed, inside a hotel room in downtown Milwaukee, discussing and making a decision to leave the life God had given us behind and embrace an entirely new one—the lifestyle of the rich and famous, ultimately. I remember telling my husband I was afraid of him going into the NBA because so many families of rich and famous people get divorced— so many families who have a person in the NBA, even. My husband told me not to worry. I remember telling him maybe I would be okay with it if he could give me an example of someone whose marriage and family were not destroyed after getting drafted into the NBA. Kobe Bryant was the only example I was given. And although Kobe and his wife had a stellar reputation in their relationship then, I remember thinking, out of all the men and married couples who came into the NBA, and the lifestyle of the rich and famous, he could only give me one example. I was literally horrified and filled with fear. I was so afraid that our marriage would end and petrified that our family would be torn apart by whores, money, and fame. I am indeed a prophet. I have never wanted to be so wrong as much as I wanted to be wrong about this family not surviving. I loved our family, flaws and all, so dearly, and my greatest fear was that our family would be another casualty of the rich-and-famous lifestyle. I didn't want to lose him, and I didn't want to lose that family. I also didn't want to get in his way of having his dreams come true. Basketball seemed to make him happy too, and I wanted him to be happy. I thought about the fact that I had asked him not to go into the NBA last year, and how this was his dream coming true, and I didn't want to hold him back but help him fly.

So with a stomach filled with anxiety and a heart overwhelmed with fear, I told him, "Yes, I agree for you to go to the NBA this year." Life as we knew it was over, and everything became new. Some of this was to our benefit, but other things, coupled with sinful decisions, led to our detriment. That happens with anyone's life who makes sinful decisions, but with millions of dollars, the consequences and pleasures of sin can be vastly multiplied, and so is the damage and harm it causes.

"Old things have passed away, behold all things are new" (2 Cor. 5:17).

LIGHTS, CAMERA, ASHES!

And you shall remember the Lord your God, for it is
He who gives you power to get wealth, that He may
establish His covenant which He swore to your fathers,
as it is this day. Then it shall be, if you by any means
forget the Lord your God, and follow other gods, and
serve them and worship them, I testify against you
this day that you shall surely perish.

—Deuteronomy 8:18–19

I can honestly say regarding some of the next events in my life,
"I thought this was going to happen." I, of course, hoped it
wouldn't, but I deeply feared that it would, and unfortunately, with
a fortune, and lack of wisdom, it did just that.

Introduction
One of the worst things I have ever experienced in my life was the
feeling of seemingly having everything but really having nothing

at all. I had what outwardly appeared like everything anyone could want, but I didn't have any of what I needed—those things that money cannot afford to buy.

By the world's standards, I was "living the life." I have, however, lived in this lifestyle of "the rich and famous," and thus you can trust the truth I am about to share. It is not "living the life." It is "living the lie." I lived this lie for many years. This lie, that once someone gets rich and famous, then they will be happy, and finally matter, and then, and only then, they will have a life worth living. This lie is what I believe to be one of the greatest deceptions ever used against mankind. This deception has caused people to set out in life with a blind ambition to get as many riches as they can because, after all, as another lie goes, "money is power." The truth is; God is power! God is all-powerful, and it is God who raises up one and takes down another. Just ask any one of the multitude of people who soared to great heights, only to end up plummeting into deep depths. There is no man or amount of money out of the reach of God's just hands. God holds the very breath that we all breathe in His infinite power, and when God says, "time's up," the poor and the rich alike both go back to the dust from which they came, and all the goods they gathered and money they had are soon forgotten! . And rather, what they did with their lives, both the rich and the poor, is remembered, and that's what has the greatest lasting effect on their soul, children and their generations to come.

I have learned this and absolutely know it to be the truth: life is so much more than money and fame. We, as people, are worth so much more than money, brand-name clothes, cars, and all the fame in all the world. This is not because of who we are, but because of *whose* we are; we are children of God. God loves us and is mindful of us, and nobody can repossess that from you, or retire you from it, or supplant you with someone younger. This understanding and truth we must get as a people. It is vital. Some have sold their souls to the devil himself for a dollar, believing the lie that money is power and the way to real happiness and peace. Those are all lies, deception, and from hell itself.

Ask anyone with wealth and wisdom, "Are these lies about money true?" They will indeed tell you that it is not true at all. But if however, you ask someone who just has wealth but lacks wisdom, they will repeat the lies about money—not because they don't know the truth, but because they won't admit the truth, or don't know that the truth will make them free. So instead of being free, they stay bound by pride and pretend to the world that everything is cool with them. But they know that they are depressed, feeling completely empty inside, dependent on drugs because they can't even sleep at night, and lonely, despite the entourage around them. Many even contemplate suicide. Others have attempted it and went to great lengths to cover it up.

I can attest that money was not at all the end of my problems; it was a magnifier of already existing ones and the beginning of new problems at dimensions that I had never experienced before in my life. Money, coupled with lack of wisdom, extended me an invitation to the love of money in my life, prior marriage, and family. It was indeed a way that seemed right, but in the end it led to death, both spiritually and physically. Hollywood, fame, fortune, television cameras, and overpriced cars with oversized homes... I at one point thought I had it all. As it turns out, the so-called "dreamy" Hollywood lifestyle was in fact: "Lights, Camera, Ashes!"

Lights!

Everything was happening so fast. One day, I was a college student at Marquette University, inside the will of God with my husband and first-born child, and although I was barely making ends meet financially, my heart and life were filled with the joy of God and the peace that surpasses all understanding. The next day, I was a multimillionaire in front of television cameras at the NBA draft.

This is not a figurative testimony, I am telling you what literally happened. I'm sure at that time, many people thought I was rejoicing, having become a millionaire, but on the inside I was very scared and praying hard that my family and marriage would not be destroyed like most other marriages and families in the NBA—in Hollywood. When I say "Hollywood," I am not talking about California by the way, but a demonic spirit that God exposed to me that operates in that lifestyle of the rich and famous, taking any measures necessary to destroy those in it by destroying their relationship with God, so in turn all they are and have will be destroyed, and those who admire and follow them will as well. This is a very dangerous spirit, because those who are a part of this lifestyle tend to be influential. It's one thing to destroy one person's life by leading them astray; it is another level of tragedy to destroy millions of people by leading them in the way that seems right but ends in death.

People of influence have to be all the more mindful of their behavior, because of their ability to influence so many others. This happens with the news all the time. By way of example, when a man kills another man, it may make the news, or you might hear about it, but you may also never get wind that the murder took place even though the life taken was valuable. However, when someone harms a massive amount of people, just about everyone with ears hears about it and becomes aware because the media magnifies it. Unfortunately, these instances are where you find copy-cat crimes committed who have been influenced by the original criminal through their fame. The same is true, but greater, when the influence is good. Everyone has heard of Jesus. The Bible makes it clear Jesus fame spread throughout when He began doing good to people while on the earth. Most have heard of Martin Luther King Jr. too. Why? Because he touched, influenced, and affected the lives of many people—thankfully, for the good. I understand now the power of influence and the responsibility that comes with it, but back then the only thing that really meant anything to me was my family.

Literally, my marriage and family meant everything to me. And although this may sound like an honorable statement at first, it was erroneous. I should have not put anyone or anything before God. That lesson I learned the hard way, and I will share it with you in hopes that you will learn from my mistakes and you won't repeat them and suffer the same afflictions and sorrows that I did. So there I was, in front of television cameras, holding my son in my arms, smiling outwardly, but shaking inwardly because of worry and fear for my family and what may come of us in this lifestyle of the rich and famous. Soon after the NBA draft, they flew my family and me to Miami in a private plane. Up until that very moment, I did not know what a private plane was—or that such a thing even existed. Where I am from, the only thing really private is the security code to your alarm system, because thieves just kept breaking into people's houses! After this small plane landed, they then took us somewhere in a helicopter. I had not flown on a commercial airliner before in my life, and on day one, I experienced for the first time flying in a private plane and a helicopter. Things were happening fast, and I was experiencing many new things even faster.

At that time, my head had not swollen yet from pride, and I was sincerely just in awe. We arrived at an overpriced five-star hotel with an incredible view of the ocean. I had never seen anything as beautiful as the risen sun over the ocean with its reflection just on top of the waves. Growing up, I had splashed a few puddles as a little girl, and I had swum in a lake before, but I had not seen anything quite as beautiful as this. I remember standing on the balcony, thinking, "God, the ocean is so large I cannot see where it begins or where it ends." It wasn't until that very moment on that balcony that I felt some happiness about where we were in life and going into the NBA. Then I literally had this thought: "God, I can live like this." The momentary joy I felt then wasn't the problem, because at that time, when I stood on that balcony overlooking the ocean, I was still holding on to God's hand, and I had not forgotten Jesus—at least not yet. God never said money was the problem. In fact, God said, I will give you the power to get wealth (Deut. 8:18–19). God does say, however, "For the love of money is the root of all evil: which while some coveted after they have erred from the faith and pierced themselves through with many sorrows" (1 Tim. 6:10). I lived the truth of these words and the consequences of not taking heed of them.

Next, I was introduced to Martin Lawrence inside the Mandarin Oriental Hotel in Miami. They were filming a movie. I was very thrilled, excited like a child in a candy store, for two reasons. One, I watched the television show he was on for years and laughed until my eyes filled with tears, and two, that hotel had the greatest scent I had ever smelled in my life. Someone should have told me, like we tell children inside candy stores, "Settle down, because too much of this is bad for you." The truth is, too much of anything isn't good. In life we need a balance, and that is exactly what I would soon lack, mostly as a result of all of my reaction to all the gain.

Days later, we flew back to Chicago, and we spent the rest of the summer in a high-rise condo just off Lake Michigan. We received our first check as advanced funds in the amount of approximately $300,000. I had not seen that many zeros together before, and when I first tried to balance the checkbook, I erred several times on the calculator. What can I say? I had not ever needed to type numbers like that before. Next came my first luxury vehicle. Well, it was a Cadillac, and where I'm from, a Cadillac is considered luxury and it says "you've arrived." Arrived *where* exactly I don't know, because peer pressure never told me that part. It only told me to keep up with the Joneses by any means necessary—whoever the heck the Joneses are.

Nearing the end of that summer, and with the first basketball season in the NBA fast approaching, we went back to Florida, purchased, and moved into our first home. I had the honor of picking it out. It was in Doral, Florida. I used to love that house. I remember there were other houses in the subdivision that were larger, but I intentionally chose a more moderate home for us. I honestly felt we did not need the costs associated with those larger homes, and when I went inside the larger homes to view them, they didn't feel like a home at all. They felt more like an office building of sorts. Plus, the house God chose through me, was the biggest house we had ever lived in before anyway, but it had the benefit of still feeling like a home and not a stadium. The neighborhood amenities were like nothing I had ever seen. There was an exercise facility, a park, and beautiful pools right inside the community that looked like a resort. I remember walking inside the subdivision in Doral some days, pushing Zaire in his stroller, and taking him to our subdivision's park and pool. I would be in total awe of what God had done for us. I would walk to the front gate of the community and listen to the waterfall running off these huge rocks. It was so beautiful to me. I prayed when I was younger for God to bless me with a college degree, a good job as a professional counselor, and a nice house, but when God answered my prayers, God did what He is known for doing. He did more exceedingly and abundantly above all you can ask for, think, or imagine (Eph. 3:20). God has put me in awe of Him.

Still Grounded

Although a lot had changed, and in a very short amount of time, many things were the same. I was still who I was and still doing what I did most other days before this lifestyle change occurred. My days in Doral, Florida, were very similar to my days in Milwaukee, Wisconsin, as a wife and mother. I rose early in the morning and cooked breakfast for my family and me, helped my husband get ready for work, took Zaire to an early-education school, and spent the rest of my days cleaning the house, washing clothes, preparing the next meal, and doing more household chores. In Florida, how-ever, the household chores multiplied in size and time, because of the size of the new home. Eventually, I applied and enrolled at a college in Florida to finish getting my bachelor's degree, because when my spouse and I decided together that he would enter the NBA draft that year, I was suddenly taken away from my college education. My efforts to finish college in Miami didn't last long, however, because I took on more responsibilities at home related to our newly started business and foundation, our financial and tax-related matters, and all the endorsement deals that my spouse was contractually obligated to fulfill. I spent hours some evenings helping him, as he had what felt like thousands of basketball cards to sign. I attended meetings with him, as he highly valued my opin-ion and often told me that I was "the smart one." Balancing our checkbook was a full-time job. We didn't have any assistant, nan-ny, or housekeeper, at first, so I did everything but play basketball on an NBA court. (God knows I played basketball on the college court, practicing with my spouse many days.) I was happy to help him and Zaire, though. I loved them, and it seemed like nothing for me to lay my entire life down to serve them. Attending the basketball games continued too, and so did being the biggest fan in every arena where he played. I didn't realize it by then, but my life was becoming his life, and I was slowly losing my own identity and instead identifying with him. I traveled on the road to out-of-state games as well, and because of the type of supporter I was, they probably wanted me out of their arenas! It was more intense than any college basketball game I attended to support him. This time I could afford seats so close to the floor that when I yelled in disagreement with the refs' often bad calls, they would turn and look at me with scorn. I was having the time of my life, but I was not having a life of my own anymore. That decision to lose my identity and identify with my spouse was a costly and almost deadly mistake.

Basketball Player's Wives: Don't Judge Them

First, let me say that I am by no means referring to the women herein as "basketball wives" in the sense that they don't have an identity of their own or as if they are married to the round orange ball. I have called it such to drive home an important point for women who have been or are married to NBA players or professional athletes in general, and for those who observe them. I remember one of the first NBA games I attended. It was a home game in Florida. There was a certain family section in the arena where they seated all the basketball players' wives and family members for the games ("the family section" they called it). I remember walking carefully down the steps of the arena that day and looking over at the wives who were already seated in the family section, and I had a poisonous, judgmental, and arrogant thought. I remember thinking at that time, "I will never be like them." I went on meditating and thinking, "I will never do the things they do." My never-to-do list that I made in my own strength, and with no reliance on God, became an, I-did-it-all list. God literally says in His word, "Judge not unless you be judged and with the same measure you judge, it will be measured back to you" (Matt. 7:1–2). Well people, I judged them without knowing anything about them or the hell they were going through and had already suffered for years. The word of God proved to be true! I judged, and I was judged with a greater measure. I did end up regretting judging them, I finally got an opportunity to know them and understood their pain soon enough. And although I don't agree with everything they did, I was not their judge. I quickly found out these women who were dolled up and looking like stars on a television screen just to attend a basketball game were not dressing the part to impress any of us looking at them. There is a silent and deadly pressure that comes with that lifestyle to look and appear a certain way at all times—or suffer severe rejection, humiliation, and the very real possibility of being outcasts, even by the woman's own husband.

I ended up meeting the reality of those pressures eventually in this lifestyle, and everything about me changed, inside and out. I didn't become an arrogant diva to try to impress people or get others to envy me; I did it because I truly believed that was the only way in "Hollywood" and the way to save my marriage. I was, however, wrong. These wives had been through a lot, and some of them warned me about the vile attacks against the marriages of those playing in professional sports. I met women who had miscarried their child when they got the devastating news that their spouse had committed adultery and gotten another woman pregnant. Others had attempted suicide and had to be cared for by a doctor at their house because it posed too much risk for the public and media to find out what was really going on in the lives of the basketball players. Still others had to be separated from their husbands while they made the decision to leave them for a younger woman. Some were constantly dealing with their husbands' extramarital affairs on a regular ongoing basis. Other women totally succumbed to the pressures and permitted their husbands to have sex with other women and even live in different houses from them in order to do it. Welcome to Hollywood—the closest thing to hell on earth, yet so many people erroneously want to be a part of it.

I later understood these women married to basketball players as time went on, and we often consoled one another because we didn't really have anyone else to go to, especially given the unique challenges in the Hollywood lifestyle. Other women were either too naïve to know what was really going on in our "hell on designer heels" life, while others were the very groupies working to destroy our then-marriages and families by luring away these rich husbands with seductive speech, tight clothes, and mouths that only told them what they wanted to hear. As wives of professional athletes, we didn't have it easy like many people erroneously believed. We actually had it harder than most wives ever would. Sure, we had money, but money didn't fix that, just like it didn't fix most of the

other problems destroying us and our families. I know that some
women marry men only because they are in the NBA or rich. That
is painfully obvious, yet some men stick their heads in the sand,
pretending the prostitute they married really loves them. However,
most of the women I met were with their husbands because they
really loved them, and they were with their husbands long before
they became rich or famous, like I was. I sympathized with them.
I became them and suffered from the same pains they did. We
were not evil, stuck-up women as many judged us. We were broken
women, in pain deeper than what most people will ever have to
experience in their lives, and for the most part we were doing the
best we could playing the role Hollywood tries to give every rich
man's wife.

Remaining Supportive

I still felt as a family, like we were dodging a lot of Hollywood-
lifestyle bullets that first year, however, and things were going
fairly well in my marriage then. I was still a very supportive wife. I
was the Queen of support, encouragement, and reassurance. That
part of marriage I enjoyed especially. (I told you I wanted to be a
counselor.) I loved the fact that my spouse would confide in me.
Keeping the line of communication open was extremely important, because I figured secrets could not be good. We remained
relatively close, despite the intense NBA basketball schedule. We
made time for us to spend together. He would have me pick him
up from the local private-plane airport where the team would land
after away games. I would go to this airport at 3:00 a.m. to pick him
up after his basketball road trips. When we got home, his meal was
already cooked if he wanted to eat after traveling. All the shopping
was done, and the house was clean. He would ask me to go on the
road to away games at first, and I went, believing he needed me,
and therefore, I was going to be there for him. This also meant
I could not attend the University I originally wanted to when we

arrived in Florida earlier, or pursue a meaningful career. All I had time for was to take care of my family. I had taken care of Zaire, my spouse and the house constantly. I didn't have time to take care of me and them, and I slowly but surely was losing time to have a relationship with God. I began praying less and less, and the door to sin began to open more and more. But I was so blinded, I didn't see it coming. All I wanted was for us to be a happy family and stay together. And I was willing to do anything to make that happen. My self-efforts to keep together what I didn't join together how-ever, proved futile, as you will come to better understand later on.

With all the success and all the money, I knew something was still bothering my spouse. One day he came home after work and laid his head in my lap on the couch. He told me that no matter how hard he worked and how well he did, it seemed like other play-ers in the league were getting all the attention. Before he could tell me who they were, I knew. These two were all over the news. I listened, and when I noticed tears, my heart began to hurt for him. While he was still speaking, I silently, on the inside of me, began praying to God that he would get the fame and credit he desired. I have literally cried profusely over the results of making that prayer and it being answered.

I should have prayed the way Jesus did right before He was crucified. Jesus didn't want to suffer the pain of the cross, but He wanted our sins to be forgiven and our diseases to be healed, and the only way to do that was for him to die in our place and be beaten nearly to death to cure our infirmities. Jesus, however, was in human flesh, and the Messiah asked God three times to take that cup of affliction (the crucifixion) from Him before He was crucified. But despite His desires, He had the wisdom and humility to finish His prayer by saying, "But nevertheless, Your will be done, Father, not Mine" (Luke 22:42, emphasis mine). This is why it is important to study the Word of God for ourselves. At that time, however, I was too busy studying basketball stats to be doing anything meaningful like praying to God. I prayed for the fame, without praying for God's will to be done (which is better than any plan we can ever come up with). This mistake was costly. Indeed, God answered, and the fame came. And as it came, "us" as I knew it was being destroyed.

Camera!

I realized that once that fame came into our lives, Hollywood sank her teeth into us deeply, and because of loving the praises of men more than the praises of God, the bite was lethal. Fame, without God, opened up another gateway to hell, like nothing I had ever witnessed before. Fame by itself isn't bad—not when God calls you to be famous. Jesus is famous, so know for sure that fame isn't evil. The reasons someone has for wanting to be famous, however, can be extremely evil and thus extremely detrimental. I mean, we had experienced a taste of fame just coming into that lifestyle, but not like what was to come. I prayed that prayer that day in ignorance, and I never asked God for His wisdom to deal with fame, and fame, with Hollywood indeed dealt with me.

Dealing with Fame while Fame Dealt with Me

It's here. Fame didn't even knock at the door, it just seemed to come right in. (I suppose that prayer gave it a key to our lives.) Everything was changing again—and more drastically and more quickly. People began to notice my then-spouse everywhere we went. He was being featured on television more and more. The media began announcing how much money we had, and how we had went up the latter of success, basically glorifying us. We went from being noticed to being worshiped. And the money, coupled with fame, had strange men, and strange women, coming from every direction too. When I say, strange men or strange women, I am referring to what is often called "gold diggers" or "groupies", those seeking rich men or rich women for money. God calls it an immoral or strange woman (See Proverbs 7). For strange women, the people who are rich and famous are considered their prey. Both the male and female versions of this specific type of immoral person exist and are especially seductive and very skilled at saying the so-called "right thing" all the time. They tend to largely be yes-people, and when they do say no to anything, that is a part of the overall scheme to not look like who they really are—people who don't love any-one, not the rich man or woman, not themselves, and certainly not God. They do, however, love money. They have no regard for marriage and family, and it becomes a trophy and a point of pride for them, the more rich men they can take advantage of—destroy-ing their marriages and their children's lives in the process—with absolutely no regard for the sins they are committing or the pain they are causing. They operate in a lot of deception. They are will-ing to seduce men into affairs, but what every man and woman on earth should know, in addition to knowing Jesus, is that a strange woman who will cheat *with* you, will DEFINITELY cheat *on* you. This doesn't depend on the strange woman, either. Men don't tame strange women. They are wild, and like everything else wild, they can't be tamed. God can transform them, but without God, he or she will be someone who used to cheat *with* you, and now they cheat *on* you as long as you stay with them. I remember one day joking with God and telling God, "You and Richard Gere who starred in Pretty Woman are the only people who can change a strange woman into a house wife." Pretty Woman's the movie classic where a lady played by Julie Roberts is a prostitute and ends up a one la-dies man after meeting Richard Gere. Then God made me laugh hard because He reminded me that even in that movie, Gere didn't change that woman; they were only acting.

The only thing sadder than a strange woman or strange man is that the rich and famous often know that strange women or man is a lie, but they keep at it with these prostitutes anyway. They begin operating in the lies and deception with them, confusing deception with reality and ending up trapped with them. Some have married them, just like Richard Geer did in *Pretty Woman*, but with one difference: the woman in the movie was acting like a strange woman, but the strange women in these rich men's lives truly are immoral women who know how to act. They act like they love them, act like their jokes are funny, and even that their gas doesn't stink. Now, ladies, if a man you loved left you for a strange woman, please understand that the strange woman is what he deserves. God told me one day that a man under God's wrath is the man who ends up with the strange women (Prov. 22:14). God has said that an unfaithful man deserves to be with a strange woman and her steps lead to hell, death and poverty. The strange woman came for money, and God is saying, "money she will get," and poverty will be the unfaithful man's portion, because that man chose lusting after an immoral woman rather than loving God and his wife.

In other words, these strange women are the judgment of God. So don't pray them out of their lives; let God keep them there for as long as it takes God to judge their wickedness. God is a just God, and a just Judge (Ps. 7:11). This is God's judgment for this type of evil behavior. Remember, I'm just the messenger—don't shoot me. Be of good cheer, daughters of God, who have experienced this painful ordeal, while that is an unfaithful man's judgment, the blessing for you is this: God says you deserve better. The unfaithful man didn't leave you and go be with an immoral woman for your detriment. He left you and went into a deep grave, unless God saves him. God surely has something and someone better for you. Again, God is telling you, "You deserve better, and better I have for you." Don't ever settle for a lick off the sucker, when you can own the candy store, like my granny often says. You let God give you His best. It will make you rich even in joy, and God will add no sorrow with it (Prov. 10:22).

I noticed that when the truth sets in about fake people with ill motives who flock toward someone just because they are rich and famous, those who loved to be worshiped like a god by these phonies find out what it's like to be God, and they end up wanting out of that deal with the devil they made. I certainly did. While it's true, that people glorified God, it is also true that they crucified Him (John 12:13, 19:17–30). The same crowd of people who yelled, "Hosanna" when Jesus walked the streets of the earth are the same crowd who yelled out, "Crucify Him" to the judge sentencing Jesus to be put to a most painful death. I was trying to deal with all this newfound fame, but it was more like fame was dealing with me. All normality went out the door, and there seemed to be no door we could enter without people noticing us.

Peer Pressure Has a Pulse

I know often times people are taught that peer pressure is something dealt with in adolescent years, but after experience, I disagree. Peer pressure doesn't die after high school graduation. It has a pulse well into adulthood, and I believe its heart beats stronger against the rich and famous in the world. Once we became more famous, more peer pressure came like never before. My husband told me how, early on after he became more famous, other professional athletes would tell him how to cheat without getting caught. I remember he came home one day and shared this with me about a particular player who explained how he rented cars in someone else's name to avoid getting caught cheating on his wife. People began telling us that the cars we drove (we both had a Cadillac then) weren't good enough for where we were. Pressure came to get more expensive cars like other people in that lifestyle. We were also told we should have an everyday car, a sporty car, a luxury car, the type of car that requires a driver, a truck because those cars are small, an old-school classic type of car, and the list went on—in order to keep up with the Joneses. We changed our cars. At one point we had about twenty cars! Our driveway looked like a car dealership. Then, after we made one of the worst investment someone can make—aka buying cars—that still wasn't good enough. Because keeping up with the Joneses required rims for every vehicle. Not just any rims—imported rims that cost more than some brand-new cars did. That still wasn't enough. After all, this is the lifestyle of the NBA, right? The cars needed to be customized, because the rule from peer pressure was that nobody could have a car just like yours. Yours must stand out. So we customized cars, putting in special stitching in the headrest and seats, tinting headlights and taillights, and the list went on, but the receipts went on longer. I know the people who sold us this nonsense were so glad they met someone so young and loaded with money. Pressure came to change even where we lived and to get a multimillion-dollar house instead. Thus, we moved. And the multimillion-dollar house cost us more than the sale price. The house was literally falling apart inside. (The worst thing was that I was inside the house, falling apart.)

There was also the overwhelming pressure to wear custom-made clothes. In one month, the accountant said that approximately $100,000 was spent on custom-made suits alone. Peer pressure didn't stop there. There was also the peer pressure that you cannot wear the same thing twice if the media was there to capture what you wore. So after spending way too much money on custom-made clothes, the only answer in order to remain caught up with the Joneses (whoever they are) was to throw those costly clothes away or give them to somebody else. That is called *WASTE!* The Bible says the prodigal son wasted all his natural father gave him on the pleasures of life (Luke 15:13). I wish I could tell you that the same wasn't true for us back then, but it was. It was a lot of waste. And while we were not supposed to love money, it was a sin to waste the wealth God gave. The peer pressure hit me in the area of clothes too, with brands. Every basketball player's wife has to wear certain brands and shop at certain stores, like Saks, Louis Vuitton, Burberry, and boutiques where they make only one of a certain garment so that nobody else will have on what you are wearing. The shoes had to be designer as well, and you didn't go get your hair done in that lifestyle unless you overpaid a hair stylist to come to you. The hair had to look a certain way too. That's why you see a lot of men and women on television looking alike. It's not because they are related or even know each other; it's because the same pressure in Hollywood that one is feeling, the other suffers from also.

In that lifestyle, someone doesn't just put on makeup. Instead, they pay a professional to put it on for them, and professionals over-charge tremendously for doing so. All that makeup, two-thousand-dollar shoes, ten-thousand-dollar purses, and a dress that costs more than four mortgage payments combined to go where? To a basketball game! WAW! (What a Waste)! I ended up dressed just like the same women I judged earlier when I went to one of the first NBA basketball games and glanced over at that family section. God said it: "Judge not, lest ye be judged" (Matt. 7:1–3). And people were judging me left and right.

Oh, and in that lie-style, don't get caught in a coach seat on a plane, lest the media get hold of it and report a "they must be on the verge of bankruptcy" story in the newspapers. There is nothing wrong with buying a coach seat on an airplane, and you don't have to be nearly bankrupt to have made such a decision. You could just not want to make the airlines richer for a two hour flight! Again, there is nothing wrong with a first-class seat or an expensive gown, but there is something wrong with the mind-set of those who make people feel worthless if they don't buy it. There is something even more wrong with allowing Hollywood to make you feel worthless. But these pressures were common to the lifestyle. The people inside the lifestyle said to get the expensive stuff to matter, and people outside that lifestyle were judging that as stuck-up. Judgment and pressure was coming from every direction, and so were the cameras, watching us closely. With fame came this peer pressure I didn't even know existed when I lived a more simplified life back in Milwaukee. Unfortunately, peer pressure wasn't the only ill effect to riches and fame.

The NBA was a magnet for groupies and gold diggers, aka those seeking a handout. Some have said that prostitution is the oldest profession and due to unfaithful rich and famous men, it may very well be. They were pretty easy to spot, even from a distance. They typically were the only women in the room or arena wearing barely any clothes. I'm in law school now, and I was thinking when I reflected back on this that they must have surely known some loopholes in the laws on the crime of indecent exposure, because they are the only people I am aware of who could wear nothing in public and not be arrested for it. This seductive spirit in these women was strategic. They did whatever they had to do to get money from rich men, even if that meant coming after the wife.

One night, I went to a nightclub after a basketball game and had an encounter with a groupie like none before. In sum, she hit me in the face—and that was all, folks! When it was over, I felt I had taken her down for all the wives who ever had to deal with a groupie before. This particular groupie (who was a regular, persistently after NBA players' money—not them, but their money), was actually bold enough to hit me in my face! When she did, I almost thanked God that she did it, because I was thinking, "I am going to mop the floor with this witch, and take out on her everything that every one of these whores has caused my family and me to suffer." When I did, they almost had to shut the nightclub down because it took about five or six NBA players just to get me off that woman. When it was over, I had wiped seduction off her face, while I, however, was more de-stressed. Trying to destroy my family was one thing, but hitting me was going too far; it was the last bit of disrespect I could tolerate that day. Also, I was protective regarding my marriage and family then. It was still at that point in my life a god to me.

I realized later in my relationship with God that the real fight wasn't ever a physical one; it was spiritual. I know God told me right, because later on there were groupies and gold diggers who came to hurt me way worse than any physical wound ever could. Some did things to my marriage and children that severely wounded the children and me. It took a long time to recover from the devastating effects their transgressions had on me and on my two children. The overcoming of their hurt took spiritual warfare, and God surely gave me victory when I engaged it the way He taught me to, with prayer, faith in God's word, trust in His justice and even fasting some times. God said there are some things people will only be free from with both praying and fasting (Matt. 17:21). So right now, I pray for those women who have chosen the lifestyle of a groupie or gold digger. I pray that you will repent to God, begin to see yourself as God intends for you to be, and respect yourself, thereby causing others to respect you, in Jesus name. I pray God will forgive your sins, remember them no more, and give you a beautiful marriage and family without sorrow, and I pray that you come to know the true joys of serving God, experiencing His love, and knowing your worth in Jesus name.

Looks Aren't Everything, Are They?

All of a sudden, with the fame, the way your body looked became extremely important. This was especially true for women, and in Hollywood it is crazy! In Hollywood's mind, if a woman isn't so thin that the wind can take her away, then she is considered overweight. The pressure is incredible to be a certain weight and look a certain way. All-Star Weekend, all by itself, was proof of that. (By the way, NBA All-Star Weekend happens when some of the more skilled players in the NBA are selected to participate in the All-Star basketball game, or various other skill activities). I remember having ready what I believed I would wear and how I would look. It wasn't long after that that I was told what clothes to wear, what designer needed to have made my shoes and clothes, what jewelry had to be imported in and how many bundles of hair extensions I needed. At first glance, someone may have believed it was a dream come true. But all it did was tell me without ever having to say the words, "You, and how you are, is not good enough," and to be good enough, we have to change everything about you. This weighs heavy on a person's mind and self-esteem. I tried for a while to believe that I don't care what they think about me, but the truth was I *did* care. And because I cared, it hurt all the more.

Men in that lifestyle don't have it easy, either. Hollywood wants the man so rich that he has more than enough money to invest in cocaine and secure an overdose for himself, and whatever money is left, he can give to the strange woman, who sleeps with more men than a full-time prostitute. And when the rich man falls, Hollywood will be present right by his bedside, but not to comfort him—to criticize him, and judge him, thus personally walking him over to the ledge to encourage him to take the jump and kill himself. Hollywood has put many needles in people's arms, forced the cocaine up their nostrils, and loaded the weapon that they used to take their own lives. Then afterward, you hear Hollywood calling the death a "shocking tragedy" at the funeral. But that's a lie. Hollywood isn't shocked at all, because she played the lead role in causing the rich man and rich woman's death—and very often their divorce. Hollywood wants you to dress the part that it swears it gave you just to threaten to take it from you if you disagree with its lifestyle traits. Legislators may not have been just enough to make the evils of Hollywood unlawful, but God surely has Hollywood on trial, having found that witch guilty before the foundations of the world. And this wicked, perverse, and deceptive spirit will pay for all the blood it shed, souls it caused to be lost, lives it took, holiness it forsook, suicides it facilitated, spirits it crushed, hope it deferred, making hearts sick, overdoses it caused, lies it knowingly told, truths it vehemently covered, divorces it caused, abortions it advocated for, and overwhelming pressures it caused people throughout the years.

Know that this spirit of Hollywood is not one of those things in life where you tell yourself, "I am strong or smart enough to handle it correctly." Nor is it something someone should be prideful about and think, "It happened to them, sure, but not me." I fell into that trap of pride, and only God was able to get me out of the hole Hollywood dug for my soul, life, family, finances, and children. Believe me, this is the type of game you win by never playing it. The opponent cannot devour those who will not play with him. It is an automatic win with the wisdom of God, requiring no effort on your part, because while you rest in God, God alone fights that evil giant for you, defeating it, and giving you victory! I truly believe Jesus is the only way to win. The fight isn't about strength. There are just some wars you were never called to fight, and we need to thank God for this rather than envy those who have went into that lifestyle, only to realize to their detriment that their dream of "making it" is in actuality a nightmare from which they don't know how to awaken. All their money and all their fame has no power to awaken them from this hell...from this Hollywood. Now, although it wasn't ever my dream to be a part of this lifestyle of the rich and famous, I ended up there anyway, and I nearly died because of it. Welcome to Hollywood!

Handouts

With the fame, along came the media, making public our estimated net worth. This opened up the floodgates for problems and stress, both financially and marital.

I truly believe we were thrust into this Hollywood lifestyle with no preparation for the truth about what really happens in it. Nobody gave us any training or skills to prepare us to survive as sheep amongst the numerous wolves in this lifestyle of the rich and famous. Nobody gave us any wisdom about how to deal with hangers-on, those wanting us to hand out the wealth God had given us—to them. They were the countless so-called friends. Although there were a multitude of them, there were basically two types of them. The pure leech, take-all-they-can-take type was one. Then there were the not-so-obvious leeches, who I called "bad-deal-making buddies." That type was a bit more crafty and manipulative than the first. They constantly had some terrible idea for us to use the money God gave us. The ideas they came up with varied, but the underlying theme was always the same. Some so-called friend with absolutely no wisdom at all wanted to take a ton of our money and invest it in some "great" business idea they had! These are clever devils. They come with a speech, always promising that the rich will get richer. They get money from the wealthy by using greed to lure them in, asking them, "Don't you want more money?" They are full of it. Most of them were guys from the "hood," but some of them were basketball agents and lawyers too. Some of these devils were very educated and used their education to push fear off on us, saying, "If you don't do it now something may happen to you, how will you take care of your family?" The end goals were built on the same foundations with them all: greed. For the most part, I discerned that they were full of it. I wasn't the only one making decisions, though, so one of those deals cost us millions of dollars.

As evil as the hanger-ons manipulative behavior was, the real problem was that I succumbed to that manipulation, and I did so often and for many years. The more I gave these so-called friends, the more they took. And no matter what I gave, it was never enough. Eventually, it got to the point where I could not give any more, and they all left me. They stopped calling and stopped coming over to visit. My behavior then was a textbook example of operating in error. God said, "Owe one another nothing, except to love one another" (Rom. 13:8). Interestingly, I didn't often get asked for love—just for money and material possessions. It was very painful hearing almost everyone around me telling me they loved me, and for me to know it was a lie. That money-hungry virus infected many people whom I knew and loved, after the money and the fame came. Or more accurately, the virus was always there inside them, lying dormant, and the money coupled with the fame just drew it out. The love of money truly brings out the worst in people. It certainly did for me. And as evil as the love of money is, fame combined with it can cause people to do more evil and harm to someone than the devil himself. People often refer to success in an area as "being on fire." You may have heard someone referring to a basketball player who is making a lot of shots in a game as "he is on fire." Or maybe you have heard someone say that a person who is really passionate for God is "on fire for God." Well, in our life, a lot was on fire. We seemed to be "on fire" in riches, material possessions, and fame, but everything that really mattered in life was turning to ashes.

Ashes!

My housekeeper found a cell phone hidden inside our summer home in Matteson, Illinois. When she handed me the phone, I immediately felt something was wrong. I felt scared. As much as I wanted to just put the phone back and act like I didn't ever see it, I picked up the phone and looked inside. I found phone numbers for women in the entire phone. There was not a single contact that was male. I began dialing the numbers back. We ended up separated that summer for some time. The very foundation of the marriage had been shaken. And with each passing day, I grew more and more hurt and desperate to save my family, but things were going to get much worse before we saw a glimpse of better.

Thanksgiving

Broken but surviving, I was back in Miami to try and save that marriage, hoping and praying that our family would stay together. When I prayed to God to fix my marriage, all I felt God telling me was to follow God completely. I wanted to follow God then, but not if it meant losing my husband. So I kept on living a lie and taking long showers, lying on the floor of the shower of a multimillion-dollar house, wishing I could just die. It fills my eyes with tears almost instantly when I think about women going through this same hell, both inside and outside this lifestyle.

Holidays used to be a time of joy and gladness, but even they had turned violent. One Thanksgiving, Zaire wouldn't stop crying and "Mr. Fist" as he called himself then, punched him in the chest, and I watched my young son slide across the floor of our home ruining more than just our Thanksgiving. The love of money, the violence, the fame, evil, the strange women, they were a fire that consumed our family, leaving more ashes.

Fighting Alone and Feeling the Blows

I had gone from being the wife who was invited to attend games on the road trips, to not being allowed to go anymore. I was crushed. The rejection I began suffering was bad. I spent more nights sleeping alone than not.

The times we used to spend together when I picked up my spouse after a road trip were over. By then, limo-service drivers would go instead of me. I also was no longer needed to wash clothes because most of the clothes by then were professionally dry-cleaned, and the hired housekeeper cleaned whatever wasn't. Some may think of this as a privilege and won't at first understand my sorrow at that time. It wasn't a privilege; it was a replacement. I felt I could be replaced, and I was being replaced, slowly but surely.

The only thing I was able to make sure we didn't have was a chef, even though I was told to get one for our house as well. I refused, and I didn't obey. I kept cooking and intentionally never getting around to finding a chef. Cooking and raising my son was just about all I had left as a role in that house. Accountants came in and did some of the things I used to do, assistants were hired to run the errands I used to be responsible for, and thus, I wasn't needed for that, either. It was sad for me. I had made my family my life, and I lived to serve them. When all these things were taken from me and outsiders hired in my stead, I felt like I didn't have a life and wasn't needed. I felt very rejected and hurt. I didn't mind fighting for my family, but when I realized I was fighting alone; I was crushed.

Sowing Wild Oats

It didn't help to voice my hurt, either. In fact, that made matters worse. I got tired of being told, "I'm a grown fu——ing man, and I do what the f——k I want to do!" I was being torn down as a woman. Then I was hit with an overwhelming blow. I was told to my face, "I want to sow my wild oats, because I didn't get the chance to do so when we were younger." Those words cut me very deeply. I was literally broken. I felt like nothing. I had no self-esteem by then. I felt the pains of feeling and believing I was worthless. The disrespect had reached another dimension and was at an all-time high. I was separated from my spouse that summer too, and I spent most of my days alone with my son.

Leaving wasn't as easy as some might think. I was reminded of what had become a routine conversation: "This isn't your money, and if you leave, nobody is going to want you, and you aren't going to have anything without me. You will end up having to go back and live at your mama's house!" I tried leaving anyway. My debit and credit cards were cut off, and I didn't have access to any money for my son or me. My father had to provide for me so that I could afford to fly back to Miami and go home. One of the wives of professional athlete agreed that I could come live with them, if needed, and they even offered to lend me a car to drive. Most people had no idea of the hell I was going through "behind the scenes" in this Hollywood lifestyle. They couldn't see beyond the lights and past the cameras into the pile of ashes our lives had truly become behind closed doors. I wasn't living anymore—just existing. I was broken completely at that point.

Covering Up the Truth to Protect the Lies

I wasn't allowed to go to many places anymore, but I was often asked to go out in public for media interviews and to smile for the cameras, answering all the questions about how our marriage and family were doing great. This ended up taking a toll on me during one interview because I knew the truth. It was a media personnel who was conducting the interview asked me some sports questions for a while, and then she asked me a question about my marriage that was embedded with her own opinion, and that was it. She stood there telling me, "You must be so happy being married to him!" Right then, I had to run away and into the restroom. The tears were pouring out of me, and I could not stop crying. I had to go inside the actual stall to avoid having the other ladies inside the restroom see me cry. Needless to say, that interview was ruined.

Hollywood has many rules, but here's it's number one: Everyone must keep quiet about whatever goes on behind the scenes, no matter what the costs are because it's not about who you really are; it's about your image (who people think you are). I believed that in the Hollywood lifestyle, more time, money, and effort goes into building an image than what goes into building entire countries. As much as I would have liked to have answered God's call and allowed God to heal me at that time, I didn't. And I knew I couldn't beat them in this lifestyle. So in error, I joined them.

Desperate Times Called for Desperate Measures

I was desperate to save my marriage and was willing to do anything to make that happen. I do mean *anything.*

I wasn't a "yes" wife. Those were the wives who said yes to their rich and famous husbands, no matter what! If he said he was going to sleep with other women, they said "yes", and if he said he was going to stay out for days at a time, they said, "yes." I was different. I was a "yes," when you are right" and a "no, when you are wrong" type of wife. I was the kind of wife that kept everybody grounded whenever egos tried to take off like a Boeing 757 plane. But as the saying goes, desperate times called for desperate measures.

I was tired of fighting and feeling alone. I tried to be a "yes" wife. This however, made me feel more low and worthless than at all times before. I remember I rented a hotel room at the Mandarin Oriental in Miami and invited my husband. I seriously contemplated, and I planned to just give up and say, "I don't care if you sleep with other women." The plan was in motion, but when he got to the hotel, I couldn't do it. I really loved him, so I couldn't go this far down.

Then I just tried saying yes to whatever ideas he brought my way in every other area. I would still be honest, but I would not ever push or make any decisions anymore. In one of the deals, there were several million dollars lost. I warned him against it, but I backed off completely and let him do whatever he wanted without my pushing in any one direction.

I also tried to change the way I looked. I got breast implants and weight-loss surgery in California. (And some of you may wondered how do so many famous woman just have a baby, and then look so thin so fast? *Lipo, tummy tucks, breast lifts*—you name it, Hollywood's buying it!) I'm not judging anyone; I got some things tucked, lifted, and sucked! Truthfully, the only thing I regretted about that was the intention behind why I did it, trying to impress a man, and also the fact that I had the surgery before my second son, because once I had him gravity and nature took its course, and what went up, surely went back down! (I'm laughing now, thank God!)

I thought if I looked like the kind of woman he described to me that he liked, then I could please him and save our marriage. I had become very desperate. The hole inside of me didn't get any smaller, however; it only grew deeper.

I tried stuffing the hole with material things, and I was changing inside more and more with each passing day and the outside kept changing too. I started wearing sunglasses that were so big they provided shade for my eyes, cheeks, forehead, and a part of my upper lip, nearly! But you couldn't tell me anything though because I was dressed for the part of a basketball wife. I stopped fighting Hollywood and just became a part of it. What a waste of space and money! I bought anything I laid my eyes on that I wanted, I had hired drivers, I flew only first class and private planes became a personal favorite. I was trying to force myself to like the lifestyle I was in. I had even paid people to be my friend just to avoid being alone. Deep down I felt that they weren't really my friends, but bad company was better than being alone at that time.

I had begun looking down on others to make myself temporarily not feel like the dust on the ground. God showed me that I had done all of this because my self-esteem was nonexistent back then. I was completely empty without God, so I just kept trying to stuff the hole inside of my heart and soul where God belonged, with material possessions and even people. It was a very sad time in my former life, and getting sadder.

There I was, all the money someone could ask for, material possessions overflowing, and alone at an abortion clinic. I had not made this baby alone, but I was left alone to murder it. I sat in a room with women who probably didn't have a million dollars, but their husbands were there with them inside the waiting room, holding their hands and supporting them through that tragic and traumatic event. Amazingly, I wasn't too tired to stop fighting, but I was exhausted with fighting these important matters alone. I was exhausted with money and image meaning more than everything else in life. It was more important that the media did not get wind of the fact that two people who were well able to care for a child were aborting it instead than it was the child. After that, I couldn't take it anymore. Thank You, God, for forgiving me for such a godforsaken act. Thank You, Jesus, for dying for this sin too, and remembering it no more (Heb. 8:12).

Temptation Was Tempting

By that time, one of my so-called friends suggested to me one day to cheat on my spouse. They told me they would bring the specific guy they had in mind to me, whom they had already reached out to in case I wanted to do it. That conversation was incredibly sad to me. I figured if someone close to me had begun suggesting for me to cheat, then the marriage must have been looking pretty bad to them—which is remarkable because we had become professionals at hiding the truth from the public to avoid the loss of any endorsements and income (the love of money at its best). The temptation had not ceased and was far from over. I flew out of Chicago, where the so-called friend arranged an affair for me (the lifestyle of the rich and famous) and I flew back to Miami, but temptation was already there too waiting on me. A new basketball season had begun again, and I had grown closer with another wife of an NBA player, whose name I simply won't mention here to protect her. She had secretly been through hell with her spouse. The only people who really knew what she was suffering were her, her spouse, the mistresses he was having affairs with, and me.

She had had enough of the adultery and disrespect. She was having an affair of her own. She made a point to tell me the guy wasn't rich at all. He worked a nine-to-five job and didn't earn anywhere near what her spouse did financially, but he was there for her and treated her with some *apparent* respect and honor. That's what she wanted—to be loved, respected, and honored—and when her spouse refused to give her what he owed her, she went elsewhere and got it. She actually sounded happy again. Everything her spouse had refused to give her, she found in another man. She stopped questioning him about staying out late at night all the time, and leaving home for days without letting her know where he was. She simply gave up that fight and responded to her spouse's evil with evil of her own. She suggested that I do the same and be done with being hurt, broken, lonely, disrespected, and humiliated. Even after all of that, the temptation continued. I had a personal assistant who noticed what was going on and came to me when my spouse wasn't home. She explained to me how I could have an affair and get away with it. She even told me I would feel better and wouldn't be so sad anymore over what my spouse was doing to me and how he was treating me. She told me I would not be lonely anymore. She was extremely specific. She told me to make sure that it was a man with whom the sex would be good, and that it be the kind of sex where the only thing I would have the strength left to do when it was over, was grab a Pepsi from the nightstand and drink it. She told me if I needed a Pepsi to drink afterward, the affair was worth it. From then on, I noticed that she would, out of the blue, say to me in front of my spouse, "If you are thirsty, just grab a Pepsi." She and I knew what she was referring to, but my spouse didn't. Then, a teammate of my spouse suggested that I have an affair right after a basketball game while still inside the Miami Heat Arena. Temptation was coming from all directions all of a sudden, and I didn't know what to do. I certainly did not pray.

I intentionally tried to love another man. Being around him made me not feel as low as I did when I was around all the "big shots" in Hollywood. I was desperate, I told you. I wanted to leave my spouse, and I thought that if I could put this guy in the place in my heart where my spouse used to stay, I could avoid ending our marriage in divorce by ending the pain I was feeling. The hole and the emptiness I felt from what was happening in my marriage at that time were pushing me to divorce him. But I loved him, loved my marriage, and loved our family. I also believed that he needed me, even if he no longer said it. And on top of that I was afraid to leave.

So I stayed, and I tried to stuff the hole inside my heart a bit more so when my spouse said he wasn't coming home, it didn't hurt as much as it used to. The problem is, I wasn't healed I was avoiding the problem and pretending it wasn't hurting. And the sick solution I chose to the terrible problem I was forced to face was making everything worse, not better. This so-called love I was trying to feel was not love at all. It was sin. And the wages of sin is death (Rom. 6:23). Actions have consequences. Inactions also have consequences, so be wise, honor God, and be mindful of your actions and your inactions...because they are not without consequence. It is written, "Whatsoever a man sows that he shall also reap" (Gal. 6:7). I had sown a seed of sin to God, dishonoring God, and disregarding my marriage. I had no right to do it. I learned his wrong didn't make me right, and it certainly did not excuse what I had done. But God's hand was upon my life, no matter how much I tried to run from God, to avoid answering His clearly heard call. God caused me not to go any further with that guy, and without need of anyone else, God told me to stop now. A feeling came over me of literal dirtiness. I felt dirty and ashamed very strongly. I also remember feeling like I wanted to hide from God. As the thought of my feelings back then came to me, God reminded me about Adam and Eve in the Garden of Eden when they had sinned against God and ate from the tree in the garden. When God spoke to them, they ran, feeling naked (exposed, in other words) and ashamed. Sin has the same ill and deadly effect.

Thankfully, with Jesus Christ, we can be cleansed of all our sin and completely forgiven for every sin we ever committed (1 John 1:7). I thank God that's what I did. I went back to God and prayed for God to help me get out of the grave I had essentially dug for myself. God did just that, and he did it instantly. And God showed me clearly what I thought was love was just another desperate measures because of the love that I had for my spouse. This may happen more often than people realize or are willing to admit. Some people think they are in love with someone else in a desperate attempt to save their hurting marriage. Rather than divorce their spouse because of the spouse's neglect, they spend time and think they are in love with someone else who is able and willing to give them what they feel they're missing. This gives a false sense of "no longer missing anything." It can cause people to wrongfully believe that now they are whole, and they are getting what they desired, so they can stay and fight for their marriage in less pain—by having another person fill the hole inside of them that is causing that pain and leading to the break down of their marriage. I have been there, and that isn't the way. I especially am speaking to women. It's not the way. The only way for any of us to be whole is with Jesus Christ. God made us, so He knows how to heal and restore us, and I know from personal experience and for a fact that God wants to heal us and restore us completely. Although I am speaking about me, I feel God is especially speaking to women. God is ready to make you whole, and He has seen what broken housewives have been suffering. Please, get in the Word of God for yourself and get to know God and how much He loves you. God is waiting on you to seek Him, because it is His good pleasure to give you what He knows already that you have need of and desire. God loves you very deeply. This I know for sure too, because I have been there.

I knew God was calling me, but I was calling my husband. At that time I wasn't going anywhere without him—not going to God, not into my destiny, nowhere. I swore I did this because I loved him, but this was not love. Love cannot exist without God, because God is love. I realized later in life that I did not cling to my former husband because of so much love, but because of idolatry also. Initially, I just placed him before God, but idolatry, like any other sin, took me farther than I imagined it would. Before long, I didn't just put him before God, I had made *him* a false god to me. (I thank God for Jesus Christ who has saved me from sin and myself.) This idolatry I once had for my spouse caused me to totally and completely rely on him for emotional stability and happiness. If he wasn't happy with me, then I wasn't happy with myself either. If he didn't behave like he loved me, then I was not worthy of being loved. If he said something about my appearance, I went and got plastic surgery. If he didn't want to be with me, then I felt I should die. I put entirely too much pressure on him to make me happy and make me feel loved, beautiful, and worthy.

And the more I demanded, the more I believed I made him feel like a failure because he was called by God to do and accomplish many things in his life, but being God was, and still isn't, one of them. Wives, husbands were never meant to be your god. There is only one true and living God, and it's Jesus Christ, the Messiah—not your spouse. And if you find yourself suicidal, depressed, oppressed, feeling unworthy, and staying in a relationship while being abused by your husband, you should make certain that it is not because of idolatry. Set both you and your husband free, and repent to God right now in Jesus name for any form of idolatry for your husband or anyone else. Now is the time. Tomorrow is not promised to you, or your marriage, so be free now. And there is no way to be free but through Jesus. So pray in the name of Jesus, or don't waste time praying. Praying in Jesus's name will get you what you need. Praying in another name of a false god will get you nothing worth having. Your marriage doesn't have to end up the way my then-marriage did. If you have breath in your body and a heart to perceive the truth pouring out of me, then right now ask God to fix what you both have broken, in Jesus's name. Perhaps my former marriage died so that yours can live. Take heed to the words God is speaking through me, and just obey God.

Having Understanding and Putting It All into Perspective
I'm not saying that notoriety and money doesn't have its proper place in the world, but it should not ever have a place in your heart—or your soul, either. This is not a poverty-over-prosperity

preaching! God Himself said that He wants us to prosper and be in good health, even as our soul prospers (3 John 1:2). The key of the scripture, within the context of what we are learning here, is that God will prosper you but as your soul prospers. Which means that God does not mind providing us with earthly possessions, but not at the cost of our souls. You see, God loves you for you and not because of anything you possess, or any award bestowed upon you from man, or how educated you might be. And if God ever has to choose between you losing some things, or people, on this earth, so that He doesn't lose you for eternity, say good-bye to whatever or whoever it is that is separating you from God. God simply will have no other God before Him (Exod. 20:3), and God doesn't want to lose you, because He loves you very deeply, well beyond what any of us will ever fully understand.

You should rejoice in God's love, because God loves you enough to not allow any misplaced feelings you may have for a car, career, or a strange woman in high heels to take you to hell. Jesus said it: "Where your treasure is, there your heart will be also" (Matt. 6:21). Where are the valuable treasures Jesus placed in you being sown the most? Is it in your car, is it in a mistress you have no business being with, or is it in your own family, and not in God? This misplacement leads to displacement—out of the will of God. But there is so much hope. Thanks be to Jesus, who forgives us and restores us when we repent and ask Him for forgiveness.

Again, I do not believe it is the will of God, those lies that religious spirits tell people, such as, they must be broke in order to be humble. You don't have to be living on the streets in order to not love money. You can have money, but money cannot have you. When money has people, that's where they go wrong and astray from God. When money is controlling them, that's the curse. I have dined with entertainers and swum laps in a pool with my name etched into the bottom of it, but when my marriage was being destroyed and the best friend I had grown up with was no more, and my heart went beyond broken to completely shattered, and my reputation was ruined, and the same so-called friends I gave hundreds of thousands of dollars showed up to testify against me, and the same media person that once shook my hand, was making sure he videotaped me being hand-cuffed to try and humiliate me, I realized money and fame is a curse beyond measure without God. Money was still present, and fame had not departed from me, but I could finally see it for what it was worth—nothing at all without God!

Like God revealed one day through my sister in Christ, Martha, you can't take a dollar bill and then tape it over your broken heart like a Band-Aid, expecting it to heal or fix it, because it just won't. I tell you these truths with both conviction and credibility. I have experienced great wealth, fame, and material things in abundance, people catering to you, and having a false sense of power. I've traveled and dined with what the world called "stars." I've been sought after by Hollywood and met people I once only watched on television. I tell you, after having experienced it all, it means *nothing* without God. It is worth *nothing*! And it will always be *nothing* without God! It is an empty, dark hole many go in and never climb out of. It is the very opposite of purpose; it is vanity. It is the opposite of real; it is fake at its finest. Don't ever envy the monetarily wealthy. I think I've seen more bankrupt rich people than angels have seen wings! I learned some time ago that someone can be very wealthy in their wallet and bankrupt in their soul and character. It will never profit a person to gain even the entire world and lose his or her soul (Matt. 16:26).

I did not have the luxury of reading these truths somewhere when I so desperately needed to. Instead, I went into the trenches of the Hollywood lifestyle and suffered the excruciating pain of realizing that all those material and shallow things many people in the world are seeking after, and believing that once they have them, then they have a life worth living, are truly the definition of rock bottom, unhappiness, many sorrows, suicide, depression, and hopelessness. It is a curse that only God Himself can remove and deliver people from. Be wise with the road you choose to take in life. Mankind, and what's on television, doesn't define success. God, who created success, failure, and man—*He* defines success. And I have learned that a man or woman who has everything by the world's definition of success but doesn't have God; they still feel very empty inside, void, hopeless, and depressed. And often times for that person with that wealth, there is nobody to turn to, because likely most of the people around them don't understand their cry and their brokenness, because of their belief that nothing could be wrong with a person who has everything money can buy. This deception in people has left the broken, wealthy man and woman desolate of help and in deep despair that most people may not ever have to endure in their lifetime.

Nobody really helps the rich man (or woman) with the loneliness he feels, because an entourage surrounds him. To the eye, he appears to have many friends. The truth is, however, the wealthy man (and woman) are some of the loneliest and hurting people. It is a different kind of despair and pain to realize that, although a crowd of people surrounds you, you are alone, and none in the crowd really love you. They only love your money. A lot of times for the wealthy person, in this crowd of counterfeit lovers of money, is his or her own family—mothers, fathers, brothers, and sisters, etc. That pain only God can heal. I have been raped, I had to bury my only sibling, I got divorced and had both my children wrongfully taken from me, I lost my home and my health, my reputation was destroyed. But it was all nothing compared to pain I felt from the love of money. From that pain, I am still healing to this day. My heart goes out to the wealthy man and the wealthy woman, especially those with fame. I tell the wealthy woman and man, forgive the one who didn't hear you cry, which was at the top of your lungs, and as you got all the way to the edge to jump, they didn't bother to pray for you. They instead gossiped about you, as if you were not human, with a heart and emotions like everyone else.

To the wealthy man and woman, I give this special word from God. God hears your cry. And God wants to heal your heart like He would anybody else's. God doesn't see your house; He sees your heart. God doesn't care about your possessions; He wants to heal that pain you've been silently carrying to avoid the harsh judgment from those around you and the media. God understands that money is nothing without Him. God understands you have everything you want, but none of what you need, and God will supply your needs. For needs are what you can't do without. Material things are what you know from personal experience you can do without. God understands that you have a lot of something; that means a lot of nothing. And God knows you have come to realize this truth, and God is merciful to your pain. Your cry has come up before God, and He hears, and He cares. God wants to heal you now. You're not crazy for not being satisfied with lots of money and material things, and you are not being ungrateful. You are made in the image and likeness of God.

God showed me this powerful truth one day. The Bible says Heaven's streets are paved in gold, and in Heaven, there are many mansions, yet God was not satisfied. Not until God created mankind in His image and likeness. When God created us, God created someone for Him to love, and someone to love Him back. And when God was done making creation, God said, "It is good." God is giving me another word from Him right now. In the Bible, God said, "And though I have all faith, so that I could move mountains, but have not love, I am nothing. And though I bestow all my goods (material possessions) to feed the poor, and though I give my body to be burned, but have not love, it profits me nothing" (1 Cor. 13:2–3). The revelation of this truth, having not love, means having nothing because of not having God. God is love (1 Cor. 13:1–3). A lot of wealthy people have learned this truth in the hardest way.

So, to the hurting who have money and material things, a lot of the pain you are feeling is because if you have not love and thus you have nothing. You are feeling the pain of having nothing, while appearing to have it all, which leads to nobody feeling any compassion for you and therefore you don't have any help to deal with one of the most difficult challenges mankind could ever face while on the earth. The most has come against you, but it feels like you have the least to help you with it. You are not exaggerating, and you are not "feeling sorry for yourself." Your struggle is real. God told me this truth one day, and it set me free from something that had bound me for a long time. When I cried out for help from a four-million-dollar prison that realtors called a single-family dwelling, people basically told me, "Go to hell, spoiled girl. You don't have any real problems. And stop feeling sorry for yourself. You're ungrateful." God told me they were the ones with the problem for not seeing the truth of what I was suffering, which a lot of wealthy people have secretly suffered from. God told me these people's feelings about the wealthy were misplaced because of their love for money, which caused them to believe the lie that once someone has money, their problems go away, and then life is good and the person is happy.

Although the prison I lived in cost $4 million, it was still a god-forsaken prison. When you think about it, a lot of prisons that hold convicted criminals cost millions of dollars to build and maintain. One of them is even on an island, I've heard: Rikers Island. How many people can say they have been on an island in their lifetime? But I'm certain that if you ask any prisoner inside of the multimillion-dollar island prison, "Would you like to stay?" they would tell you, "Absolutely not!" I know you may sense a bit of humor in this truth, but some of us have been so destroyed by the love of money and the lifestyle of the rich and famous that we intentionally are finding ways to laugh to keep from so much crying. I cried hard even as I wrote this, because I relived this truth as I reflected back on it. I thought about my future husband a lot too, as I wrote this. God feels your pain, has heard your cry, and surely God is healing you. I love you.

In sum, I had never in my life felt true emptiness until my bank account was full. And I know I am not alone in this feeling, as I have encountered countless people rich in their monetary possessions, and impoverished in their relationship with God, and other areas of life, that really matter. Understand that well before I ever was a millionaire, I had everything I could ever want or need. After the million dollars came, then all my dreams were crushed. It wasn't until I climbed the so-called ladder of success that I fell and hit rock bottom. I would have never guessed these places were one and the same before becoming wealthy and having fame. You see, the truth is that we are all alike, both rich and poor. There is no cure for cancer for the rich or the poor. And Jesus is the way for both the rich and the poor alike, and both the poor and the rich have a heart that can be broken. We've all felt grief, and we all feel joy. We've all felt afraid, and we all have been courageous. We all have lacked faith, and we all have dared to believe. We all have wants, and we all have needs. We have more in common that matters than we don't. So we should all stop looking down on one another, because we all do so from a position on the floor, compared to God's position!

I know the hard, cold truth now, and it cost me everything that ever meant anything to learn this lesson. If it wasn't for the pure love of God and His mercy for me, and the love God has for you all, who God knew would read this book, I would have been dead a long time ago, and you would have been reading the headline of a newspaper announcing that death. Right now when I was writing, I thought, it's as if money makes you choose. It's as if money won't let you have both. Choose money or choose God, your family, and the other things that matter in life. God came immediately and let me know, and had me tell you, it's not as if money wants you to choose, but a choice has to be made. You see, in the Word of God, Jesus says, "No one can serve two masters, for either he will hate the one and love the other, or else he will be loyal to the one and despise the other. You cannot serve God and mammon" (Matt. 6:24). Mammon is money. This revelation of having to make a choice is not imagined, it is very real. So a lot of wealthy people have gained the world and lost their souls, and that has profited them *nothing*.

When I tell you not to chase after riches, fame, and that lifestyle, I am essentially telling you to stop chasing after vanity, despair, and the excruciating pain that come with the realities of the lifestyle of the rich and famous. I'm saying chase after God, and let Him make you rich and add no sorrow with it (Prov. 10:22). I was learning this lesson slowly, but surely. I was learning there is a way that seems very right, but it can be deadly to a person and their relationship with God, when the way isn't God's way.

"There is a way that seems right to a man, but in the end that way leads to death" (Prov. 16:25).

IDENTITY CRISIS WITH
IDOLATROUS ROOTS

*There is a way that seems right to a man,
but in the end, it leads to death.*

—Proverbs 14:12

This identity crisis I had, and the revelation that God gave me while delivering me from it, is so powerful that it warrants its own chapter.

At that time, I thought that I just loved my husband very deeply. And I thought that the way I loved him, specifically, the way that I laid down my life for him, was right. But in the end, it led to death. What I experienced happens to a lot more people than I realized. This idolatry resembles love so closely that it can be very deceptive, having people tramped without even realizing they are held captive. Being imprisoned can be a terrible ordeal; however, being in prison without realizing you're there can be worse and even deadly.

At least the person in prison who realizes they are there can pray for release and freedom; however, someone who is held captive but thinks they are free will never pray or even allow someone to lead them out of bondage because, for them, the captivity doesn't exist. When I speak of prison and jail here, I am referring to the worst kind of bondage: spiritual bondage. This type of imprisonment extends well beyond the walls of Rikers Island, and it chains and binds the very soul of an individual, ruining their life from the inside out. It is much worse than any natural prison. There are plenty of people locked up behind the bars of a natural jail cell, but they are as free as Jesus Christ Himself! And there are people who walk outside on the streets daily but are completely bound and handcuffed to destructive habits, destroying their relationship with God, themselves, and everyone around them. God had me expose myself here, and what happened to me, so that those in need of freedom in this area of their life can be free to love God as well as others the way God calls us to, and not in the destructive way so many have done because of unrealized internal issues or society's so-called norms.

Idolatry is putting someone or something in the place in our lives where only God should be. It is a sin against God, and in a society that uses the word *idol* to bestow honor, many have been led astray believing that idolatry is honor (Exod. 20:3). Idolatry is, in fact, the exact opposite of honor; it is dishonor toward God and an invitation for destruction to the life and soul of anyone bound by its snares. Being in idolatry is a sure way to bring chaos and destruction into your life, because idolatry is rooted in disorder itself. Idolatry is an internal way of displacing God in our lives from the position He has tailor-made for Himself and then trying to get someone or something to fit into God's position. Nobody and nothing fits into that place, the number-one spot in our lives, except for God. Idolatry is a lethal attempt to dethrone God in our lives. God is a king. Now imagine what would happen to someone who went into the palace in Nigeria and tried to dethrone the king. This wouldn't be any ordinary mistake; it would be a most costly one, the kind that people pay for with their lives. The attempt to take God's throne is not just dangerous because it's crazy to try to dethrone God, who is all-powerful. It is dangerous and lethal because God is all love. God's place in our lives, and His being enthroned as King of kings in our lives, guards and protects the gates of our lives from evil people and evil spirits. (Yes, there are evil spirits, which is often what is operating in a person who does evil things.) God being in His rightful place in our lives—which is first place—protects us, blesses us, and divinely leads us and our families into salvation, causing us to fulfill our destinies in life and producing a satisfaction and fulfillment in us that nothing and nobody else on earth is capable of doing. This is why you will often hear people say they feel empty, even though they have the career they always wanted, money, a wife or husband, children, an education, and much more. What they are missing, what is causing that void, is that God is absent from their lives entirely, or they have not allowed God to be in His rightful place in their lives. This doesn't happen because God is weak and can't stop you from moving Him out of your life as God. It happens because God gives us all the ability to choose Him (Josh. 24:15). And isn't that what we all want—someone to love us unconditionally, and not because we forced them to do so? Whatever is forced won't last, but when people use the gift of God, which is their free will, to make a conscious decision to love God (love is a choice), then it is lasting and not fair-weather, false love. Ask the people who have loved and been through the excruciating pain of a divorce: is it better to have fair-weather, false love, whereby, when the times get tough, the tough get going? Or a love that is mature, selfless, and "a mind made up to love and stay no matter what"? That, dear, is a rhetorical question, because we all know the answer deep down inside. God wants us to love Him with all our heart, mind, soul, and strength (Luke 10:25–28). To do this, it will take both God's grace, us getting to know God and how deeply He loves and cares for us and us allowing God to be in His rightful position in our lives: first. God's position is tailor-made for Him only, a custom fit in our lives, hearts, minds, and souls. Again, idolatry is the deadly attempt to force someone or something else to fit into God's place. Sometimes that someone can be our own selves. You see, idolatry takes on many different forms. Some people idolize themselves, their spouse, their children, their families, their bodies, their jobs, their education and degrees, money, fame, sex, drugs, alcohol, other people—and the list goes on. And although idolatry takes on many forms, the result is always the same: death and destruction. And I don't just mean a physical death, for death has many forms as well. I am talking about the kind of death in which a person still has a pulse, for whatever it's worth, but they want to die because death has come to their relationship with God—causing destruction to their destiny their health marriage; the relationship they once had with their children; their finances, and much more. I thank God for Jesus Christ who is the Resurrection and the Life, able to raise the dead, no matter what form of death has come (John 11:25). For me, the idolatry came in the form of my spouse, to whom I am no longer married, and then in the form of my children. It led to death.

Let me begin by clarifying something. There was nothing wrong with my believing in my former spouse's dreams to become a professional basketball player. It was, however, a fatal mistake to allow his dreams to become mine, because that had the effect of causing me to stop dreaming myself. I forgot my own dreams, goals, and aspirations. When my marriage ended, I remember thinking, "What did I want to do in life again?" I could not remember. I could not recall what I had wanted to do in my own life anymore. I remember trying very hard to remember and my mind was drawing a blank. This was one of the most awakening moments of my life. I knew I had gone seriously wrong. Idolatry had locked up the leader inside of me and thrown away the key. (But Jesus was watching and saw where he put it! And this book is evidence that Jesus has indeed restored those keys unto me).

My dream seemed dead at that point, because I couldn't even remember what it was. But I thank God, because although I forgot God and my dreams, God didn't forget me, or my dreams either. (I am crying right now, people, as I remember God remembering me. Oh, the depth of God's everlasting love and His tender mercies that endures forever.) I sincerely thought I was being a loving and supportive wife, but as it turned out, I was sincerely mistaken. I had allowed my husband's dreams to become my own, and his goals became my goals. Thus, when he accomplished something, I felt accomplished too. And when he believed he lost, I lost too. And wherever he went, naturally or spiritually, I followed. I had allowed my former spouse to become my god—a false god. Consequently, my identity became his identity. This inward identity crisis grew worse as the media and those in that same "rich and famous lifestyle" only referred to me as someone's wife. People didn't even call me by my name anymore. I don't believe a lot of them bothered knowing my name. That wasn't the worst of it, though. The worst part is that when people and the media called me just someone's wife, I answered to it. I should have corrected them or ignored them, but I was bound by idolatry and operating in error myself, so I couldn't. It was so deceptive, because I was certain I was just being a good wife. I laid down my life for my husband and just lived life through him instead. I dropped out of college to help him pursue his dream of playing in the NBA—and to raise our child. I did this with joy. He never had to ask me; I just did it. It came like an instinct. I loved this man more than life itself, more than myself, more than anything. More than God. There was nothing I would not have done for him—lawful or not. I remember that in high school, he couldn't afford basketball shoes, and the only ones

he owned had holes in them. Therefore, he couldn't play basketball anymore. I saw the sadness in his eyes as he told me. All I kept
thinking while he was talking was what I could do to help him. I
went into a store, put on men's basketball shoes over the top of my
own shoes, and walked out of the store with them on. I thought it
was love, but I was lost. God let me know later that some of it was a
measure of love that God gave me for him, but there was also a lot
of foolishness and pride in me. God showed me that the idolatry I
had for my former spouse is the proof that nothing I ever did even
as that marriage was breaking and facing divorce, was from an
intent to harm him. One of the most difficult things I ever had to
do in my life was be on the other side of the "vs." from my former
spouse in a divorce court. During our marriage, and well before it,
all I did and knew to do was to fight for him. I swore he needed me,
and I wouldn't let anyone stop me from being there for him—not
any lawyers, and not God either, even times where he was wrong.
This was foolishness by definition. No worries, however, because
I have learned my lesson, albeit the hard way, because the same
false god I made an idol and placed before the only true and living
God rejected me so severely and wounded me so deeply in every
way imaginable, and all I had left was the real God I had rejected.
Divorce already hurts and causes some of the deepest pains, even
in marriages free from idolatry; however, when someone gets divorced and their spouse is their god, it kills them in the worst way,
and sometimes they do commit suicide because all they had to live
for no longer wants to live with them anymore. They married their
spouse their life, and so when they get divorced, their life as they
know it ends too. Many have committed suicide because, for them,
the shame was unbearable.

God's love and forgiveness toward me changed my life forever, and it changed God's place in my heart, mind, and soul forever as well, because He went from no place to eternal first place.
God willing, I won't have to ever learn this lesson again or idolize

anyone or anything except for the only One who is worthy of being called God: Jesus Christ.

Before and during my entire marriage, many times, my then husband didn't take something from me; I laid it down because the love and idolatry in me ran very deep. Police have been called, furniture broken, and my heart shattered. I've had internal and external scars. I admit it, I've been battered. But even still, I continued to love. In 2007, when my former marriage came to a crashing end, I never thought I would say these words, but they are nevertheless true: I am glad that the idol didn't love me anymore. I am glad that it got so bad, that I had nothing left to do but face reality. I could hide my scars and refuse to tell a doctor what really happened, but when the day came that I could not hide the truth from myself anymore, I was free. The truth was, and still is, that I was worth more than what I even admitted, and that I deserved better than to be one woman among many—it hurt, but it was necessary and liberating. Now I am free to love and be loved for real, to put away Ishmael and ready for Isaac. (If you read Genesis, you will be very blessed and understand exactly what God means when He speaks these words through me regarding Ishmael and Isaac.) Now that God has set me free from this idolatry, I can say this with joy, but prior to my getting to this point, I made one last desperate attempt to build another idol and put it in the place of God.

When I didn't have my then spouse as an idol to idolize anymore, I did what most do who are bound by idolatry: I found another idol. It was my children. Instead of fulfilling my destiny, I put my children in the place of God, and I put my children first. Instead of doing what God created me to do and fulfilling my divine purpose in life, I just gave my all to helping Zion and Zaire work toward fulfilling their destinies. (God showed me later that this pattern of idolatry was because, deep down inside, I feared fulfilling my own destiny; I feared greatness. I feared the responsibility that comes along with what God has destined me to do, including writing this book.) I went to every parent-teacher conference, I didn't miss any activities my children participated in, I volunteered at their school, provided their tutoring, and taught them Sunday School too. I didn't miss a practice or a pep talk, a doctor's visit or a trip to the dentist. I baked brownies, and nightly I breathed out bedtime stories. I was the field-trip chaperone and a member of the PTA. I didn't miss a haircut or a home-cooked meal with these boys. I got up every day, and I lived for them instead of living for God. I became what I proudly thought of as "super mom," but it was actually super stupid, deceiving, and extremely tiring. God showed me later that my overly occupied schedule and busy days were excuses I used to keep myself from fulfilling my destiny. I had what I thought was a legitimate excuse for not doing what God called me to do. After all, I was a mother, just "busy trying to help my children."

Oh yes, I was a busy woman, but I wasn't fulfilling my purpose. I learned quickly, however, that being busy and fulfilling your purpose can be two very different things. A hamster is busy. All day, the hamster runs on the hamster wheel, but sadly, he isn't going anywhere. And that is the effect idolatry has. It keeps people busy, but they aren't really going anywhere but in circles, because they are not fulfilling their purpose and the God-given destiny for which they were created. I engaged in this God-forsaken behavior, rationalizing that my children needed me. The truth is my children really needed me as I am now, the woman God called me to be—a woman who seeks God first and then all things are added, a woman with wisdom, a woman without fear, a woman who prays for her children and whose cry God hears and answers. Now my children have what they need from me as a mother, because I have what I need in God. I'm no longer just a mother; I am a mother with meaning, a mother with a divine purpose in the life of her children. This is what God wants for all mothers and fathers, and with Jesus, it is absolutely possible. My life is the evidence of that truth.

Idolatry is folly! This idolatry proved to be detrimental to my relationship with God, the most important relationship I will ever have. It also became harmful to my marriage and almost fatal to my own destiny and purpose. In time, God allowed me to see the error of my ways, and out of pure love, God corrected me. God corrects whom He loves (Heb. 12:5–6). Now, don't get me wrong, I'm not saying anything is wrong with loving someone, especially your spouse. In fact, God says, "Love one another deeply" (1 Pet. 4:8). We have to love one another deeply, because if we just love superficially with what I call "surface love," then at the first offense, we will run out, and run down to the valley of the shadow of divorce, where people give their lawyer *all* of their money to avoid giving their spouse just *some* of the money! (It's okay to laugh, even if you're the one who gave it all to the lawyer.)

You see, in loving a man this deeply, there was nothing I would not do; I did it all. There was nothing I would not give up or give; I gave my very own life, and I ceased to live. So I gave up my life in exchange for his. I laid down my dreams too, and I became just a wife with children, when God created me to be much more. For the cameras, I played the role, recited the lines, and looked the part. But on the inside of me was the deepest sorrow, and in a million pieces was my shattered heart. No name, no face, and I was fading fast, thinking it's no real need for me individually, because my marriage will last. I soon realized, as I looked beyond his eyes, that the me, inside of him was also fading fast. But there was nothing I could not forgive, overlooking violence time and time again. I was self-defeated, just to see my abuser win. I hit rock bottom; I was in the darkest place. Life became unbearable and death looked like a way of escape.

This is where I called on Jesus, and I was saved by His grace. I finally remembered God, the One who created me. And in His mercy, He healed me and gave me destiny. And He promised me, "It's not too late. You will be who I called you to be, and your sins

won't determine your fate." This promise God has kept, and because of His love, I've wept. But these are tears of joy, and I finally
have peace. My life hasn't been the same. Surely Jesus delivered
me. I know, if it weren't for Jesus Christ, I would have taken my
own life. And so His intervention, I don't fail to mention, every
chance I can. Jesus's love has caused me to lay down idolatry for
man, and instead lift up my heart in worship to God and be His
number-one fan. My heart is filled with God's pure love, and that
love has set me free. I have a purpose, I have worth, I have Jesus
Christ's identity!

I cried as I wrote during this chapter and prayed to God that
He will not ever allow me to go back to the place where I live for a
man, rather than for meaning. Because God is the only one who
can give your life meaning. God, the Creator, is the one who knows
what purpose He created you for. Know, indeed, that God has a
purpose for your life. You see, your life isn't happenstance, a co-
incidence, or luck. You've been bought with the highest price, the
blood of Jesus. Just like the life and death of Jesus was not an accident, and when you understand the purpose of His life, you know
that your life, likewise, isn't an accident. God has never had an accident. God is a God of purpose, intention, and plans—plans that
are good and not evil, giving you hope and a future. If you feel you
haven't had the best past, you can tell the hell itself that has come
against you, "but God has a glorious future for me!"

God did for me what He always does when I get into a mess. He
turned it into a miracle. God turned what was meant for my death
into my destiny! I learned a lot from God about what love is and
what it is not. I didn't get this from a therapit. (That spelling is not
a typo, sometimes the therapist can be a *theraPIT*, only treating
and never healing but collecting money all along-putting clients in
a financial pit, hard to get out of. This keeps the client unhealed
and in need of more therapy, while the therapit keeps getting paid
more and more money.) *I'm not saying all therapists are bad*; I am

just saying, seek God first in all things (Matt. 6:33). God doesn't want you free from spiritual debt, just to end up in financial debt, because Jesus died and shed blood for you to be free from *all* debt (Eph. 1:7). Again, God used this identity crisis I was bound by, along with the bondage of idolatry, to teach me the truth about love. Married couples, and those who want to get married, take extra notes, because this is going to bless you especially.

And to the Married, God Says...

First, God let me know that love is not a feeling. Love can cause you to feel a certain way, but the feeling itself is not love. Feelings are very secondary and subordinate to love. God told me that love is the cause, and feelings are an effect from that cause. Love is deep, while feelings are up-and-down, back-and-forth. Feelings are by definition shallow and superficial. For instance, have you ever *felt* like you really loved someone and would do anything for them? And then have you ever *felt* like you don't ever want to see that person again in life—all in the same day? Those are feelings— hot and then cold, on and then off. I believe that a lot more marriages would survive and last, if, first of all, Jesus is Lord over the people and their marriage, and also if people didn't give the credence they do to their feelings. To help avoid this and a worst fate, like ending a marriage with God (God calls our relationship with Christ a marriage), we would all be wise to do what God commanded: "Submit your emotions under the mighty hand of God" (1 Pet. 5:6). This "giving first place to my feelings" mind-set is nothing less than a covenant-breaking, relationship-destroying trap from the devil himself. The good news is that Jesus is the deliverer from even the most deceptive traps. God says love should be first place in your relationship with God, your relationship with all others, yourself, and your entire life. Why? Because, God is love (1 John 4:8). God said you are to love Him with all your heart, mind, soul, and strength and have no other god besides Him. (These gods that the only God is referring to can be a job, spouse, children, money, drugs, food, fame, etc. God is referring to any idol. We have to stay close to God, people, because God is the only one who can instruct us and deliver us from these hidden traps that ruin marriages, friendships, jobs, and finances, etc.) Now, in addition to loving God with all our heart, mind, soul, and strength, Jesus said to love one another deeply. Doing this will bless you and cause you to succeed in both this life and in the next.

Love is the fulfillment of God's entire law, so when you love the way God says to love, you have indeed obeyed every command (Rom. 13:10). We have to come out of our feelings and love so deeply that we *become* love. God desires to take us to the place where we not only love, but we become love, like Jesus is love. How, you might ask? God can fulfill this most beautiful phenomenon. God said, "Love is patient, love is kind, and love keeps no record of wrongs" etc. (See, 1 Cor. 13:4-8). When we allow God to produce the fruit of patience in us, causing us to be patient, we become love. Likewise, when we allow God to produce the fruit of kindness in us, we become kind, and thus we become love. Love must be something we become, and we must get away from or steer clear of love being something as weak and wavering as a feeling. Becoming love is the way. Let's walk in it, because we do want a beautiful relationship with God and with each other.

Our Destinies are of Great Importance to Us and the World
God calls married people to become one (Gen. 2:24). But God has a destiny for each individual person on earth—the married and the unmarried. Imagine the deadly effect of forfeiting your destiny for anybody else's. God gave me this example to teach me the severity of the consequences: imagine a husband who is a lawyer, and a wife who drops out of school and quits pursuing or even thinking about becoming the medical doctor she dreamed of becoming so that she can stay at home, have children with her husband, and

help him reach and fulfill *his* destiny and purpose. Now, one day, this woman is out in public when a man falls down ill in the street and needs medical attention because he can't breathe—something this woman would have easily known how to fix at this point in her life if she would have pursued and reached her own destiny. Very easily, she could have performed mouth-to-mouth resuscitation and revived this man in need, but she doesn't know how. She doesn't have the medical training to do so. She lacks the ability to help, not because she doesn't want to help him, but because she can't—because she stopped pursuing the very dream that would have saved this man's life, and she did it so that her husband could fulfill his destiny. Ironically, her husband's law degree, which she gave up her destiny for, can't save this dying man, either. It was never intended by God to do so; her destiny was. So in effect, the man didn't make it, because a vital part of her purpose in life was to save his life. That man died when her destiny did. People, our destiny is never just about us; our destiny is always bigger than us, and it will always bless and reach beyond us and our blood-line family members. And God has given each of us a purpose and a destiny to fulfill. None of them are small or insignificant, because our Creator isn't small and is so wonderfully great that He cannot do anything insignificant.

You matter, and your purpose matters, and we all need you to fulfill it. I don't know if God's destiny for you is to be a medical doctor and resuscitate people in that natural sense, like the woman in the example above; however, I know your destiny is equally important. God reveals this truth in His word when He teaches us all about being a part of the body of Christ Jesus (1 Cor. 12:27). God showed me that the word *resuscitation* means, "revival" or "resurrection." Some of you are called by God to revive and resurrect people emotionally, spiritually, financially, in relationships, health, or in their destiny and purpose. Some of you are created by God to take people from hopeless to hopeful, from fear to courage, from depressed to joyful, and from suicidal to lively. Some of you are literally called by God to talk the man from the ledge who is ready to jump off the ledge literally—or to talk to those who ready to jump off the ledge figuratively-like jumping from their marriage, or to children ready to jump from finishing their education. This is resurrection and revival power. And the ability is in the medical doctor, treating a certain type of death or life-threatening factor, but it is also in those of us who aren't medical doctors, to deliver people from every other kind of death and life-threatening factor. Glory to God! So come on, people, let's fulfill our destiny with God, and even if we feel afraid, feelings are no longer in first place to dictate our day or our destiny! We won't be controlled by our feelings, and I decree that our future is free from every evil fear, manipulation, and control, in Jesus's name. Let's mount up on wings like the eagle and soar, because we don't have to be a plane to fly. We were created by God Almighty for this very purpose: to soar into and fulfill our destiny! You see, God does have a plan for your marriage, but God has a plan for you too. God says, "I know the plans I have for *you* declares the Lord, plans to prosper you, and not to harm you; plans to give you hope and a future" (Jer. 29:11). Your destiny is a plan of God's that is tied directly to your relationship with God, and your marriage is a plan of God's, in addition to, or a part of, your individual life and God-given destiny and purpose. And remember, God will have no other god before Him—women, including your marriage, and men, including your money. Your marriage, spouse, children, money and career should be an *addition* to your destiny, not a distraction from it. I say this especially to women, if you feel like you have to choose between your destiny and your spouse, or you have already chosen the latter or believe you have to choose between your destiny and your marriage, you must seek God now for the solution to this problem and submit your will to God's will, whatever it may be.

Putting and Keeping God First

God also taught me that, although idolatry has bound some men too, this type of idolatry, seeming like love, has mostly bound women. Men tend to fall into an idolatrous trap relating to money, jobs, careers, and accomplishments, while women tended to have their husbands as idols. God showed me this one night in a dream. In the dream, I was inside a classroom with other women, and there was one man inside the classroom, whom I believed was an angel. God was teaching a class on marriage. God was speaking and saying scriptures on marriage that are in the Bible, and everything God said was true and from the Bible; however, something was wrong with the decisions the students made after class. After the women in the class heard the Bible verses on marriage that God said, they left the classroom and all began running in the same direction outside the classroom, and they were running very fast. I got ready to leave class too, and I was going to go in the same direction the other women had run, all except one woman, and that one male student. (I think both of them were angels.) I overheard them speaking to one another, saying how those women who ran out of the classroom after class did not understand what God was teaching them. God was not telling them, to go in the direction they went, even though God honors marriage. They had gone in the direction that put their husbands and marriages in the place of God. When I heard this, I didn't leave the classroom, but rather, I waited around to see what God and those people I overheard speaking would do. Come to find out, there was another class right after than one, in which God continued to teach about what His will is concerning marriage, and God certainly never intended for people to put their spouse as a god! God meant what He said: He will have no other god before Him, the true and living God (Exod. 20:3).

Women of worth, always remember that God has ways of doing things for our good and while we chase after God, God supplies all of our needs, causes goodness and kindness to pursue us, and gives us the desires of our heart. God clearly says, "delight yourself in the Lord, and He will give you the desires of your heart" (Ps. 37:4). Understand what God is telling you here, because it is powerful and good news that gives you rest. You will not have to work for the desires of your heart, convince the desires of your heart to come into your life, or denounce God for them. God will *give* you the desires of your heart. God will not make you work for a gift; He gives it.

A Deeper Look at Feelings

Let's go a bit deeper regarding feelings, because they have been lethal to marriages and relationships for far too long. It ends now, in Jesus's name! Let's expose feelings for what they truly are, because once that is done, I am certain there will be nobody who knows the truth who will want them to ever have first place again—not in any area of their life. We will do this by taking a look at the things that have been thought to "feel good."

Have you ever gone to a fast-food place to eat with a tell-all name like "Fat Fanny's," and right after eating their leading cause of death, what Fat Fanny's calls a number two on their menu, but heart surgeons call heart disease, and said something like, "Oh, I feel so good"? Now, we all know heart disease is far from good; it's deadly, in fact. Eating the wrong things, often feeling good, is a leading factor in causing heart disease. I have been blessed to eat some pretty good food in my life, especially my granny's. home cooked food. However, her cooking is actually healthy. I have also had the chance to eat at some very tasty restaurants. But I have not had any food in my life that was worth dying for. Feeling good and being good can be wholly different. We have to allow God to get us to the place in our lives where we do what *is* good and not what *feels* good if they conflict. There is no greater feeling of goodness than knowing you have done the will of God.

Giving this a bit more thought should cause us all to want to do away with putting our feelings first and doing whatever feels good to us, rather than what is actually good for us.

There are people who felt like killing someone, and the law tried them as a murderer. Their feelings never showed up to testify at trial on their behalf, and their feelings failed to exonerate them from life sentences and lethal injection. But if these people repented and were forgiven by God, that is because love was there. And while the natural laws have no room for love, and very little for forgiveness, God is love (1 John 4:8). There are drunk drivers who felt like drinking and then felt like driving home, and they killed someone on the way. There are men who felt like raping a woman, scarring her inside and out. There are racist people who felt like killing and enslaving entire races of people. Adolf Hitler felt like killing Jews, and the people who passed Jim Crow laws felt like mentally and emotionally enslaving African-Americans. And the devil feels like keeping us in our feelings, to get us to destroy our life here on earth—and our eternal life. But thanks be to Jesus Christ, who, although He didn't feel like dying for our sins, He did and made it possible for us to be free from every bondage, including idolatry (Luke 22:42).

Now, I am not stating that the idolatry I was bound by concerning my former spouse was in any way the sole reason the marriage ended. I am, however, saying this is where I went gravely wrong in that marriage. If it were a movie, I am admitting that I was starring in the same film as him. I had lines too, and I played my part in it also. If anyone reading has made this same mistake, be of good cheer, because God works together all things for the good of those who love Him and are called according to His purpose (Rom. 8:28).

In Closing

Take away this truth with you, among all others: God never intended to give you a marriage in exchange for your destiny. You

see, God said it, and He means it: "You shall have no other god besides me" (Exod. 20:3). That includes your husband, wife, money,
children, career, car, education, looks, notoriety, and reputation. It
includes everything. Your marriage matters, but there is no higher
calling than fulfilling the destiny Jesus has for you. You can likely
tell that I am very passionate about people not having an identity
in anything or anyone other than Jesus, their Creator. It is because
I know the cost of this sin all too well. As you will see, I nearly paid
with my life.

"It is no longer I who lives, but Christ who lives in me" (Gal. 2:20).

THE BEGINNING OF THE END

*God is close to the brokenhearted and saves
such a one with a contrite spirit.*

—Psalm 34:18

Introduction

I want to begin by saying that being separated from a spouse is not
the worst separation. Neither is being separated from children the
worst separation, nor being separated from loved ones, or people
you thought were your friends. I can truly attest to the loss of them
all. And what I have learned is this: being separated from God
is, by definition, hell itself, and by far the worst separation anyone could experience. The hell God warns us of in His Word is
eternal separation from God, which is torment and suffering with
consuming fire that's never put out (Rev. 21:8). The gift of God is
eternal life, which can save us from this hell (Rom. 6:23).

Being separated from God while on earth is a type of hell,
manifested right here on earth that is also filled with suffering and

torment. While there might not be a fire blazing in hell on earth, there certainly is pain, suffering, and anguish of the soul when someone is separated from God, which for some is commensurate with the pain of being on fire. This is all the more certain to occur with those who knew God and then knew Him no more (2 Pet. 2:21). That is the worst separation, and the worst thing that can happen to any of us while here on earth. This separation is what Jesus experienced for us all when He was being crucified and He cried out, "Father, why have you forsaken me?" just before He died on the cross (Matt. 27:46).

Notably, Jesus had suffered extreme pain, suffering, and betrayals in the hours leading up to that moment. A friend of His had turned on him, someone who walked with him and ate with Him daily—and He turned on Jesus for money! In exchange for thirty pieces of silver (they use shekels for money there), Judas told the people, who were looking for Jesus in order to murder Him, exactly where to find Jesus. Then Judas personally escorted them to where Jesus was, and he gave Jesus evil for all the good He had done for all mankind, even for Judas, because Jesus died for us all, including Judas (2 Cor. 5:15).

Some people have been erroneously taught that Jesus died to save the holy, or the "Christian," but that's not true. Jesus died to save us all because God does not desire that one person perish (2 Pet. 3:9). Some wait for their behavior to change to give their life to Jesus, but this is an error also. Jesus came for the sinner, not the saint (Luke 5:32). Jesus came for all of us broken people who have tried it on our own and still failed, those of us who realize we are sinners and in need of a Savior who will have mercy on us and not condemn us (1 Tim. 2:4). That Savior is Jesus.

Jesus also was falsely accused of crimes He never committed, and then He was arrested and wrongfully imprisoned. Afterward, He was beaten all night long until His face was disfigured and unrecognizable. He had a crown of thorns crushed into His skull and holes pierced in both His hands and feet in front of an enormous crowd that included His mother. Jesus did not fight, even though He had access to weapons (John 8:11). Jesus didn't defend Himself either when He was falsely imprisoned by a judge who knew Jesus was innocent, but because of political reasons kept Jesus in jail and sentenced Him to death anyway, after being warned not to do so (John 19:12–16). Unfortunately, Judges sentencing innocent people to jail, and judgments that the judge knows are wrong, but because of political pressure, the judge harms the innocent anyway; is still happening today, as it did with Jesus. Jesus didn't yell at Judas for betraying Him, and He never once used His power to harm those He knew were about to kill Him. In fact, He didn't say a word (Isa. 53:7). But when Jesus experienced separation from God, Jesus finally opened His mouth, and as Matthew 27:46 tells us, Jesus cried out, with a loud voice, "Father, why have You forsaken Me?"

Jesus experienced hell on earth (separation from God) so that we don't have to. And Jesus did this for us all, regardless of what we've done or what religion someone is associated with. For with Jesus there is neither Jew nor gentile, black nor white, male nor female; we are all one in Jesus (Gal. 3:28). What made Jesus speak out is very telling. Jesus had been separated from His friends, His family, His reputation, but He was able to bear all of that and in silence. But when Jesus was separated from God, He could not hold His peace any longer. That was Jesus's response to being separated from God. How much more does being separated from God harm and cause anguish in us, if it made Jesus cry out in anguish?

This sort of separation, however, happens too often in people's lives—and often because it is subtle. But it is still better than eternal hell, because people still have an opportunity to repent and receive God's promised forgiveness. It seems to be worse, however, in the sense that it is more deceptive than the eternal hell described as a lake of fire. Every soul in the lake-of-fire hell knows they are separated from God, and that they are being judged. But those, however, who are experiencing hell on earth don't seek God because they are likely not even aware of their separation from God and the fact that they are being judged. I have witnessed this truth in my life, as well as in others, and it often causes people to believe that all is well in their lives concerning God. This is one of the greatest deceptions I have ever witnessed and personally experienced in my lifetime. God showed me that the deception occurs for two main reasons.

First, God is good, and God's goodness does this. God is merciful to both the thankful and the unthankful, and He rains on the just, as well as the unjust. God causes His sun to rise on both the wicked and the good, and God gives gifts without repentance to both (Matt. 5:45). So this causes people who are desperately wicked to be amazingly talented and successful in life, because they are operating in the gifts and talents that God has given them, without having any relationship with God whatsoever. God gives gifts to mankind without repentance (Rom. 11:28). So people can operate in the gifts and talents given by God but be separated from God. This causes deception, because those separated from God on earth still have wealth, live in fine homes, enjoy health, and sometimes have untainted reputations. This does not mean they are not in serious trouble, though. For the wages of sin is death, and only the gift of God, Jesus Christ, is eternal life (Rom. 6:23). God is still a just judge (Ps. 7:11), and the only way to escape the well-justified judgment of God for sin is to be saved by Jesus. Being saved by Jesus is not complicated for us, because God has made it easy for those of us who are willing to be saved. The Word of God says, "if you confess with your mouth the Lord Jesus and believe in your heart that God has raised Him from the dead, you will be saved," and, "For with the heart one believes unto righteousness, and with the mouth confession is made unto salvation" (Rom. 10:10). For the scripture says, "Whoever believes on Him will not be put to shame," and, "For there is no distinction between Jew and Greek, for the same Lord over all is rich to all who call upon Him," and "For *whoever* calls on the name of the Lord shall be saved" (See Rom. 10:9–13). Salvation through Jesus Christ alone exempts mankind from the judgment of God for sin. It is both what we need and *all* we need!

Secondly, the devil gives people wealth too and nearly untainted notoriety (Matt. 4:8–9). The difference is that God does it because He is loving and good, even though we can be evil and unthankful. The devil does it because he wants to kill, steal, and destroy everyone he can (John 10:10). Repentance is something that needs to take place in order to leave this place of separation from God, and be reconciled with Him, through what Jesus Christ already did for us all by dying on the cross (2 Cor. 5:18). We are acknowledging we need God to do it, and we need Jesus's righteousness in order to be righteous before God (Rom. 3:22–26). It's not hard; Jesus did the hard part for you and me. Repentance requires acknowledgment that you have done something wrong, humbling yourself, asking God for forgiveness, and allowing God to change your mind toward God, and your behavior also. This is not complicated, because God is doing the work and forgiving us for the wrong we do along the way in life. Sin still has consequences, but it won't be hell, and it will not be loss of the love of God when you give your life to Jesus Christ.

However, as simple as it is to be saved by Jesus, this is *almost* impossible for someone filled with riches and possessions—and most of all, filled with pride (Matt. 19:24–26). For them, everything is *good*, and so their logic follows that "everything has to be good with them and God." They are self-dependent and wrapped up in their own good deeds, believing that makes them righteous. Allowing their wealth and possessions to be proof, albeit false, of their erroneous belief that all is well with them and God. This, however, is the wrong way of thinking for both the rich and poor. There is one way to God and it is through His Son, Jesus (John 14:6). It's not through our good works, charitable donations, family relations, the prayers of others who are saved, or our own selves (Eph. 2:8). Neither good works, good success, or anything else measure up to God's grace, which is the only thing sufficient to save us from our sins—and even save us from ourselves when needed (2 Cor. 12:9). All the things I am about to bravely share with you, I had to suffer before I realized the simple yet powerful truths mentioned above. Hopefully, after reading about my life, you won't have to endure these hardships.

The Beginning of the End as I Knew It

I woke up from my sleep in the middle of the morning, around 3:00 a.m. For some time I thought I woke up because I had been very sick at the time. Later, I understood that it was God who woke me out of my sleep that early morning, both physically and spiritually. When I awoke, I noticed right away that I had been sleeping alone. Initially, I didn't panic. My other half must be somewhere in the house, I thought, or perhaps he couldn't sleep himself and didn't want to wake me. These were all rational thoughts, but the truth that was unfolding would be anything but rational. I searched the entire house, the garages, and outside, and I still didn't find him. Then I began feeling something was wrong, but I didn't feel worried about his well-being. So, I did what a lot of you are thinking right now: I got my cell phone and I called him. In fact, I called, and I called, and I called again. But I got no answer.

Finally, our house phone rang, and I just knew it would be him, because who else would be calling our house at that hour? But it was odd to me because it was the house phone ringing, and we rarely called one another on the house phone. I remember my hands were cold and sweaty as I nervously answered the phone. Surprisingly, on the other end of the phone, it was the voice of a woman who began to tell me right away how she had been with my former spouse and had just had sex with him. She went on about how she could prove it, giving vivid details of a sexual encounter and the location, and even a description of the underwear he was wearing. So much was on my mind, miraculously, that I didn't feel the fact that I was sick at all anymore. A worse affliction had come upon me at that point. I let that woman on the phone have it! [Where I was raised, that means I gave her a serious tongue-lashing!] . I also let her know that if she thought calling me and giving me all those details would make me leave my spouse, she was sadly mistaken! I told her that because of her, I would stay with him just to spite her. I'm pretty sure I called her a prostitute on the prowl for hurting me. This woman didn't call to help me; she called to destroy me. Her intentions in hurting me were more evil than the extramarital affair she confessed to having.

By then, hours had gone by, and the next day had begun. It wasn't until 10:30 a.m. that the door to my house finally opened. I was certain I would receive an apology, along with a legitimate excuse for such an illegitimate act. But I was completely wrong. What I got instead was one conflicting story after another. I was told, "I am a grown man, and I do what the f—ck I want to do." Later I was told, "I just went out with my friends." Several stories followed that one, with a lot of stuttering in between. It was the final story I got, however, that caused something to die inside me regarding that marriage. I was told, "Oh, I was at L's house, comforting him because he just lost his child." That was it. I was still married, but something was ending at that very moment. The lie wasn't even what caused me to throw my hands up and say, "I'm leaving." It was the content of it that did it. L had just suffered the loss of his child, and that is obviously extremely painful for any parent to endure. (Just ask my mother.) The fact that this man's tragedy was used to try and cover up what was evidently going on for real—that did it for me. At that moment, a part of me was done. I do believe that something inside me died regarding that marriage. The next events, however, were the most shocking of them of all.

I thought that after everything I had just had to suffer because of another's indiscretion, I would be the one infuriated. But again, I was wrong. This time, however, the error nearly cost me my life and the life of my unborn child. When I said I was done and that I was leaving, I was faced with some of the worst violence ever in my life. I was pregnant with my second son at the time, when I was picked up and violently thrown down with so much force onto the ottoman furniture inside our master bathroom that the impact of my body being thrown into it, broke the furniture into four pieces. My head and back went through the furniture and onto the marble floor. I blacked out. When I came to, I ran for the phone inside the bathroom to call 911. I didn't make it. He snatched the phone from my hand and threw the phone against my body, breaking the phone into pieces against my body. I ran toward the bathroom door to escape, but he had locked the door to the bathroom so that I couldn't get out. I was literally trapped and had no way out, unless I risked dying by jumping out the second-story window of the bathroom. I went for the gun I knew he kept in the closet of the bathroom, but I never made it to that gun. I was picked up again and slammed to the floor, but this time he sat on top of my stomach and chest and held me down. It was very hard to breathe. Finally, someone came over to visit and heard my cry for help, and they began beating on the bathroom door. He then got off me, and I was able to leave.

My Body Speaks

I spent about seven days in the hospital following this episode of violence. Because of fear and shame, however, I did so all the way in Illinois. I was so weak, I didn't leave the airport once the plane landed. I checked into the Hilton Hotel at Chicago's O'Hare Airport, and I there alone and in darkness, seriously contemplating death. I didn't want to live anymore—at least not like that. I tried to get myself together because I was going to my mom's house, and I did not want her to know. I tried not to tell anyone, not even her, what had happened. It was very humiliating and shameful for me, and so I tried my best to hide it. It was also terrifying for me to tell anyone what had happened because, during that violence, when I tried to call the police, it got worse for me. I also didn't know if I was leaving him, and I didn't want anyone else deciding that for me. But I couldn't hide it any longer. When I refused to open my mouth and speak about what was happening to me behind closed doors, my body began to talk for me. Shortly after arriving at my mom's house in Illinois, I fainted in her kitchen and had to be rushed to the emergency room of Christ Hospital. Notably, Christ Hospital is where I gave birth to my first child, and there I was, millions of dollars and some fame later, inside that same hospital where my second child could have died.

Hospital

It is amazing how the trained staff at the hospital asked me several times if I was a victim of domestic violence almost immediately after getting in the hospital. At the time, I honestly did not know that I was. At that time, I didn't know what "domestic violence" meant; I only knew what I thought it was. I later found out I had been suffering from domestic violence for years, according to medical and domestic-violence professionals. I told the staff I was not a victim of domestic violence. And when they asked me if any-one had caused my bruises, I refused to tell them. Instead, I covered it up with makeup and lack of confession. I lay there in that hospital bed and cried for hours. Nevertheless, these professionals sent someone in to speak to me about it. One of them, I know God sent. He was like an angel to me. I remember him telling me these words, which I don't believe I will ever forget: "Suicide is a permanent solution to a temporary problem." It was like he knew in my heart I was giving up the will to live. But I still kept quiet and suffered silently.

Later, I discovered that my reaction to the hospital staff who were trying to help me was normal in domestic violence. While domestic violence is the leading cause of injury to women, above all other harms, it is also termed by some experts as, a "silent epidemic." This isn't news to many, as they have suffered from domestic violence themselves, or know of someone who has. Many heard of brave women coming forward about the violence they suffered such as Robin Givens, the former spouse of Mike Tyson; Tina Turner, the former spouse of Ike Turner Halle Berry; and so many more.

I was already feeling terrible physically, and emotionally I was in a bad space, but when I got a phone call from the one who helped put me in the hospital—and it was not to apologize or see how I was doing, but instead was to instruct me not to tell anyone what happened to me—at that moment I am sure something else died inside of me, and I felt more worthless than ever before. I lay there on that hospital bed, bruised and completely broken. And as much pain as I was in physically, the pain and brokenness of my heart and on the inside of me was unbearable. I cried for hours, and I refused to be comforted. There I was, willing to die for a man who had not even asked me how I was doing, but instead just making sure I didn't tell the hospital what happened. I had allowed a man to break me all the way down. I had allowed another human being to nearly destroy me completely. I wanted to die. I did not want to live like that anymore.

I lay there with tears pouring from my eyes, literally praying that God would take my life. It had become too much to live a life of poverty concerning the presence of God and real joy while clothed in richness and material possessions. It had become too much, with everyone saying how lucky I was to be married to their sport's hero, while the million-dollar house had become hell, and was like a house of horrors. I learned you can put a mess inside a mansion, and it is still just a mess! Money doesn't convert messes into miracles; only God has the power to do that! Trust me, I know this. While I had all that money, the mess was still there. And later when they wrongfully took my money from me, God performed a miracle in and around me. Again, money doesn't perform miracles, God does, and He does so freely.

I was tired of Hollywood and the "liestyle" of the rich and famous (that's not a typo—most everything about it is a lie!). It had truly become way too much—the weight of Hollywood, that lifestyle, where abused women are pressured to keep their mouths shut about the abuse they suffer from their spouses, just because it could affect the money coming in. This makes no sense. A dead woman can't spend money, even if it's billions of dollars. Dead people don't shop! At least not people who are *literally* dead. Now, those who are dead spiritually and emotionally shop a lot; Fifth Avenue, Beverly Hills and Miami Beach are probably flooded with them. And I'm not talking about the dead whose remains are inside a casket, but the dead who are working on Wall Street and attending Award shows, televised red-carpet events, and inside some of the most well-known music studios in the world—the spiritual and emotionally dead, that is. We have to be careful not to envy people or secretly want their life, because with their life could come every curse and desire to die right along with their riches. There are no material possessions on this earth worth your relationship with God, or your salvation, or your life.

I certainly know what it is like to feel worthless, but I also know what it is like when God gives you the wisdom to know that since a man did not give you your worth, he cannot take it from you. Don't ever let someone or something convince you that you are worthless. That is too much power to give anyone over your life—even yourself. God gave you your worth and your value, and therefore, only God can tell you what you are worth, or remove it from you, which God will not do. Nobody else has that power, women (I feel that God is especially talking to women). I didn't know then, however, what I know now, and so I continued to suffer and continued to believe that I was worthless whenever he told me I was, or whenever he treated me as if I were nothing.

He was wrong for this, but I should never have given him the power to make me feel that way or cause me to believe those lies. That part I take full responsibility for, but for what he did to me all those years, he is responsible. I know now that I didn't make him do it. God asked me, "Siohvaughn, if you had the power to make him do evil, wouldn't you have used that same power to make him do good?" I told God, "Yes." Then God asked me, "But you couldn't make him do good, right?" I responded, "I couldn't." God asked, "As much as you wanted and longed for him to do right, you couldn't make him, correct?" I responded again, "Yes." God told me, "It is because you didn't have the power to make him do good or evil, because if you did have that kind of power, you would have used it to make him do good." Ever since that day, I was totally set free from the lie that somehow it was my fault he behaved that way, and the violence was something I made him do. I am free, and I thank God with everything in me because of this freedom!

After about seven days, I was finally released from the hospital, and after some time, I went back home to Miami. And although my external bruises were healing and no longer visible, the wounds and scars on the inside of me were still very painful and present. Despite all the pain and humiliation I had suffered, I still wanted to save my family and marriage. So when I got home and my spouse asked me to have sex, I did it.

I don't remember the sex we had on our wedding night, but I remember with clarity the sex we had that day. I remember the words spoken during sex, and how they seemed to cut me. I literally had to turn my face because I could not stop the tears from pouring from my eyes. Afterward, I felt like showering the entire encounter off me. I stayed in the shower for the longest time, because I felt literal disgust. I felt worse than I ever did after being raped as a child. I was at an all-time low. I had allowed myself to be trampled on, used, and abused. The feeling of worthlessness had set in. I couldn't live any longer without God. My life was filling more and more with darkness, but God in His mercy and love for me had blessed me with life inside my womb, which brought some light into my life.

"Weeping may endure for a night, but joy comes in the morning" (Ps. 30:5).

LET NO MAN TEAR ASUNDER

Therefore what God has joined together,
let no man tear asunder.

—*Mark 10:9*

I stayed. After all I had gone through, I stayed. It takes a woman who has been the victim of domestic violence seven attempts, on average, before she actually leaves. The truth has shed so much light on the decisions I made in my life. I wanted that marriage to get better and work. I wanted that family to stay together and our children to be raised by both their parents together. So, I stayed.

I began praying and seeking God again at that time. But I was still not fully following God. I knew that God was calling me, but I didn't want to answer God's call until I knew that my husband was going with me wherever in life God was taking me. At that time, I was still bound by idolatry. Married people are certainly one flesh when they join together, but we are still all responsible for working out our own individual salvation, and we all have an individual choice to serve and follow God, or not. I had one foot in the door with God and one hanging out, in case my spouse changed his mind and wanted to join me. I didn't want to go where God was taking me alone. I really wanted my husband to go with me. So I religiously followed God, but I ran from having intimate contact with Him.

I also began attending church services in Florida, along with my son. Around that time God also allowed me to begin nurturing A Woman's Worth Foundation, Inc., a non-profit Christian organization, which He founded through me. I went on as best I could, trying not to think about what I had been suffering and pretending like it never happened, but that proved to be impossible for me. I was coming along in my pregnancy with Zion, my second son, and while this was surely some light in the dark tunnel I felt I was in, I was still broken. I still felt humiliated and ashamed about what had happened to me. Feelings of worthlessness were still present. But at that time for me it was better than getting divorced. When I got married, I intended to stay married. On top of that, I was afraid to leave. I was afraid of every threat made to me—especially the one about being separated from my children. (A lot of them eventually did come true.)

Pregnancy: Some Light in the Tunnel
My pregnancy with Zion seemed to be normal at first, aside from the violence he was subjected to early on as a result of the violence against me. A couple of months along in my pregnancy, however, I received devastating news after what began as a normal prenatal doctor's visit. In short, there were complications with my pregnancy that was life threatening to the child and myself. They found a tumor. I was given a serious choice that day to either have an abortion or go forward with the pregnancy and risk having it kill me.

I remember, after I left the doctor's office that day, getting into my car that I had parked on the roof of the doctor's building, and looking up to the sky, praying to God while weeping. I was very saddened by the news I'd just received, but I was sadder about the reaction I got. I called to let my spouse know but the response wasn't the loving and supportive one I had hoped for. I felt so alone. I called a pastor, who prayed for me, which helped me a lot in that moment. Ultimately, God made the decision through me and with me alone. Now, I realize that even back then I had faith in God. I prayed to God in Jesus name to save the child and my life—to spare us both. My days of aborting the purpose of God were over. God had saved me from that sin, and He saved my life and Zion's. God healed me completely, and He supernaturally removed the tumor from my body without the need of medication or chemo treatment. I had left God before, but it was obvious that God had not left me. People, God really is faithful, even if we are unfaithful (2 Tim. 2:13).

From then on, I went along in my pregnancy with Zion complication-free. I tiptoed around in my marriage, however, as if walking on a land mine, praying I didn't say or do anything to cause another explosion. Despite this, I began enjoying my pregnancy. At the baby shower for Zion, my house was filled with people and filled with gifts. I remember being very grateful to have received such wonderful gifts. Some gifts were so expensive that, when I saw them, I was thinking, "I would not have even bought that for myself." I was grateful, and in awe, because after God had blessed me financially, I didn't seem to get gifts anymore. I suppose people felt I didn't need them, or maybe they didn't feel I would appreciate it. I really don't know, but I know that when someone receives a gift, long before they open it up, they are blessed, because to give a gift to someone is not about the content of the gift, it is about the gift of being mindful of the person to whom it is given. Wealthy people need to know also that someone is thinking of them or appreciates them. Being wealthy doesn't change the fact that you are human. Again, it truly isn't about the content of the gift, it is about the quality of the heart of the giver. Believe me, I know this is true. I have been battered and given the gift of a luxury vehicle. The gift was demeaning. Luxury vehicles don't heal broken hearts, and to give the gift to pacify such a serious wound is demeaning, hurtful, and insulting.

Before having a lot of money, I remember receiving letters from my spouse (not even a greeting card, because it was too expensive). I often got handwritten letters as a gift while dating in high school. And when I moved into the multimillion-dollar house with a pool, I had a special, beautiful box filled with all those handwritten letters. To me, those were some of the best gifts I had ever gotten. They were more valuable to me than any car I was ever given to drive or any house I ever lived in. They were more than letters; the content was love. And love is and always will be, without question or doubt, much more valuable than all the money or material possessions in the world. Everyone needs love. God is love.

But that day at the baby shower, out of all the gifts I received, I remember one in particular that stood out to me. The woman who was married at the time to a coach for the NBA team in Florida gave me a book. The title was *The Power of a Praying Wife*. She seemed to be one of the only people who seemed to have even an inkling of the hell I was suffering—not that it was anyone's responsibility to notice, but I sure wish someone would have been there for me during those difficult times. To this day, I still have a copy of that book. The other gifts, the expensive ones, are all gone now. They have largely been given away. But the word of God that woman gave me through that book is still in my possession today. Others gave me what I wanted. God will bless them for it, I know. But God used this woman to give me what I needed. And for that, I pray God goes beyond a blessing for her life and marriage, in Jesus name. By the way, if that woman is reading this book, thank you.

A New Beginning?

Before Zion was born, we purchased a new home in South Holland, Illinois. It was beautiful. It had everything my former spouse wanted, down to the basketball court. Things were looking up—as long as we didn't kick up the rug that all those repressed problems were swept under. I think at this point in time in my life I redefined "walking on pins and needles." I could feel that when serious issues of violence and affairs were not addressed and dealt with, it was dangerous. It was the equivalent of putting pearls on a pig. The pearls can be beautiful and even valuable, but it doesn't change the fact that it's a pig they are hung on. We had the beautiful house and baby, but it didn't change what was going on in our lives. But I kept at it in faith that it would someday change. I thought, "Maybe even once he retires from the NBA, things will get better then." A wife of an NBA player told me very early on how her spouse had several affairs while playing in the NBA, and how he treated her like garbage. However, once he retired and was no longer in the limelight, and most people were not around him anymore since he didn't make that kind of money anymore, everything in him changed. And it had changed him for the better. She also said that at one point, he became depressed. He was a better husband to her after his retirement, though. Reality had likely sat back in for him.

So, it was in remembering her story, that I just kept thinking, "If I can stay with this, maybe by the time he retires, things will get better again." I didn't make it. And as sad as that was for me initially, I realize now that it was absolutely for my good, for the good of my children, and for many others, including some of you who are reading this now.

Back then, I was still hopeful, though, and I was not about to give up. With a new baby and a new home, I was really hoping and praying for a new beginning. I wanted us to go to marriage counseling together, but I attended alone because he wouldn't go with me. I was disappointed to be alone, but I was hoping that my going, even without my spouse, would still be enough to help our marriage and family stay together. I kept attending church services alone too. I did everything I could to work on myself and better myself. I kept taking care of and raising my babies, and I did so without complaint. I did a lot of reflecting then. I thought about the things I was told were the reasons for his anger, and I tried to do the opposite. For example, I was always the type of woman and wife who would tell my spouse the truth about whether or not I believed something was wise or unwise to do. I stopped doing that. I distinctly remember someone approaching him about a business deal to open up a restaurant, and instead of me pushing against it, I said once that I didn't agree, but then I said, "The decision is yours, and I will support you." Inside, I knew it was going to be a disaster. I could clearly see the error in it. (Years later, the people from that business deal took millions of dollars.) I also stopped insisting on going to games or attending road trips, because I wanted to avoid the pain that any rejection could possibly bring me. I just wanted things to get better, even if it meant that I kept suffering silently.

As a part of my efforts to bless my marriage and family, I went out and bought my spouse several gifts that I knew would bless him. I just wanted to show him that despite it all, I still loved him and supported him. I made a gift basket and filled it with sentimental gifts. I also arranged a romantic getaway. Everything seemed to be going well. But on the way home from the hotel after our romantic getaway, I found pictures and instant messages from a lot of women inside of his phone. The messages were graphic, detailed encounters of a spouse's worst nightmare. Fear came all over me. For some reason, I wasn't angry, but I was very afraid. I waited until we got home, and then I went into my eldest son's room and knelt at the foot of his bed to quickly pray to God. In seconds, I was up and ready to confront my spouse about what I had found in his phone. I thought I would be met with apologies or maybe even denials, but instead I was first called crazy, and then I was told that this is the lifestyle, and I should just be grateful for having the house I have and not complain about it. I was told to wake up! This is the real world—connoting, I suppose, acceptance of this kind of behavior in that lifestyle. I was being yelled at, "You don't know who the f—ck I am! I'm a grown man. I do what the f—ck, I want to do. You don't know me." Initially, those words made me angry. With all I found, I wasn't angry until I heard those words. But at some point, after hearing it several times, I wasn't angry anymore. I became deeply wounded, because in that very moment I realized he was right. I didn't know him. That was the day we separated.

What I Needed Wasn't What I Wanted

I did what I had done before with God concerning that marriage, and I prayed that God would put us back together. This time was different, however. Many times before I would pray and ask God for something, and He would answer me right away with what I wanted. We will call these my prayers to put a Band-Aid over the problem. Surgery, getting to the root of the problem, was too invasive, painful, and time-consuming, so I just asked God to fix the surface issues—to bless my husband and me to get along better, for example. But I never asked God to get to the root issues of why we weren't getting along in the first place. And more gravely wrong, I didn't ask God to make things right with each of us, and God before that time. Terrible mistake! God showed me one day when I pulled up in front of the house in Illinois, that many marriages were ending because of this same error. People were interested in and prayed plenty about their marriages with their spouses getting better, but they did not pray for their marriage with God, and their spouse's marriage with God, to get better. This caused many marriages to die, because prayers like those are prayers for the fruit and not the root. And fruit on a tree cannot bear more fruit in and of itself; it must be attached to the tree, and the tree must have roots. And whatever comes from root will become the fruit. Also, there can be no fruit without the root. Jesus explains this concept for *every* area of our lives in the Bible Jesus is our Vine and we are the branches (John 15). A branch cannot bear fruit unless it *abides* in the Vine (John 15).

God created marriage, and is the foundation of it. When people keep God out of their lives or their marriages, it is only a matter of time before they fail outwardly in divorce, or inwardly in a hell behind closed doors, masked with a public appearance of happiness. Either way, they fail. God is the glue that holds together every successful marriage and all healthy relationships. Remove God, and you remove the very thing that kept the relationship or marriage together in the first place. I know experts report what the leading cause of divorce is, but I am telling you God Himself has told me what is destroying marriages. And while the statistics can be telling about the manifestations of the fall of a marriage, God has exposed to us the root problem of it. This means God loves marriages and wants them to succeed. God is telling married people the root problem, so they can get the perfect solution: God! I'm not talking about a false god. I'm talking about the true and living God, Jesus. Don't waste time staring at a statue that, if someone walks by and bumps into it, the false god tumbles to the floor and into pieces. Talk to the real God, Jesus, who, although He was broken and beaten, was raised even from the dead! Those statues won't glue themselves back together; they need human intervention. But when Jesus died, He was resurrected without need of human help. That's God! And if someone's life or marriage is suffering the way I did or my previous marriage did, you don't need to play, you need power—and power belongs to God! My marriage, however, had reached a point of no return, and I learned that what I wanted was not what I needed.

One day I was praying, and for the first time I could ever remember, God didn't give me what I asked for regarding that marriage. Instead, and out of love, God gave me what I so desperately needed. God gave me Himself; He gave me Jesus. And with Jesus came everything I needed. My life has changed and not ever been the same since, and it has been for my good. I had become spoiled. I was used to God giving me whatever I asked Him to. This time— and it was on time—God put His foot down as a loving Father and gave me what He knew I really needed. I cried and was extremely angry with God as I endured the pain of the already-broken pieces of my old life, and as I watched that marriage I once loved dearly fall completely away. I wanted God to fix it, heal it, and make it better. But that time, with that man, the answer was no.

The Dark Days

The dark days were the most painful days of my entire life. I have not felt such depths of pain and sorrow as during these days. Never has life been more dark to me. But never has the Light of Jesus shone so bright either. God has turned these dark days I am going to tell you about into light for me that still to this day is lighting my path and leading me and my children—and many others.

Not long after the separation, none of the people I thought were my real friends were there for me. The people I had supported in so many ways for so long were long gone. Not one of them remained. Instead, God used people I least expected to be there for me, or those I never expected at all, such as a lawyer from Florida who actually understood what was really going on, and some women God had just introduced me to. These women were instrumental in helping me. They were also strangers. I don't dispose of someone just because they are a stranger. Judas was not a stranger to Jesus; Judas was supposed to be His friend. Simon, who helped Jesus carry the cross when Jesus couldn't anymore, was more of a stranger than Judas, but when Jesus needed help, it was the stranger who was there for Jesus! All of Jesus's close friends left him and ran off. The one friend, who followed Jesus at a distance when He was arrested, denied even knowing Jesus multiple times. Those who know what happened to Joseph in Genesis know that it was Joseph's own brothers who had Joseph enslaved. And the same motivation behind Joseph's enslavement and Jesus's betrayal was the force driving against me too—the love of money, and jealousy. My granny warned me of this when God initially blessed me with financial blessings of riches, but I didn't take heed to the wisdom of God in her. Instead, I defended the very people I thought were my friends, who later ended up being false witnesses against me.

There I was, alone. I had nobody. Before this, I was surrounded by people, especially whenever going to All-Star Weekends, Disney World, and shopping malls, but when I hit what the world calls "rock bottom," nobody was really there for me but my mother. I didn't feel comfortable speaking to my dad about it—or my granny either. For some reason, I felt comfortable being ashamed in front of my mother. And my mother wasn't like some other people who did try to come around me, telling me, "You'd better get a private investigator and a lawyer." Their words cut deep and hurt me worse. I wanted my marriage to be saved, not destroyed. But *reconciliation*, even when I spoke that word in English to those who spoke English, seemed to be a foreign language to them. It was just my children and I in that house, or at least that's what it felt like at first. But the fact that we survived tells me God was in that dark place with us and closer to us than ever before during each of those dark days.

It was hard to sleep then. My mind was going a hundred miles an hour with thoughts of the hell that broke loose in that family and marriage. But nighttime was better than the days, because at least when I was asleep for a moment, all the pain seemed to go away. I had begun to look forward to nighttime. Mornings were the worst. I swear, it was like a demon sat on the end of my bed, and every morning during those dark days, he made sure that, before I could hear anything else when I arose, he would list off to me everything that was going wrong in my marriage and my life. Later on, I visited another part of Florida, and God used a woman

I had never met before to pray for me that the demon that sat on my bed would be removed, in Jesus name. I slept back in that bed again, but when I woke up, none of those evil thoughts came to my mind anymore. People, that is the power of God! Sometimes we look for God to do a miracle like open blind eyes because, for us, this is a miracle. But when you have been in the hell I lived in, you know very well that real miracles are of the nature I just described: Jesus setting somebody free from something tormenting with just a simple word! That, people, is the power of God.

The power of God amazed me in many ways at that time. Despite what I had suffered, I continued to live like a wife. Whenever my spouse did decide to come home, I cooked dinner for him just as if he were living at home. I kept myself pure and in the presence of God. I was fulfilling my wifely duties, though I had every reason not to. At that time I had told God that my spouse did not deserve the way I was treating him; however, God corrected me. (God corrects whomever He loves.) God told me something that is powerful for any couple that made vows to God in getting married. God told me I made my vows to love, honor, and be faithful to God, so regardless of a man's behavior, I was to keep those vows I made to God. God showed me later on that I was being like Jesus. I was being faithful despite unfaithfulness. I realized then that marriage is much bigger than the two people saying, "I do." I was and still am amazed at the power of God to keep me loving, honorable, and faithful during such dark days and trying times.

Clothed in Humiliation and Shame

I put on humiliation and shame like garments of clothing. I was literally dressed and covered in them. Everywhere I went I just figured people knew what had happened, or that they had heard what the media was reporting. The media began releasing news that my spouse was with another woman, and that he was seen with her, and the media would release all of this news publicly of course. I remember going to the store and not wanting to use my credit card because the cashier would ask for ID, and once they got my ID, they often said, "Hey, you are Siohvaughn. Your husband is in the NBA, right?" They were usually smiling as they asked, but on the inside I was going cold from fear that they would say, "You know, I heard your husband was with so-and-so, and that he did so-and-so to you..." I literally began to wear big weaves, sunglasses, and a hat most of the time when I was outside in public. I didn't want anyone to recognize me. I was so ashamed.

It became a difficult task even to take my eldest child to school. Again, I figured everyone had heard by then what the media was reporting about affairs. I remember racing every time I dropped him off for school and rushing when I picked him up. I didn't want anyone to ask me anything about what was happening in my marriage or about what the media were reporting. I figured if I got out of that school fast enough, people would not have time to ask me anything or say anything harsh to me, which at that point I felt might be the thing to finally finish me off. I was already hang-ing on by a thread, so to speak. I felt I was barely making it. I had just enough strength to pray and take care of my children. After I dropped Zaire off for school in the mornings, I came back home and spent almost the entire day in my room. I felt bad for Zion because his mommy was sad like that at the time, and it was hard to even enjoy the gift of life that God had given me. I felt I was sur-rounded by darkness and death at that time. When I had to chap-erone for Zaire's school, I went with my head held down. I couldn't wear my disguise around the other parents and school staff; they all knew of me anyway. I endured those field trips, very sadly. One mother noticed that I had lost a lot of weight. She wanted to know what I had done to lose so much weight. It was no diet, however; I was depressed and oppressed. Even when people have to deal with only one of these things, they have given up and died, but both were up against me, and I was left to raise my two children alone.

It was extremely difficult for me. My mother wanted to be there for me, but she couldn't. She lived and worked in another state. Plus, only God could heal the pain and brokenness inside of me. There are people so broken that an encouraging word or steadfast counseling won't do it; they need the power of God. That is what I needed without question. I was so ashamed, I didn't even want to talk to my own family members. I even hid from them. Even when someone tried to comfort me because of what was going on in my life, it only reminded me of the shame and humiliation I was experiencing. The media, and people, just spoke about my marriage and family as if it were nothing, as if I had no feelings or children. It was horrible—nothing I would wish on those who did it to me. That dark place is that bad. I told God, my life had not hit the floor, it went through it. Rock bottom was my ceiling!

I remember at one point before all of this, I was very arrogant and prideful about who I was married to. I was really proud of it. But not after those dark days. It had become my greatest failure, my biggest shame. I used to like being in the limelight before. It made me feel special. The cameras of Hollywood had become a nightmare to me. I was terrified of them. I didn't want anyone to see me. I remember wishing I could disappear. Wow, what a turnaround! The Bible says the proud shall be humbled and the humble exalted (Matt. 23:12).

I Can't Save Them; Only God Saves

The Bible says that God alone saves (Isa. 43:11). I am good with that Word from God now, but at that time, I refused to accept it. In my mind my spouse was in trouble and he couldn't see it because of the riches of this world, and my children were devastated by a broken family, so I was going to do what any good mother and wife does: I was going to fix it. The funny thing is, I couldn't save myself, but I thought I could save my spouse and save my children from the pain and negative effects of a broken family.

I thank God that Zion was so young during this time. I believe it was the mercy of God on him. Zion was around three months old when his dad decided to leave, so Zion hadn't had the chance to bond with him as much as Zaire yet, and he didn't feel the pain that Zaire felt then. Zion also went several months consecutively without seeing or spending time with his dad, so when he did see him again, Zion was afraid and would cry profusely. I tried to fix this too. I would call his dad's cell phone and beg him to just speak some words to Zion, while I held my cell phone to Zion's ear. That way, Zion would at least recognize his dad's voice. That, however, did not work. Zion still so infrequently heard from and saw his dad that he just cried and tried to get out of his arms when he did see him. This was painful for me to watch. I could see with my eyes and feel the pain in my heart of a broken family, of a marriage ending. We were hurting.

I remember my eldest son being very broken about the separation of his parents. He cried daily for so long. I remember trying to make him feel better by buying him things. I think I bought more toys for that boy during those dark days than every birthday celebration combined. This was a fatal mistake. I remember driving down US 1 in Miami, and I saw in the rearview mirror that Zaire was sitting in the back seat crying, missing the family he once had. By then God had told me to stop buying him things, because the toys and material possessions were not healing him. They were at best a brief distraction. I literally told God as I saw Zaire crying, "God, I am just going to buy one more toy." I stopped at a toy store on US 1 and bought him and Zion more toys. That same day, he was back in tears and broken. That was it for me. I stopped trying to heal my children with toys. I learned quickly that there was another reason God wanted me to stop trying to stuff the hole of emptiness Zaire felt when his dad left.

Eventually, I noticed that God was healing Zaire. I also began noticing that Zaire used the fact that he knew I was very concerned for him to manipulate me and obtain all sorts of material posses-sions from me. Then I had to forgive myself because I blamed my-self for some of his behaviors. God taught me soon, however, that every one of us has a choice to make, to do the right or the wrong thing. That decision is ours alone and we can't blame others for our own actions-good or evil.

You have likely heard the old saying, "You can lead a horse to water, but you can't make him drink it." I discovered at this time in my life that whenever you are dealing with a human being and pride, you can't even lead them to water, let alone make them drink it. I learned a painful lesson: only Jesus saves! God never intended the lesson to be painful, but I kept going in my self-efforts to try to save my spouse and children, my marriage and family. The pain came from the disappointment when I realized that no matter what I did, I could not save them. No matter how much I wanted to, I can't save. Only Jesus saves! I was a mate, not the Messiah, and I learned the difference the hard way, with many tears.

I felt at that time that I had tried it all. I tried to beg my hus-band to do what I believed was the right thing to do. I tried to rea-son him into doing what was right; reminding him of the effects sin can have on his life and soul. I kept sleeping with him, but after the sex, the brokenness remained. I tried reminding him of his own past pain that he had shared with me and that he attributed to a broken family. But all to no avail.

I was faced with the reality of my weakness and humanity as I tried and failed over and over again in my human self-efforts to save my marriage and put the broken pieces of a once-beautiful family back together—all to no avail. My pride was wounded. But I needed to be delivered from pride and be humble anyway. I had become very tired and worn down because I was still trying to carry something that God never called me to carry. It was never my cross to bear. I am not the Savior. God gave me this under-standing, which I desperately needed; one day after He gave me a vision that completely clarified things and put them into perspective for me.

Having Understanding

In this vision, I was on a dead-end street. I had raced down this street, and at the end of it was a cliff so deep that it seemed literally bottomless. But I had driven so fast down that dead-end street that even if I had wanted to, I couldn't stop before crashing and going off the cliff and into the chasm below. Miraculously, after the crash, I was still alive. God obviously had taken me out of that deep hole, but I was still wounded severely as a result of the crash. I was bleeding and bruised, and I walked with a limp then. My scars were evident. As I limped in the opposite direction of the dead-end street and back toward the direction from which I had come, I saw my former spouse coming down the same dead-end road, but he was driving even faster than I was before I crashed. I flagged him down with whatever strength I had left. I remember that he rolled down the window of his car just enough to hear me, but he looked irritated at the fact that I had even stopped him. I warned him that the road ahead was a dead-end road, and the bridge at the end was out, and there was a deep hole just over the cliff ahead. He didn't listen; he cursed at me and rolled up his window and drove away faster than he was driving before.

God explained this vision to me, and I want to share it with you. God showed me that the speed at which I was going, and at which I saw others going, symbolizes what is referred to as "living life in the fast lane." Living life in the fast lane represents living a life of sin. Sin likes to take people really fast, so that, by the time they realize the bridge is out and the crash is ahead, they have too much momentum to stop. With sin, it is like they are bound to keep going, and it will take God to stop them. God showed me that the street was a dead end because there is one place sin takes people to, and that is to death. This doesn't have to be a physical death, although for some it is. It can also be the premature death of a marriage, death to someone's health, death to their finances, or death to their relationship with their children etc. And no matter what type of death it is, the reasons are all the same: separation from God.

God showed me that I was the driver of that car. I was responsible for my own sin, and likewise my spouse was the driver of his own sin. We were married at the time God gave me the vision, but we were in separate cars, signifying a married couple's individual responsibility to obey God, and their individual accountability to God if they do not obey. At the end of the street, the ground was missing and there was a big, very deep hole with a bunch of boulders and concrete blocks of street pavement, rocks, dirt, and debris, where I had fallen over into that hole. The hole was deep—so deep that only God could deliver me out of it. That's sin—a deep hole, that nobody can get themselves out of. They need a deliverer to deliver them from the hole of sin, and my Deliverer, who delivered me from the deep, seemingly endless hole, was Jesus Christ. And that is the heart of God, that even if we willingly choose to go into a hole of sin, God sent Jesus to die, paying the price to have us eternally extracted from that hole, forgiving us of all our sins and remembering them no more (Isa. 43:25). God also showed me my heart toward my spouse in the vision. Regardless of what had happened, in my heart was deep love. With whatever strength I had left, I tried to use it to save him. God also showed me that I couldn't save him; he actually went away, driving even faster in the same direction from which I had just come.

This is when I realized I wasn't attempting to save him at all. I was hurting him and myself in the process, by trying to be a god to him, and by having him as a god to me. You see, the truth is, I didn't get to where I needed to be in life until I went down that road, all the way to the end of it, and crashed hard. We must stop fearing the crash. (I feel God speaking to parents who are worrying over their children because of the child's choices and conduct. "Fear not," I feel God saying.) No matter how bad or severe the crash is, it is not greater than my God, who is love and who is good. No matter how severe the wounds, they could never out-hurt the healing power of Jesus Christ, and His desire and full willingness to heal you and make you whole in every area of your life. Look at my life for the truth of that message from God.

The devastation of that crash became my deliverance in that vision and in my life. Sometimes that is the road people must take to be saved. That can be hard for others who love them to watch happen, but try to keep your mind focused on God and the fact that God is good and well able to take the worst crash in life and turn it into a beautiful destiny and purpose. God is not shocked by the decisions we make; God is in control. You must know and trust this, because life at times will seem out of control, or loved ones may seem out of control. Have no fear; God is in control. And God's plans for us are good, and not evil (Jer. 1:17). Now, understand that God's being good does not always mean the absence of bad being present in our lives. Thinking otherwise is error and usually from the devil himself, or immaturity. It tries to cause people to judge God and to question His goodness and love toward them. God's goodness is seen best when, despite the evil, God still blesses you, keeps you, provides for you, forgives you, heals you, delivers you, and restores you. Sometimes we want all the evil to be gone, but God doesn't mind blessing your life with your evil enemies watching closely. You can see this truth in Psalm 23, which is often read at funerals—for what reason, I don't know. There is so much life in Psalm 23. The psalmist mentions death once, and it's been to more funerals than dead bodies it seems. I don't get it, but I don't want it read at mine. I'm telling my family now: pick a different Bible verse! Pardon me, I just felt the need to get that off my chest and share that with you as well. Now, in Psalm 23, God promises to prepare a table before us in the presence of our enemies. Take notice that God does not say in the *absence* of our enemies but in their *presence*. God has a plan even for your enemies who are breathing down your neck so close you can feel them. Don't panic. God has a plan for your life, and it is good and not evil. God wants to give you hope and a future, the opposite of death (Jer. 29:11).

Finally, I came to the end of myself, and from that moment forward I have been realizing over and over again that God truly is all you need and all you will ever have need of. It's not just that God is a provider, only supplying your natural needs. God is provision, supplying all things needed and desired. God is the source for everything you could ever need and even desire. Now that I know this truth, I rest so much more in my mind, emotions, and physical body. I have so much more peace and so much more joy! This truth has indeed set me free, and whomever Jesus sets free is free indeed (John 8:36). The roads of my own self-efforts were the painful way that I chose to take in order to learn these valuable lifesaving and life-changing lessons. But you however, can just take heed of the truth and the wisdom of God, without enduring the sorrow that I did in order to gain this wisdom.

Renewing My Vows with Jesus Christ

Jesus loves us with an everlasting love, and God forgives our sins abundantly. I never knew this to be so true as when I needed it— until I found myself feeling completely empty and devoid of love and in serious need of God's forgiveness. I went back to Jesus, my first love. And instead of Jesus telling me, "I told you so!" or calling me "dumb," Jesus forgave me and loved me with open arms and love and compassion, as if I had never done anything wrong. People, this is the love of God. This is the grace of God. Jesus didn't even mention what I did wrong; He just forgave me and loved me more than ever before. Jesus was to me what I was not to Him; Jesus was faithful. This love and grace Jesus has shown me has not made me want to sin and abuse His love and forgiveness, but rather it has made me love Jesus more than ever before. It has caused me to draw nearer to Jesus than ever before. Jesus has saved my life more than once, and this time when He did, He gave me the life worth living, that He had for me all along, and for that, I am very grateful.

Jesus alone helped me through these dark days. Jesus is the only reason I didn't kill myself. Jesus is the only reason I was able to parent my children with my heart in pieces, my mind racing, and my entire life having become a public shame. I hid in Jesus Christ, and I found refuge and safety. In Jesus I found deliverance from the things that had held me captive for many years. Jesus dug deep and delivered me from all the years of abuse and the way I allowed myself to be subjected to it. God took my head that was hanging down in shame, humiliation, and worthlessness, and He lifted it up with love and instilled in me the truth about who I am by revealing to me, whose I am. I have not been the same. My entire life has been transformed. I'm no longer just alive. I am living an abundant life, the life that is worth living. I am free from everything that used to bind me. And whomever the Son of God sets free, is free indeed (John 8:36). And I am free indeed, because Jesus set me free!

Mending a Broken Heart

God showed me that the process of His healing my broken heart was like a patient with a broken arm who is in excruciating pain. The patient goes to the hospital and asks for a doctor for the sole purpose of being healed, but when the doctor reaches out to begin the healing process by examining the arm, the patient screams at the doctor, "Don't touch me!" I, like the patient with the broken arm, wanted healing, but I didn't want God, the Healer, to touch me, because I didn't want anyone to hurt me more.

Likewise, the patient with the broken bone very naturally pulls away from the doctor and doesn't want the doctor to touch it, because it already hurts bad enough. The patient doesn't want to run any risk of the doctor hurting the wound more. But the doctor must be allowed to get close enough and to touch the painful arm in order to help heal the patient. Sometimes the doctor has to take the brokenness, the broken arm, and snap it back into place—causing more pain, but it's temporary pain and its—in order to heal the brokenness. The doctor's intention is not to hurt the patient; it is to heal the hurting. If we can trust the doctor even when it hurts, we know surely we can trust God.

There is no mistake or malpractice with God, but doctors err often, because they are human beings under their white coats, and a medical degree won't change that. God is God, and He is flawless! He is perfect and He loves you, so you can trust God and His healing touch. Now, being touched by the Healer may hurt sometimes, but only temporarily. It is for healing purposes only and, not to hurt you. Sometimes being healed requires the Healer to touch the brokenness. Sometimes you have to come in contact with the Healer to be healed. (Not all the time, as sometimes God heals you with just His Word!) Other times, we need a touch from God. The lady with the issue of blood was healed when she touched the hem of Jesus's garment (Luke 8:42–48). Jesus healed one man by spitting and then touching the man's blind eyes so that he could finally see (Mark 8:23). God wanted to heal me, but I wouldn't let God do it. I didn't want God to touch me because the pain was so severe. This seeming self-preservation was indeed deceitful and fruitless, however, because it didn't preserve me at all. It was causing me to perish in that pain. This is because, if I didn't let God touch it and risk feeling hurt in the process, He couldn't heal me. I desperately needed for God to heal me, no matter the cost, but I was so scared of being hurt again that I didn't let Him really heal me the way He wanted—and the way He knew I needed—for some time.

I was, in essence, afraid of the very healing I needed. This I believe has happened to many others, whether consciously or not. I had cried out and prayed to God for healing, and when the Healer showed up to heal and mend my broken heart, I cried out, "Don't touch me!" God let me know I was screaming inside for Him not to touch me. The pain was that deep. I trusted no one with it, not even God. At that point, I was only willing to even let God get a *little* close to me. After all, look at what happened with the over-whelming majority of the people I had trusted previously. Almost all of the people I loved deeply and trusted had betrayed me, hurt-ing both my boys and me beyond measure. The depth of the pain I was in at that time was river-deep pain.

In fact, the emotional pain was so deep at that time that it hurt me physically. My chest and stomach would be in severe pain. At times, it hurt to breath. I had stomach pains also that were so pro-fuse that I would just lie in a fetal position on the floor, balled up, and cry. These wounds were very severe, and I have no doubt that when the devil himself led in doing this to me, he intended to kill me by having me kill myself because of the pain and humiliation.

I struggled during that time with the belief that God could heal me. I honestly didn't *believe* that He could heal me. I just didn't be-lieve that it was possible. I told God, "I have had a broken heart be-fore, but nothing like this. God, my heart is shattered into pieces, not just broken. For God, if my heart were just broken, you could take the two broken pieces and mend them. But God, my heart is broken like someone went to the top of the highest building and dropped my heart off the top of it. When my heart hit the ground, it was shattered into pieces. God, even if you can put some of the pieces back together, because my heart is shattered, You won't be able to find all the pieces. My heart is in a million tiny pieces. God, such is my heart after this. How can you heal that?" I was giving up. BUT JESUS!

But God didn't give up on me, even when I gave up on myself. He instead patiently waited and loved me daily until I trusted Him enough to take all the pain I was in upon Himself and heal me, even if the healing process hurt. Thankfully, I finally trusted God. That is a decision I don't ever regret making. God can be trusted. He can be trusted to be who He says He is, and trusted to do all He says He will do. For I have not found this with mankind—not in myself either—but I have found this faithfulness in God, in Jesus, and in the Holy Spirit of God.

You were not there literally with me behind the scenes when all this was happening in my life, but as best as God has allowed me, I have taken you behind there with me through this book, by God's grace. Now that you can see what I see, you very likely know what I know: only God saved, healed, restored, helped, and made me whole again. I was shattered to pieces in complete brokenness. Not all the best therapists collectively could have helped me, and no medication in the entire world would have healed me, because the pain was entirely too deep, and the crisis and trauma too severe. And for the glory of God, God healed me completely without the need of either. Jesus healed me. Jesus, I publicly acknowledge Your infinite power, and I declare without any shame that You alone, Jesus, healed me. And when all seemed to forsake me, Lord, You never left me. Jesus, I love You, and I thank You eternally because, instead of judgment, You forgave me, and instead of condemning me, You restored and healed me. And You alone are the reason why I live. Again, thank You, Jesus.

The very depth of my brokenness I have shared with you, the very intimate parts of me. I have done so believing that God will use all this to heal and to restore those of you reading this who are in need of healing and restoration.

Now, one of the greatest miracles I have ever witnessed in my life is the power of God to heal my heart, emotions, and life. I have experienced the very power of God to heal the most impossible wounds and brokenness. Jesus's walking on water is impressive and glorious, but the power of Jesus to heal me from the depths of the pain, sorrow, and mourning I was once in is more powerful than raising the dead and walking on water combined. I was glad Jesus was healing me, and I was better in so many ways. The inflicting of wounds and causing of pain was far from over; but the love and power of Christ Jesus to heal me wasn't over either.

Home Not-So-Sweet Home

I began traveling from Miami to Chicago with the boys at that time. I would walk through the airport, trying my best not to cry, but every so often, the tears would just pour out. I remember wondering, as I looked at all the people who surrounded me in the airport and on the plane, whether any of them noticed that I was in this pain. Nobody ever hugged me or just told me, "Ma'am, everything is going to be all right." Everyone just went along about their day. That didn't make me bitter, though; it made me better. I have consciously prayed for people in houses just as I drove by, running errands, and especially houses that are very expensive, because I assume the wealthy live there. I have stopped and asked people if they are all right. I have heard God speak something to me about some stranger I am in a building with, and I've told them what God said, and they've thanked me profusely and exclaimed, "God bless you, ma'am!" I laid my hands on and prayed for healing for an older woman coming out of Chase Bank one day. I didn't know that woman was ill, but God in me knew what she needed.

Now when I walk through the world I am conscious of those around me, and when God prompts me, I take notice of their problem or pain, and I stop whatever I am busy doing to love people and bless them and encourage them. I give to them what I needed so deeply in those dark days. I have become in a lot of ways the change I wanted to see. But back in those times, Miami had become a graveyard to me. It was a place in which I became deeply sad and heavy whenever I returned there.

Eventually, God showed me I was going to leave Miami and go back to Illinois. I prayed, and when God released me, I called my spouse and asked him to please come to the house so that I could speak to him about something very important. When I asked him if he was okay with my moving to Illinois with the boys, he said yes. That was all I needed to know. God surely called me to leave. Shortly thereafter, the boys and I went back to Illinois to live. We had a home there already in South Holland, Illinois, so in some ways we went home. This was also a relief because my mom was in the Chicago area and able to help me with the boys and be there for us during these very trying times. But home without the family I once prayed for made "home sweet home" not so sweet.

God gave me supernatural strength to press on, though, through all the hell. I had the house in Florida kept clean and all the bills paid. I cut a lot of expenses from that house, but I kept it so that I could bring the children back to Florida to spend time with their dad, and they would have a place to go. (After my spouse filed for divorce, however, the court made me sell that home in Florida, and when I brought the children to Florida after that point to see their father, we didn't have a home to return to, so I would have to stay at the houses of other people from the church I attended in Florida.)

Zion's birthday was nearing, and I wanted to do something special for him. I had a hotel room rented at an indoor water park in Illinois. I invited the children's dad and gave him the address where we would be. That day—Zion's birthday—was one of the first days in a very long time that we spent time together like a family. We played board games and actually laughed together and gave gifts to Zion and ate together. God had used Zion to bring the family back together, in peace, even if only for a moment.

Torn Asunder

Soon after getting back to the house in Illinois, FedEx came to the house. I accepted the envelope, and when I opened it, I soon realized that a divorce petition was inside. The air seemed to go out of me. The very thing that I was terrified of—getting divorced—was in my hands that spring day. I was very scared. I did not know at all what to do. I knew how to be married, but I didn't know how to divorce. I had suffered a lot of pain already, and I was broken, but when I got that divorce petition in the mail, I died all over again. After all, we had been in the sanctuary of God together, spent several years together, cried together, broken bread together, hustled together, prayed together, laughed together, worked together, had faith together, lost hope together, had two children together, built our lives together with God, seen poverty together, and sat under the rain of wealth as God poured it from Heaven on us together. And yet, it was the FedEx man who delivered the news of divorce to me.

Millions of dollars, and none of them could help me. Oh, how I loathed money. I remember going into my closet for something, and as I looked around at all the "stuff" I had, my heart seemed to fill with rage. I was looking at all the designer clothes, shoes, and handbags, and none of it could help my hurting children or me. Good for nothing! This wounded me more severely. You see, the money never meant anything to me. I always wanted a family. So when I looked up and saw that I had money and material possessions, but I did not have the one thing I truly desired, my pain grew even deeper. To understand some of the effects the destruction of this marriage had on me, it is important to understand what was going on inside of me back then. My husband was an idol to me then, so when my marriage was destroyed, I did not believe I was going to make it. I literally thought I was dying—the pain was so deep. Nothing had hurt me in my life as much as this did. I felt like I loved my husband more than any other human being, including myself. In my lifetime, I have been raped repeatedly—both systematically and individually—and discriminated against because of my race. I have lost the only sibling I had, and I have been abused physically, emotionally, and financially. I have been lied about, publicly humiliated, falsely accused, falsely arrested, and imprisoned for days. I have buried one of my parents, and both my children were taken away from me on the same day. Yet none of that hurt and suffering caused me as much anguish and deep sorrow as the ending of my marriage back then. The ending of that marriage was the ending of my family, as I knew it, the acceptance of the death of the man I once married, and because of the identity crisis I was in, it was also the end of me. Back then all I was a rich man's wife. That is how the world identified me, and it is how I identified myself. Thus, at that time when my marriage ended, my life ended too.

But God allowed who I had become—let's call her the "old woman"—to die, to perish with that marriage. God did for me what I was too weak to do for myself. He saved and delivered me from just accepting being trampled over, abused, used, and completely taken for granted, just to say I was somebody's wife. God delivered me from me. Because at those times in my life I would rather have someone, even if they were destroying me, than feel like I didn't have anyone at all. God also delivered me from fear of what would happen to me if I did leave. God delivered me from all my fears. By the time all was said and done, when the devil came back trying to scare me and threatening to take someone else or something else from me, instead of fearing, I was willing to hold the door open for him while he carried it out. I had not given up. I had given it all to God. I decided that I was no longer going to be crushed under the weight of carrying something that God never intended for me to carry. Wise people know what battles they are called to fight—and which ones they are called to completely turn over to God. Who, after all, created them, their enemy, and the fight! The wisdom of God will tell you when to punch and when to peel out, when to rage and when to run, when to strike and when to submit. Every fight just isn't my fight, and I am okay with that, because God is and always will be my victory. That makes perfect sense to me now. It amazes me how it was like a foreign language to me for so many years. I thank Jesus for redemption, deliverance, and His wisdom.

Be the Change You Hope to See

I don't even remember how, or who, helped me to find a divorce lawyer, but I eventually found one. I went to her office. It was a horrifying experience. This lady was telling me how to get divorced as if she were explaining how to change oil in a vehicle. There wasn't the least bit of compassion in her. I remember her talking and her voice slowly fading from me as I began to look around her office. I saw a picture in her office with her, her husband, and their children in the photo, smiling and appearing very happy. I burned with anger inside, because this lady had a family, so presumably she knew the importance of it; however, she instantly and very willingly was ready to destroy mine without ever even asking, "What do you want?" or "Are you okay?" or "Can I recommend any counseling for you and your children, since times like these are devastating?" None of that. Even her tone seemed harsh. I needed more than a divorce lawyer; I needed someone who had compassion along with their education and law license. I wish I could tell you I found the compassion I needed in a divorce lawyer, but I didn't. I found it in Jesus. This developed compassion in me. You see, I knew what it was like to be dragged across a floor, choked until I could not breathe, physically assaulted. I knew what it was like to be manipulated by being told that nobody would ever want me, and that I wouldn't have any money if I left that person, and that my children would be taken from me. I knew what it was like to have someone without any compassion look mercilessly at me, as if I were a fool, and ask, "Why didn't you just leave, then?" when I finally got the courage to tell of the violence I suffered. I didn't "just leave" for the same reason anyone else bound by something doesn't "just leave." Bound people need a deliverer to set them free. This is why Jesus refers to people in sin as being "captive," and why God has appointed Jesus as our Savior and Deliverer, because we need to be saved from any sin that binds us and holds us captive. And whomever Jesus sets free is free indeed (John 8:36). But even with all the abuse I had suffered silently all those years, the abusive, and unjust ways of the judicial system and those involved was way worse. Systematic injustice and abuse are by far worse than any abuse an individual man or woman could produce. Systematic injustice also does significantly more damage than any one abusive man or woman could ever accomplish on their own, and in their individual capacity. Systematic abuse has the force of the law

"I will never leave you nor forsake you" (Deut. 31:6).

THE LEGAL INJUSTICE SYSTEM

*"Do as they ask, but solemnly warn them about the way
a king will reign over them." So Samuel passed on the
Lord's warning to the people who were asking him for a
king. "This is how a king will reign over you... "The king
will draft your sons and assign them...[and] some will be
forced to plow in his fields...The king will take away the
best of your fields and...give them to his own officials...
and you will be his slaves."*

—1 Samuel 8:9–17

It was after this chapter in my life that I realized just how wise
we would be to take heed to what Jesus said about running into
court. Jesus said, "Be quick to agree with your adversary and settle
your disputes while on your way to court" (Matt. 5:25). Jesus even
said, "If anyone wants to sue you and take away your tunic, let him
have your cloak also" (Matt. 5:40). This doesn't mean you are weak;
it means you are wise—wise enough to know when it is worth it to

engage the enemy, and when it is not to. Ask military officials, who plan for battles and wars, and I am certain they will tell you they don't engage in every battle, nor do they pursue every rescue mission. Knowing when to fight is as important, if not more important than, knowing how to fight. God gives us victory in the battles He ordained for us to fight, not the ones chosen by us. God won't put on us more than we can bear (1 Cor. 10:13). I asked God one day, "Why then do people commit suicide?" God told me, "I said I will not put on you more than you can bear." God continued, "I didn't say people don't put more on themselves than what they can bear." We don't want to be crushed under the weight of a fight that we were never called by God to be involved in. Jesus knew when it was time for Him to respond and engage the enemy, and when it was time for Him to literally run (Mark 5:23). We know Jesus has all authority over hell itself, but even Jesus Himself sometimes fled. Why would Jesus do this? Because Jesus knew the will of God for His life, and when Jesus knew God was telling Him to fight, He fought, and when He knew God was telling Him to flee, He was wise and humble enough to listen to and obey God, and thus, He began to run! R-U-N stands for Rejecting Unnecessary Nonsense. So we would be wise also to reject unnecessary nonsense and run whenever God warns us to do so! Jesus was too wise to attend a fight He knew God had not led Him into. And yes, God did lead Jesus sometimes into serious battles, but because God led Him, Jesus was always victorious (Matt. 4:1–16). The same is true for you and me. Remember, discerning what battles to fight or from which to take flight does not make you weak; it makes you wise.

We must learn to follow Jesus's wise guidance, and *run* from the court system when we can do so. Jesus's warning is because of the terrible things that can happen in court, and He says that plainly. Jesus warns us about the possibility of going to jail also. Notably, He didn't say we had to be guilty to end up there! I'm sure people have thought, that won't happen to them, but I am sure if we ask the last twenty thousand people who were wrongfully convicted and imprisoned, they will say they didn't think it would happen to them either. Let's take heed to Jesus's wisdom.

Jesus also warns us about corrupt lawyers. Jesus said plainly how some lawyers love people with burdens hard to bear (Luke 11:46). I have found this to be true, and not just because of my faith in Jesus, but because I experienced it. I watched lawyers lie to me, manipulate me, and literally try to scare me, because they only got paid if there was a problem. So when there was no problem, they manipulated me with fear to try to justify their running into court and charging nearly $600 per hour! When there was an actual problem, they lied and exaggerated it so that they could justify why they spent so much time trying to resolve it—and at nearly $600 per hour, of course! In short, lawyers only get paid those high fees when there is a problem, and the more "complicated" the problem, the more time they spend allegedly resolving it, and that means the more they take money from their client and make themselves rich. Divorce court and other courts can be wholly losing battles, costing the most priceless of things to seemingly come out better than the opposing side but never actually winning a thing. The purported winners are the corrupted lawyers, but even they have not won, because people reap what they sow (Galatians 6:7-9). Like I said, there are no winners. It costs to be contentious and quarrelsome! God's wisdom is free. You choose.

The Bible is rich and filled with both the wisdom and the knowledge of God about legal matters. God is a just Judge, and Jesus is an Advocate and Mediator. Thus, you can learn a lot about the legal system from reading the Bible, and you should. God is not like some of the natural judges that I've encountered. God is a just Judge, who is merciful and righteous, and He hates bribery and will not pervert the ways of justice, but rather, God executes justice for all who are oppressed! And in my personal opinion, He should be the only judge, as He said in the beginning (1 Sam.

9–17). Jesus is also called the Wonderful Counselor (lawyers are called counselors). And Jesus should be the first Counselor you go to if you have a legal problem. Let Him lead you from there, because Christ will not steer you wrong, and Jesus does not want to take money from you. He gave up being rich in order to prosper you financially and He can be trusted (2 Cor. 8:9).

If you are faced with a legal battle, He will tell you when fighting is the way to victory and when refraining secures your win and avoids your defeat. This will take God's wisdom, discernment, and maturity, all of which Jesus is certainly ready to provide to you. In fact, God says, "If you ask for wisdom, I will give it to you freely without finding fault" (James 1:5). I encourage you to pray to God for His wisdom, not the wisdom of this world, but God's infinite, perfect wisdom, in Jesus name. Jesus warns us to not run the risk of the corruptions inside of court if we can avoid it. Sometimes, however, it is inevitable, as in the divorce case I was in. I didn't file it, but I had to fight it. I did learn, however, that not every battle within, even a war you didn't choose, is meant to be fought, and that part we can decide. I'm okay with the fact that I learned this the hard way, because I was blessed to learn it. I know Jesus's warning is worth heeding, not just because of my faith in Christ but because of my experience with the court system.

Justifying Injustice: Corruption in the Court System

Unfortunately, what I'm about to share with you is not rare, foreign, or tailor-made to fit my life. Injustice is an infestation that has been hidden in the legal system, has plagued the people, and has been passed down for generations by judges, legislators, elected officials, and law-enforcement officers. The legal system has constantly justified injustice through corruption. Just a few examples of legal injustice in the American legal system are slavery, segregation, rape, sexism, and murder—all of them legal at some point. Unfortunately, injustice is not just something that negatively affected history; it still plagues the so-called justice system. Hopefully this chapter will shed some God-needed light on this darkness operating in the court system through some of my experiences in it.

The case was initially filed in November 2007, and it didn't end until February 3, 2016—over nine years later. During this time, a lot occurred in the case, but it suffices to share the experiences below in order to take you behind the closed doors of that courtroom in order to share with you the truth. It is likely that if I would not have shared the truth with you, it would have not been told. I say this because of the frequent measures taken to hide it. One of the most common ways used was undoubtedly unlawful. When I watched it unfold countless times throughout the case's history, I had inner discernment that it was wrong; however, after I got accepted into law school and began an in-depth study of the law, I knew it was unlawful. I want to give you a little background so that you will know, if you don't already, what the process is supposed to be like for hearing a court case, whether you are a party to the case or the public in general and want to sit in the courtroom and hear for yourself what is going on. Almost always prior to a court hearing, the parties to the case—the plaintiff/defendant or petitioner/respondent—will be given a time when their case will be called and they will be heard by the judge. Once the parties or their lawyers actually arrive in court, they check in with the judge's clerk. This then becomes a "first-come first-served" basis for those within their pre-designated time frame. This is the way it worked in Cook County, Illinois, at the Daley Center, at least. It is also the way it is supposed to work in Miami-Dade courtrooms. I have had experiences in them both, but this chapter will focus on Illinois, because that is where my former spouse filed the divorce case and where I first became exposed to the injustice in the justice system. Also, court cases are public record, and court hearings and trials are also open to the public. This law requiring transparency of court proceedings is for good reasons. Opening the courtroom doors and allowing the public to hear and see what goes on in court cases helps ensure that the law will be executed justly. People are less likely to do wrong in the open and with others watching. I noticed that, for the majority of times during court hearings in my case, even though we would arrive to court first and check in first or very early, the judge would not call our case until last, when the courtroom was completely cleared out. Eventually, I understood why this was happening. Every other person (the public) who could witness what was happening behind the closed doors of that courtroom was gone—and that's when some of the most corrupted events took place. So, as I said, I will open up the doors of these courtrooms through the truth and take you inside in order to shine light on the darkness of injustice.

When the case first began, I had an elderly lawyer whose husband was sick (and eventually died during the case), and so I needed co-counsel. This led to my having several lawyers from both law firms on my case. Hence, that was the beginning of why I had multiple lawyers on the case. It didn't take long before some of those representing me, as well as I myself, realized that something had gone wrong with some of the judges involved in the case. We knew this because there are a lot of common things that happen in just about every civil court case, including divorce cases. In fact, often lawyers will use the same documents for each case. Very commonly in divorce cases there are temporary orders entered for support, whether spousal or child support. This protects individuals and children from not having their needs met because the working spouse refuses to give them access to their money. (Money in marriage is shared for the most part.) In my case, however, something much different occurred. When it came to spousal support, whether temporary or permanent, I never received it. I supported my children and myself with whatever savings I had, and when that ran out, I went to my parents, and when they did all they could, I borrowed from a friend, and when that didn't last, I got into debt just to survive. All the while, our family had millions of dollars. And with millions of dollars, my children and I survived by the grace of God alone.

When I realized the court was not going to give me temporary spousal support, or any for that matter, I did try to at least get monetary support for Zaire and Zion. The court refused to do that too. Years went by, and millions of dollars were available, yet the court had not entered a single order of child support for our children. Not one! Not one hundred dollars, not fifty dollars, not ten dollars—nothing! We lived off the savings I had left, but it dwindled down and eventually was gone. It was also impossible to get a job during this time. Very often, my former spouse's lawyers and the court would require that I be in court, in person, or otherwise go to jail. I spent many days inside courtrooms and away from my children to avoid going to jail. I spent the good part of the workday, and sometimes every day of the workweek, inside of that courtroom. By the time court concluded, it was time for me to pick up my children from school, help them with homework, and prepare dinner for us. I was also the parent responsible for taking our children to their doctor appointments and extracurricular activities, and I wasn't giving that up willingly for anyone. Court became consuming. And the injustice became blatant.

I can't count the number of times men who worked nine-to-five jobs, with no celebrity status, came in to court, and for being only weeks behind on paying spousal support, they were put in jail or threatened with jail if they did not pay everything owed—and this was done by the same judges who heard my case. But not so in my case. I was a wife who went without receiving any spousal or child support for years, even though there were millions of dollars from which to pay, and the same court told me time after time, "Ms. Wade, we are going to give him more time to pay." God used my mother to buy clothes and shoes for Zion and Zaire, because they had outgrown the old ones, and I couldn't afford it, and the Cook County courts told me for years that they were going to give the multimillionaire more time to pay, but they put the middle-class man in jail for being a couple of weeks behind in paying, right before my very eyes! Injustice is real, people, and corruption is all too common, especially in Chicago, Illinois. By the grace of God, I learned what many civil rights leaders who died in the fight against injustice knew: "Justice delayed, is justice denied," as Dr. Martin Luther King Jr. said.

Even though the law provided that I was entitled to spousal support, I stopped asking for it altogether. I began seeking only child support for my two children, which the law also clearly mandated my children were entitled to. The court didn't give Zion and Zaire that either, though, despite the fact that there were millions of dollars available. Obviously, the children didn't need millions of dollars, but they did need food to eat, clothes to wear, and their educational expenses paid for, just like every other child does. The judge again said, "Wait." This wait turned into years. The children had needs like food, clothing, medical, and educational expenses that could not wait. I had needs as well. Eventually, my debts totaled well over hundreds of thousands of dollars, the one car went up for repossession, and the other one broke down and I could not afford to have it fixed. Again: "Justice delayed is justice denied." After asking for child support, they did, however, ask me to take a DNA test. I almost raced to take that test, because I figured this was yet again another delay/denial tactic, and two small children were suffering already because of this injustice. Even after taking the test, however, and proving what they already knew—that my former spouse fathered our son—they still did not enter an order for child support. Even after I went through this humiliating DNA-testing process and waiting for years, the court told me again to wait for child support for my two children. Unfortunately, this was not the first time injustice perpetrated, and plagued, this case, and it certainly wasn't the last.

Due Process Long Overdue

I learned quickly that the injustice occurring in my case was not happening because of one particular judge being unjust. If it were, perhaps I could have withstood it without the need to voice the truth. But it was nearly every judge who was on my case. At that particular time, the original judge I was in front of gave the case to a subordinate judge to make decisions in the case. And although this judge had a different name, the same injustice flowed through her. In fact, it became all the more clear why the judges didn't want anyone from the public inside the courtroom while they ruled on my case.

At that particular time, I didn't have a lawyer, and I had to represent myself. I suppose this judge thought she would really hit me hard with lawlessness then, since she didn't see any legal advocate there with me. What she failed to realize is that God was with me, and Jesus too, who is an Advocate above all advocates. When I didn't have a natural lawyer, however, they commanded me to come in to court on an emergency basis. They asked the judge to take Zion and Zaire from me right then and there. I had no natural lawyer, they had no evidence and no witnesses, and we had not had any hearing; yet they wanted to take my two children just by requesting to do so. As crazy as this may seem, what is really bizarre was this judge's response. Now, this judge knew very well that everyone is entitled to due process. Even if someone is not a citizen of the United States, they are entitled to due process.

Due process is a constitutional right to fairness in substance and procedure in courts of law and outside of them. Due process is why police have to have probable cause before they can even temporarily affect your freedom and pull you over while driving a car. Due process is why police have to read someone their Miranda rights—especially telling them they have the right to a lawyer—upon arrest. One of the most fundamental due process rights inside of a courtroom is the right to be heard. People have been guilty of crimes, admittedly, and the entire case was still thrown out. The guilty were allowed to go free because the judge, or some other government official involved, violated their due process rights! Due process is supposed to be at the center of justice in the law. Before a court can take away someone's freedom or property or children or any of their rights, they have to allow the accused person to be heard. This is true in civil court as well as criminal court. This is a check on the government, to bring balance and avoid tyranny by judicial officials. In my case, however, and in front of this judge, the constitution was made void, and justice was a victim of death. This judge told me to my face that I was not allowed to talk, present evidence, or have any witnesses! She then told me she was going to take the children from me immediately! She was going to take my two children, according to her own words, and without allowing me to present any evidence or call any witnesses, and without allowing me to take the witness stand and defend myself. She allowed my former rich-celebrity spouse, however, to have his entire argument heard. I remember thinking, what was the purpose of even having constitutional or any legal rights when the judge refused to acknowledge I had them. I had rights on paper, but in reality, I had nothing. I was a US citizen without any constitutional rights! That is by definition an oxymoron. Unfortunately, this was common in America's legal system. For example, African-Americans had been freed from slavery for many years but couldn't educate themselves or ride public transportation as they saw fit: Thus they had rights that essentially had no effect! Welcome to the corrupted court system.

I thank God, for being just! At that moment, God came to my rescue. A lawyer who was not on my case came inside the courtroom for something unrelated to my case. When he heard what was going on, he spoke up, and that's when everyone noticed he was in the courtroom. He told the judge that he understood that he was not my lawyer, but he heard what she was saying to me and just wanted to remind her, as "a friend of the court," that she was violating my constitutional right to due process, because I had a right to be heard, whether I had a lawyer or was representing myself in the case. The judge went off on him and tried to get him out of the courtroom, but by that time his partner had come into the courtroom too, presumably looking for him, and they both began to defend me. One of them whispered in my ear exactly what to say to the judge, and to ask her for a chance to be heard pursuant to my constitutional rights.

This judge didn't care, though. She instructed the lawyer to leave her courtroom and shut up unless he was my lawyer. This lawyer literally pulled me to the side and asked to be my lawyer right then. I agreed, and he asked her to allow him fifteen minutes, and he would officially have it on file that he was my new lawyer. That day, God saved me from this unjust judge—and just in time. She never allowed me the opportunity to speak on my behalf and be heard, though. And the injustice didn't stop there.

As I mentioned earlier, very often the judges would mandate that I come to court or be held in contempt and go to jail. And indeed, that is exactly what happened the one day when I didn't come to court. My lawyer at the time was in a car accident, totaling her car on the Stevenson Expressway in Chicago. I was just outside the court building when I was told that the court hearing for that day was cancelled because my lawyer had to seek immediate medical attention. I guess the judge didn't care if my lawyer could have been killed and needed to see a doctor, and the judge certainly didn't care that I was instructed by my lawyer to go home. She issued a warrant for my arrest, had me arrested, and said the only way I was going to get out of jail was by posting a ten-thousand-dollar bond. This was the same judge I went before for several years, asking for financial support I was entitled to, and she kept denying me and my children, saying, "Wait." This judge, out of all the judges, knew I didn't have ten thousand pennies, let alone ten thousand dollars. Injustice has teeth, and they sank deep into me as this unjustified judge bit right into me with her fangs of unchecked power. But God once again saved me, and God delivered me. God had someone post my bond for me, and I was out of jail within hours! This, my love, is a miracle from Jesus!

A striking contrast was how the judges treated my former spouse when he failed to appear in court numerous times. I lost count of the number of times my lawyers, issued "237 notices," which compelled my former spouse to come to court in person so they could obtain his testimony. In nine years, he came to court all of approximately four times, and not one time did the judge have him arrested, throw him in jail, or require him to post bail. They didn't even so much as threaten to do so. They did, however, speak to him over and over about his NBA basketball games. If we were on a basketball court, I would have understood the prejudice and bias coming from these judges, but we were in a court of law, where justice is supposed to be executed regardless of whether you are rich or poor, male or female, famous or never appeared on television. Just the opposite occurred.

I remember the media reached out to me—specifically it was E! Television—in order to do an interview with me, which I did conduct, but not without opposition from the court! When they found out I was doing an interview and possibly sharing with the world what was occurring in the court case, I was required to come to court by the judge. This judge instructed me that I could not allow my children to speak at all to the media. The judge said she did this because she was old-fashioned and did not believe that children should be in the media. Interesting, to say the least, because my ex-husband had the children appear in various commercials, on the front cover of a magazine, and in an array of worldwide media! The judge, however, never said a single word about that! This same judge had issued a court order forbidding me to do things with my children in the media, before anything ever could air on television, but with my former rich spouse, she did and said nothing! I suppose the "old-fashioned" judge was new-age contemporary with the rich-and-famous basketball player, but she was "old-fashioned" indeed for the poor housewife!

I remember when I first spoke out about the domestic violence I had suffered for many years, I was unjustly and ignorantly asked, "If that is true, why didn't you say anything until now?" Just when I thought it could not get worse inside of that corrupt court of lawlessness, the judge hit me with the blow of her erroneous mentality that has been the same straw breaking the backs of many rape victims in courts across America: "Why did you wear that, if you didn't want to be raped?" People, this type of foolishness is real, and it would have been something I could have held my peace about if it were just an ignorant neighbor, but these are actual judges making decisions that affect people's lives and children! My God, this is why you said don't ask for a king to rule over us! It is clear to me why God gave us this warning. God knew this sort of thing would happen when unjust men and women held positions as judges. I have suffered the living proof of that. Asking a victim of domestic violence why didn't she say she was being abused sooner is the same as asking a victim of rape why she wore a particular garment on the day she was raped. The better question is, why are we asking the *victim* anything? The victim is not the one who broke the law! The focus is completely misplaced. What next, if the court continues on with this mentality and thought process? Should we ask the owner of a nice car that is stolen, "Why did you buy such a nice car if you didn't want it stolen?" And should we ask the person whose house is broken into, "Why didn't you buy extra locks and put them on your door if you really didn't want the house broken into?" The way this judge treated me was horrible, but what made it worse was that she never questioned the one who did these horrific things to me.

I remember another time I was in court, and shortly after I approached the judge's bench, I noticed that several of the other judges were sitting beside the judge. Literally, one judge was sitting in the witness seat, and another judge was sitting in the seat where the clerk normally sits. They were staring at me with looks of pure intimidation. The lawyer I had at the time told me that he had practiced law in Illinois for well over a decade, but he had never seen judges behave the way they did with my case. He told me what the judges did to me that day reminded him of bullies who gang up together to intimidate another child. I met so many women subsequent to my court case, women from all over the United States, who suffered the same injustices as my children and I did, and even worse.

On another occasion one of my lawyers was very troubled by the judges behavior and explained to me that judges are generally not permitted to talk to other judges about a court case. These judges, however, were doing whatever they wanted to do behind the closed doors of those courtrooms, including speaking about the case to each other. Sometimes I felt like I could not take the injustice anymore. The case was no longer about my former spouse. Something bigger than both of us was at work, and the judges made that abundantly clear. The judges' behavior made this case no longer *Wade v. Wade*; it was *The Rich Man v. The Poor Housewife*, and soon after, it became *Injustice v. The Voice Exposing It*. Indeed it is true: "Silence is the enemy of the truth."

Only Jesus Saves

It certainly was not just me who realized the injustice that was coming from the court system in my case. A lawyer from one of the most well-known, top law firms in all of Illinois was representing me in the case. After a *single* hearing in front of the same judge who violated my constitutional rights, the lawyer snapped! I had been through hell because of these judges and their injustice, but I had not snapped. After one hearing, however, this seasoned lawyer went off! He began literally yelling at the judge, and he rebuked her to her face. This man told this judge that what she was doing to me was unlawful, and that her lawlessness put him in a position as my lawyer whereby he could not do anything to help me, because she had made up her own rules to benefit the rich celebrity party in the case. He went on and told her that everything he ever learned in law school was for nothing, because she was changing the law as she went along. This lawyer was enraged and had turned completely red. After that, he quit, and he withdrew from being my lawyer on the case. I wasn't mad at this lawyer for quitting, because he realized what I already knew: that with all the knowledge in the entire world, he could not help me if the judges were hell-bent on doing injustice. I knew this long before he figured it out. I was actually proud of him for telling this judge the truth about her unjust behavior toward me. But because of the way the legal system works in America, it is a system of precedent—I should more correctly say, toward you and me. It goes without saying that in a legal system of precedent, what affects one affects all.

Another lawyer I hired, who said he could help me just after reading the case files and seeing what the judges were doing in my case, also changed his mind and said there was nothing he could do to help me. He quit too. Another attorney from Florida told me that the judges on my case had written a new constitution for the Wade case; he too withdrew from my case shortly thereafter.

I had another lawyer who actually became a witness to the abuse; however, the law requires that if a lawyer is a witness for his or her client, the lawyer needs to withdraw from the case to avoid a conflict of interest. This lawyer had the choice between earning more money by keeping my case or withdrawing and testifying to the truth about what my children had suffered behind closed doors. She chose, by the grace of God, to take the witness stand and testify for Zion and Zaire's sake. This also meant she had to withdraw from being my lawyer.

I had other lawyers too. Several of them were sued by my former spouse, and since that created a conflict of interest, they too withdrew from my case and were forced to quit as my lawyer. Another one was diagnosed with cancer and was receiving chemo while she helped me with the case, but that didn't last long either. Another had a husband who died during the case. My former spouse sued her too, and thus she also quit being my lawyer. Another lawyer I had exposed some of the injustice in my case that spread from Illinois, and to the judge in Florida who picked up right where the injustice left off, and she was persecuted for it. They tried to get her law license revoked. Right after that, she withdrew from my case too. But at least she had shed some light on the darkness of injustice that was operating in the court. That didn't change any of the injustice, but it was a relief to know that I wasn't the only one who knew that this so-called celebrity case was submerged in injustice and lawlessness coming directly from the court. And as much as I wanted God to take me out of that situation, God allowed me to go through it instead, and He blessed me right in the mist of it. God did not cause the sufferings I went through, but God did allow it. God allowed for nobody else to help me truly, so that God would be all I had. When God was all I had, then I realized the truth: God is all I need. I learned a priceless lesson during these difficult times: only Jesus saves!

Divine Provision from God: Rivers in the Desert

Some of you may be wondering how my children and I made it financially during this time. The answer, in sum, is Jesus. How He did it was amazing. It taught me that Jesus is truly our provider, providing everything we will ever need. One night, Jesus gave a dream. Inside the dream, God was clearly saying to freeze the bank accounts. The law calls the freezing of accounts, as well as other types of equitable relief (nonmonetary) and injunction. Every lawyer I had at that time told me that an injunction would never be granted by the judge. They assured me that an injunction was extremely difficult to obtain, especially given the large amount of money my former spouse was earning. Nevertheless, I had faith in God and believed that if God showed it to me, it was because God was going to make the way for it to happen. The lawyer warned me once more, letting me know that it would cost a lot in attorneys' fees to fight to obtain an injunction, and they didn't believe I would be granted one. (I can understand this doubt for other reasons. The judges had not granted to me what the law clearly stated I was entitled to.) But even so, this dream was not from a human judge; it was from the Judge of all judges—God Himself. The Messiah had spoken, and that, my love, sealed the deal! I directed my lawyers to file an injunction on an emergency basis, and to all of their surprise, the injunction was granted. God used this injunction, which eventually became permanent, to provide some funds to me and my children, and we lived off that money for years. We didn't have the things we wanted, but we had what we needed.

I was supposed to get funds from this injunction on an ongoing basis, but the same judge who refused to allow me to be heard terminated the injunction. Then when she was ordered by the Appellate Court to make sure I was given all of the money owed to me pursuant to the injunction, and to restore me to the status quo and they also found her to have abused her discretion in my case. But instead of making sure I was given the funds that were owed to me so that I could provide for my children, and myself she recused herself, (removing herself from my case). Then the replacement judge told me that I would have to begin the process over again because that judge removed herself from my case. It was one of the most unjust cases I have even known about, and I have read at least hundreds of court-case opinions. I was back to having no income, but God turned this evil into good. I learned a lot about God as a provider during these times, and I know God taught me for my benefit as well as yours. I learned that God can do the impossible. Remember, every lawyer I had at the time said getting that injunction was not possible. But I believed that God gave that dream, and what was impossible for man is always possible for God, for Jesus spoke the truth, telling us, "With God nothing is impossible" (Matt. 19:26).

The whole truth is, however, that when I saw that savings (the means by which God had been providing for my children and me), going away and dwindling down, I panicked in fear, rather than responding in faith. My car had went up for repossession, and the truck I had was so broken down that, twice, my children and I ended up stranded, and we had to walk home. I couldn't afford to pay for the house we had lived in in South Holland, and eventually our home went into foreclosure. I began giving people our possessions in exchange for money, in order to pay the bills, but eventually I ran out of possessions to give away. Eventually, the lights were turned off, and the water and gas too. And when I was forced to move out of that house, I had to go and live with my mother again. I have nobody to thank for those hardships but the Cook County, Illinois, family court in Chicago. And I have nobody to thank for our deliverance but Jesus! And again, God was turning what was meant for evil into good.

I would often say, after that experience with God giving me that dream and providing for Zion, Zaire, and me through that injunction, that, "I look to the hills from which comes my help, my help comes from the Lord" (Ps. 121:1–2). One day God showed me, however, that the trust and faith I thought I had in God, my Provider was actually in His provision—and there is a big difference. When people trust in God, they do keep the eyes of their heart set on God, because He is the One who provides the supply for all their needs. However, when someone trusts and depends on the *provision* (the substance), they keep the eyes of their heart on that provision. And if that *provision* (e.g., money, stocks, a job, wages, etc.) begins to go away or change, they panic.

God asked me a simple question that gave me profound understanding: did I trust the amount of money I had, or did I trust Him as my Provider? I realized the truth about what I really believed at that time as I honestly answered the question within myself. I was scared. And it wasn't fear of not living the "lifestyle" that I feared. I had not shopped Fendi and had cut coupons to shop Family Dollar, so this was not about material things at all. I had long ago learned to do without material things by then. This was more serious than anything material. I even ate less, because I was worried about Zion and Zaire not having enough to eat. At that point in my life, I was trusting in the provision (the money), not God the Provider. But God came right into the dry place I was in, and He brought rivers to serve me. God promises to supply all of our needs according to the richness of His grace (Phil. 4:19). God's grace is so rich that, yes, it does include money, but it extends well beyond money, and even beyond full human comprehension, I believe. God has proven this to me.

With those savings having gone nearly completely away, I was paying attention to the cost of goods that we needed. I noticed specifically at that time that the cost of paper goods had gone up extremely high. Paper goods are also a necessity. Let's face it, we all need tissue! I remember telling God, "God, it is very expensive the things we need, like paper plates and tissue. God, have mercy, please, and help me, God, for you promised to provide for me and Father, be it unto me according to your word, in Jesus name."

One night, while I was driving because of a visitation issue with the court, God did a miracle in the middle of that mess. It was extremely dark outside, but in the darkness, I could see what looked like white papers flying across the ground on the highway, and so I slowed down a little bit to see more clearly. Once I realized what it was, I pulled over. On the ground were stacks of brand-new paper plates, napkins, and paper goods. I was in a truck, and so I was able to pick up all of these brand-new packages of paper goods, plates, and napkins, and to load up the truck to full capacity. It was so much that I loaded up the truck until I literally couldn't fit any more in it. God had given me so much supply that I was able to give a lot of it away and still keep a lot of it for us to use. That happened well over four years ago, and to this day, I still have some of those plates and napkins! That evinces just how much God gave. When God blesses you, people, it is more than enough! God had supernaturally provided for us, and I was able to get the things we had need of and could not afford, without ever having to pay any money for them.

I learned it to be true that God will indeed make rivers in the desert (Isa. 43:19). This means God will make a way out of no way. The desert is a very dry place, where water is scarce or nonexistent. Water is important; it is causes things to grow. Rivers are water in abundance. God is telling us that He will put a river in a desert situation. This means also that God is not promising to always just deliver us out of the desert; He brings the provision to the desert and not just any provision, abundant flowing river type provision. Now, I say with certainty that God does not do this to scare us, so don't panic in the desert. God allows deserts to teach us that God is indeed a provider, and He provides for us regardless of the situation. There is no desert or dry place in your life that God cannot bring the rivers of overflowing abundant provision to you, and provide for you right where you are. This is what makes God, God! If we could do it all, we would be our own god! (Some people still are). I pray that you and I always remember that it cost money to buy those paper goods, and at the time, it cost a lot of money, but God gave them to us abundantly and for free. Sometimes when people don't have the money to buy something, they believe they will go without it, but God will bring the river to the desert. He will do the impossible, and He will do it well! Also, the paper goods that God gave us, without the need for any money, were among the most costly of all paper goods.

I learned a priceless lesson: God is my provider—not money, not man, and not myself. My help comes from God, and my help is good! And know that if God did it for my children and me, God will provide for you and your children. God is not a respecter of persons (Acts 10:34). God told me that the provision He gave me was not about me; it is about God. That is who God is; He is a provider. The judges meant what they did for our harm, but God allowed it for our good.

Precedential Effect

I learned some of the hardest lessons of my life during the time of this court case. Sometimes judges are corrupt, and lawyers are thieves. Sometimes lawmakers do more *law-breaking* than they do *lawmaking*. It was wholly unjust, and often unlawful, what happened to my children and me. And although this injustice happened to us during this case, I believe that God still had me share this truth with you, and He even allowed all the media attention surrounding the case for your benefit. This case may not have had your name on the front page as a petitioner or a respondent, but the injustice affects us all. Let me explain it to you the way God has shown me this is true, from both a legal and spiritual standpoint.

The American legal system uses a concept called *precedent* in lawmaking. *Precedent* is defined as "A decided case that furnishes a basis for determining later cases involving similar facts or issues." In other words, when judges make decisions on one case, they are actually creating laws through that case, and consequently, subsequent cases with similar facts as that one must follow the law of the previous case (what is called "case law"). Thus, an injustice in one case is like a virus of injustice spreading to and infecting every other similar case coming after it.

Unfortunately, it had already begun spreading from the case I was in. A previous lawyer of mine called me one day, explaining to me how he was in court on a totally different case, and he watched as another lawyer was using the case law from my case. He explained to me how the opposing counsel in that case he was watching was arguing with the judge, saying how the judges in my case should have never decided the Wade case the way they did in the first place. He was arguing that the judge in my case literally changed the law when she ruled the way she did in my case. Several more lawyers after that began reaching out too as they noticed the negative effect this precedent was having in other people's lives.

Many lawyers in Illinois and in Florida have reached out to me, telling me just how unlawful and unjust most of the decisions were in my case. Many of them even showed me the law in order to prove to me that it had been broken in order for the judges to rule the way they did in my case. I read the law for myself, but by it was a confirmation of what I already knew: that case was plagued with injustice, and it was coming from the bench. Many after my case have been upset, and for good reason, because they have seen the negative and damaging effects the unjust decisions of judges in my case have had on others after me. But God showed me one day how injustice reaches even beyond the law to have negative effects.

Spiritually speaking, God also showed me that injustice affects us all collectively as well, regardless of the name appearing on the court's order, and it does so for the same reason it does so legally: "Injustice anywhere is a threat to justice everywhere." To teach me how, God used the following illustration: African-Americans (like many other races) were not allowed to be educated because of their race. That denial negatively affected the African-American directly, but it also affected everyone else—and directly! For example, God taught me by saying imagine an African-American child that unjust lawmakers forbade from learning how to read because of his or her race was actually ordained by God to be a doctor and to find the a cure for cancer. But because injustice through the law stopped him from learning, he didn't get the opportunity to fulfill his destiny. Many people, regardless of their race, have died of cancer. It was as if God asked me questions after showing me this illustration: In this illustration, what actually killed the victims of cancer? Was it really cancer? Or was it the "legal injustice system" that caused those deaths? The answer is clearly the unjust lawmakers, because they are ones who forbade the person called to discover the cure for cancer from ever doing so, and solely because of racism. If these lawmakers are afflicted with a deadly cancer, they will have effectively killed themselves too.

Indeed, God warned about judges and rulers being corrupted if they were allowed to rule over us, and Jesus sternly warned against being quick to run into court. Obviously, they did so for good reasons! And although I did not start this court case but rather had to endure it, I am glad God used it to expose to me the injustice of the court system, especially in family law. God has indeed turned all that was meant for harm into good for me, as you will see. I even believe God will bless those judges with deliverance and righteousness, and enable them to do the will of God, and not their own anymore, in Jesus name.

Justice Aborted

I really hoped I could have ended this particular chapter with some inspiring story about how the judges turned their hearts toward God during my case and began executing justice pursuant to the law, but that's not how the case ended with them.

Eventually, a bifurcation was entered by the judge in my case, which allowed my former spouse to divorce me but without my receiving any money, child support for my two children, or property of any kind. Approximately two weeks later, my former spouse signed a contract for roughly $100 million. Yet the court had not ordered him to pay even one hundred dollars to help me take care of our children. It wasn't even about the money; it was about the injustice. That hurt more than the financial situation at that time. What do you do when your bully is a lawmaker and a law enforcer? That is the question that engulfed my mind, causing me to miss meals and keeping me awake some nights. Looking back, on all of this, I can say that up until this point, justice was perverted, but the next chapter of my life was when justice was altogether aborted.

"Agree with your adversary quickly, while you are on the way with him, lest your adversary deliver you to the judge..." (Matt. 5:25)

THE CUSTODY TRIAL: TRIAL BY FIRE

You will be brought before kings and rulers for My name's sake. But it will turn out for you as an occasion for testimony. Therefore settle it in your hearts not to meditate beforehand on what you will answer, for I will give you a mouth and wisdom which all your adversaries will not be able to contradict or resist.

—Luke 21:12–15

Special Dedication

I want to dedicate this chapter to all the women survivors of domestic violence and let you all know that you are most precious and valuable in the sight of God, and your cry has not gone unheard. God hears your cry. Pray to God, because, God is a Deliverer (Ps. 34:4). God wants to deliver, heal, and restore you completely and give you wisdom to get out. God calls you a "WOW Woman." That is, you are a woman of worth, a woman of wisdom, and a woman of wealth. You are exactly who God says you are and who God called you to be. God doesn't make mistakes, and God made you, and thus, you are not a mistake. And when God made you, He made you fearfully and wonderfully (Ps. 139:14). WOW woman, you are a wonder! And you are nothing less than God's very best!

I also want to dedicate this chapter to the mothers and fathers and family members who lost their loved ones due to domestic violence. May God heal every brokenness and deeply rooted pain, in Jesus name. May God bind up every wound, and put back together the fragmented pieces of your heart, mind, soul, and life, in Jesus name. And may God completely restore you, and make you whole again without void or emptiness, in Jesus Name. My mother is a parent who faced the grief of the loss of a child, when my sister was killed in a car accident. God did for my mom what we thought couldn't be done, and that is: God completely healed her and restored her. God even gave her another daughter. What God has done for my mother, I pray He does the same for you—and even greater, in Jesus name.

Lastly, but certainly not least, I want to dedicate this chapter to those of us who have suffered from injustice and the devastating blow of corruption. If you are going through it now, my prayers are with you for justice from God. God is just, and justice can only come from God (Ps. 7:11). An unjust judge or person cannot give justice, because they don't have it to give. But God is holy, just, and righteous, and my prayer is for those of you in need. I pray that God will give you justice, and I pray that God will do so speedily, in Jesus's name.

People Are Destroyed for Lack of Knowledge
God makes it abundantly clear the importance of having knowledge and the dire consequences of not obtaining it (Hosea 4:6). Thus, I want to begin with important facts regarding domestic

violence. One in every four women are victims of domestic violence in their lifetime. Domestic violence is more than just physical violence. It includes a dynamic of power and control running so deep that many victims of it, have been murdered without ever having escaped or even spoken a word to anyone about the mental and emotional prison the abuser put them in. Breaking the silence about violence sounds easy at first. We have all likely been told at some point in our lives before, "Speak your mind," or, "Just say what's on your mind." This isn't easy, however, for victims of domestic violence, and it is instead often terrifying, because the person abusing them is manipulating and controlling them with fear and intimidation, so that they will keep silent and remain afraid to speak to anyone about the abuse. When we understand domestic violence, we understand this devastating effect it has on victims of it.

Experts define *domestic violence* as "a pattern of physical and psychological abuse, threats, intimidation, isolation, or economic coercion used by one person to exert power and control over another person in the context of a dating, family, or household relationship. Domestic violence is maintained by societal and cultural attitudes, institutions, and laws which are not consistent in naming this violence as wrong." Additionally, most victims of domestic violence are women. Domestic violence affects a multitude of women of all different races, ages, educational backgrounds, socioeconomic statuses, nationalities, and cultures. The one thing, however, that almost *all* victims of domestic violence have in common is: they are women. Very often, victims of domestic violence are referred to as "battered women." And although the term *battered woman* gives the impression of just physical abuse, domestic violence is so much more than that. The depth of this particular evil goes well beyond surface pain, such as black eyes, stab wounds, and bruises, as bad as they are. It reaches to the deepest place inside, where no ice packs, medical bandages, or doctors can reach.

Domestic violence has deep roots and involves psychological, physical, emotional, financial, and sexual abuse, or threats of such abuse, and using fear in order to control the victim of the abuse. These deep roots cause deep pain and anguish, especially since domestic violence is a crime committed by someone the victim often loves very much, such as a spouse.

Studies have consistently shown that the worst form of abuse in domestic violence has been reported by survivors of it as being the emotional and psychological abuse. Notably, it's not the physical abuse that those who actually suffered from it say is the worst. The abuse to those places where a bandage can't cover and medicine can't heal is where domestic violence cuts the deepest. And unfortunately, in my experience, it is where most survivors have found the least sympathy from the community and the court system, further victimizing the woman.

Also, despite the fact that those who have suffered from domestic violence come from all different racial, ethnic, social, and economic backgrounds, those victimized by this type of abuse almost always suffer the same dynamics and patterns of abuse. This is because the abusers share identical or very similar behaviors and characteristics. Let's shed light on this darkness, because often times women who are suffering from domestic violence don't even realize they are. They think their spouse or partner is just harsh sometimes, and even more often the abuser has convinced them that *they* are the reason the abuser treats them, and the children, the way he does. Being able to detect this early and knowing the signs are vital to not allowing your own life to be destroyed, or even lost, due to domestic violence.

Abusers are often charismatic and/or charming, but they also have (often times secretly) ideals about women being inferior to men. Sometimes they refer to themselves as "just old-fashioned." And while calling an abuser "old-fashioned" has some merit, especially since the history of our nation made it lawful for a man to physically and emotionally abuse his wife, and rape his wife also, it does not begin to describe the horror within them, and the evil they unleash against their partners (majority of the times, behind closed doors).

Again, abusive people often engage in identical, or nearly identical, abusive behaviors. Not always, but sometimes, abusers will not want a woman to work. This is not because he wants to sweep her off her feet and take care of her, but rather it is so that he can control the money, and thus control her. Since he controls the money, he makes it either extremely difficult to leave or impossible, because the woman cannot support herself or her children. Women in these common situations are often left wondering how they will support themselves and their children with no money of their own. People may judge them, shunning them with questions like, "why don't they just leave with nothing then?" Leaving seems to be a surety that they won't die from the abuse, but not having the resources to support their children financially has meant for some that their children are taken from them. These mothers love their children like most every other mother, and they would often rather die than to have their children taken from them. These become real fears for women in these situations, and albeit this fear is not rationale to some outsiders, it is real for the victim, and often the worse fear for them.

There are often subtle but damaging insults and demeaning comments in domestic violence also. For example, telling a woman something like, she should try to lose some weight, or after a woman has gotten all dressed up and beautiful, he might search for something to insult her about. This can wear a woman's worth down to the point that she eventually feels and believes that she is worthless.

Abusers also very often use the people a woman loves the most to hurt her and to control her. For women who are also mothers, it is often their children. Abused women are often taken to court for custody of their children when the relationship ends or when the abuser fears it is ending. An abuser's hope is that a loving and devoted mother will do anything to protect her children. They will especially use the children and custody when they know that their spouse or partner has witnessed them being abusive to the children. An abused woman knows how bad the abuser has hurt her, so she wants to protect her children from the abuse, often by any means necessary, including staying with an abusive man, *whom she is afraid of,* and made to feel completely worthless by.

After an abuser subjects a woman to abuse, and often times abusing her children also, the abuser will very often defame the woman, saying she's crazy because of her reaction to the abuse. One day while I was in court, defending my reaction to abuse, God set me free from the madness coming from some judges regarding my response. I listened and watched as judge after judge acted as if abuse were no big deal, and literally making excuses for it, like, "Oh, he was mad." They did it so often that I began questioning myself. Maybe I did something wrong, or maybe I *was* wrong. One day, however, God told me the truth, and I have been free from that moment. God told me that if there were nothing wrong with the verbal, emotional, and physical abuse that I suffered, then the judges would be okay with him doing the same thing to them or to their children. God asked me "What do you think would happen if he called the judge the same curse words he called you?" What if he slammed the judge down right now in her own courtroom, like you were slammed down in your own home?" God asked me, "What do you think she would do?" God answered me before I could answer, and He let me know: "She would have him arrested. No questions!" The problem was not that I was not abused, or even that the judges knew the truth, because the evidence was in front of them. The problem was they did not value my life or the life of my children. That was their problem. They valued money and fame, more than morals, the law, and human life. Unfortunately, this response from judges is also a common attribute in domestic violence.

Another very common characteristic of abusers is that they are often times jealous. Even abusers, who don't outwardly show that they are jealous in a direct manner, do so subtly. Abusers are professionals at concealing things. Remember, they are manipulating. That is why they often get a woman to marry them. Some women see subtle signs, but the monster is unleashed only after the abuser feels the woman is emotionally or financially attached and dependent upon them. Then, and often only then, will a woman see the abusers true colors. An abuser's jealousy is most often made manifest by the fact that they verbally and emotionally abuse the woman. These abusers will often tell women that "nobody will ever want them" or things like, "nobody else will put up with you." Abusers also find ways to let the victim know that the abuser doesn't think she is beautiful, or they will purposely compare them with other women, often pointing out physical traits that a woman couldn't change about herself, even if she wanted to. For example, an abuser may say, "Your breasts are small, and I like a woman with big breasts or a woman who is taller." All of these things the abuser says to the victim are intentional, because the abuser wants to control the woman, and a key way abusers do this is by making the woman feel so low and unworthy that she will not even attempt to leave the abuser. The psychological and emotional abuse is like an extremely heavy weight that the abuser puts on the woman, weighing her down in her mind, spirit, and emotions. And whenever someone is weighed down in their mind, spirit, and emotions, they are physically put down too. That is why the word *depression* has the word *press* and *de* in it, meaning "pressed down." This is also why someone suffering from depression—which is a battle in their mind, emotions, and spirit—will not have the strength to get out of bed, comb their hair, eat, or even shower. I have suffered from depression before, and for good reason, so I understand this devil.

When an abuser weighs the victim down in her mind, emotions, and spirit, her physical body stays weighed down in their toxic relationship, and she lacks the strength to leave. Oppression is the same. People who were enslaved were oppressed in their mind, spirit, and emotions first, and once the slave owner accomplished this, he didn't even have to bind the slave in chains anymore. The prison was on the inside of the slave. The same happens to victims of domestic violence. They are enslaved from the inside out. All of these behaviors and characteristics of abusers, whether subtle or blatantly obvious, have the same goal: to control the victim.

Sometimes abusers, in addition to subtle jealousy, will have flat-out outbursts of jealous rage. I once had to try and jump out of a moving car in a parking lot of a Loews Movie Theater, because the jealous rage became so intense. But I experienced more of the subtle, yet deadly, emotional abuse described herein, which was clearly rooted in jealousy. The efforts of an abuser to convince the woman that she is worthless are because of the abuser's deep-rooted fear, insecurity, and jealousy, making them believe that this woman could indeed be with someone else—and someone else better. Abusers often are very insecure men, having been abused themselves as children, which is where the insecurity likely took root in them. I'm not saying this to make excuses for them at all. I was abused as a child, but God has kept me from abusing children. I risked my life to protect my oldest child from physical violence at that home. Thus, there is no excuse.

Domestic violence has what is called, cycles of violence. One of the cycles is the honeymoon phase. This takes place after an episode of violence. This phase is another reason why victims stay in the relationship. The honeymoon phase brings a false hope, as the abuser promises (I mean every time, just about) that he will not behave the way he did anymore towards the victim. Often an abuser, especially during the honeymoon phase, will behave very lovingly toward the woman, making her feel really high emotionally, and loved and desired—just to take her down really hard, and make her feel more worthless than before. The reason for the high and the extreme low are the same, as are all the reasons for all this demonic behavior of an abuser. The abuser wants to be in control. He wants to decide when the victim feels good, and when she feels worthless. This is not the will of God, and it is not what God desires for any of His daughters. Let God be the source of your joy, because it's free of manipulation and fear. Believe me, I know.

Also abusers are manipulative. They are crafty and skilled at making a woman believe she is the reason they behave and treat her the way that they do. Manipulation! Manipulation! Manipulation! Women don't *make* the abuser do anything, because if she had the power to make the abuser do something, she would first make him stop hurting her emotionally and physically, controlling her financially, taking her to court for custody to hurt and control her more, and sleeping with other women, which does its own emotional and spiritual damage (to married people).

Last, but certainly not least, is the fact that abusers often use the court system to re-victimize their partner all over again. Once a woman leaves the abusive relationship and has taken control of her life from him, abusers will often use the court system as a means of controlling and abusing the woman more than in times past. Abusers have to be in control. They use the long- arm of the court system to reach the fleeing victim, and then they use any judge who is willing to use his or her authority to hurt these women in the most devastating ways, often by wrongfully taking her children from her. Abusers are notorious for using something called parental alienation syndrome (PAS), to accomplish this great evil. PAS is an unfounded and non-scientific theory that in sum states that abused women, and abused children, are lying on the abuser about the violence suffered, causing the child to be alienated from the abusive parent and it was developed by Richard Gardner. This catastrophe of an attempt to diagnosis, often women, with "parental alienation syndrome" is flawed, as evidenced by its title. First, it is not a syndrome at all! It is a theory this one man came up with, without research to support it, and then he attached the term *syndrome* to the end of his fleeting thoughts, so it would appear to have clinical importance. But it doesn't. In fact, the American Psychological Association and the American Medical Association don't recognize it, and it has been rejected as a diagnosis in the *Diagnostic and Statistical Manual of Mental Disorders.* They refuse to support some man's theory, even if he does attach the word *syndrome* at the end of it. In fact, one expert stated, "PAS [*parental alienation syndrome*] is essentially composed of unsubstantiated claims; there's no science behind it."

Second, the inventor of this miscarriage of justice is not a doctor or a psychiatrist qualified to diagnose anyone with his "theory." As ignorant as I believe Richard Gardner was for creating this theory, the injustice lies in the judge's reliance on a theory to remove children from mothers who have suffered from domestic violence when they expose the abuse or try to protect their children from the abuse. Some judges have sided with Richard Gardner's unscientific theory to discredit mothers suffering from domestic violence that is recognized in the very law that judges are mandated to uphold. This magnitude of injustice gives evil a pulse inside these courtrooms. Doctors, scientists, Psychiatrist, Senators and the House of Representatives recognize domestic violence and abuse as violent crimes, but judges have made legally binding court decisions based on an unmerited, nonscientific theory. Judges have sided with this Gardner guy, suggesting that mothers who allege domestic violence may be making it up, and children who have been abused may be faking also, because of being "brainwashed" by the mother. But here are the facts about Domestic Violence, without use of any nonscientific opinions:

- *One in four women are victims of domestic violence in their lifetime.*
- *Battering is the single major cause of injury to women, exceeding rapes, muggings, and auto accidents combined.*

- *A woman is **more likely** to be killed by a male partner (or former partner) **than any other person.***
- *About 4,000 women die each year due to domestic violence.*
- *Of the total domestic violence homicides, about 75 percent of the victims were killed as they attempted to leave the relationship or after the relationship had ended.*
- *Women of all races are equally vulnerable to violence by an intimate partner.*
- *On average, more than three women are murdered by their husbands or partners in this country **every day.***
- *Intimate partner violence is a crime that largely affects women. In 1999, women accounted for **85 percent** of the victims of intimate partner violence.*
- *On average, a woman will leave an abusive relationship seven times before she leaves for good.*
- *Approximately **75 percent** of women who are killed by their batterers are murdered when they attempt to leave or after they have left an abusive relationship.*

These are the facts people. What Richard Gardner came up with is a theory. Richard Gardner's theory, and his blasphemous accusation, which some corrupted lawyers have used to call survivors of domestic violence "brainwashers" of their own children, is despicable and evil. This theory has been a weapon in the hands of the devil himself, through lawyers, as a means by which abusive men continue to abuse, control and wreak havoc against women, through the court system long enough! These surviving women are not trying to separate their children from their dad; they are trying to protect their children from violence. It would be evil for a parent to see their child in danger, or potential danger, and do nothing. But some judges, acting in lawlessness and sexism against women have continued to subscribe to the magazine of lies, that this deceased theorist, Richard Gardner, called a *syndrome*.

Richard Gardner, who attempted to diagnose women suffering from domestic violence and protecting their children from violence, with parental alienation syndrome (an alleged mental syndrome), committed suicide, a certified mental syndrome. Nevertheless, some judges across the United States have relied on Richard Gardner's nonscientific, so-called *syndrome* to take children away from protective mothers and give the children to abusive fathers. Corrupted lawyers have become this dead man's hand, to reach out as a means by which abusive men continue to further abuse women and children, subjecting them to the worst violence yet: systematic violence and abuse.

Those experts disputing the validity of parental alienation syndrome theory know that "the theory is biased against women... and that it is used as a weapon by lawyers seeking to undermine a mother's credibility in court." Richard Gardner may be dead, but his "theory" lives, and many judges use it to the detriment of a substantial amount of women. It is important for lawyers representing clients in domestic violence to know the fact that its currently acknowledged by some judges, and women suffering from domestic violence need to know too, for the same reason. Lawyers need to know how to navigate through the muddy waters of PAS that have flooded family courtrooms and also know that sometimes it is wise to use what is within the guise of the law until it changes in order to bring about justice for the abused.

Protection is not Parental Alienation

It is not parental alienation syndrome for an abused parent to want to protect her child from the abuse that very often both she and the child have suffered. It is protection absent abuse. Nor does this protection alienate an abused child from their abusive parent. What causes parental alienation, if anything, is the abusive parent, who through their harsh behavior has caused their own child to be afraid of them. That is parental alienation syndrome. Now, judges, this is common sense to consider in an abusive context: a parent who abuses a child in any way, or who abuses the child's mother in front of the child, will cause that child to be afraid of that abusive parent, reluctant to be around them, and to likely react by running from them, rather than drawing nearer to them; and that child's reaction is a result of that abusive parent's behavior. The mother is not alienating anyone, she is responding to abuse, and the child is not being brainwashed they are also responding to the abuse. So execute justice, judges and stop taking children from protective parents and placing them with abusers!

In the law, protection in every other aspect is expected and praised, despite the value of what is being protected. People put alarms on their houses, and nobody ever takes their home from them for protecting it from a burglar! If someone has the right to protect a piece of property, how much more shall they have the right to protect their children from harm, regardless of who is causing the harm to them. Children are of the utmost value and deserve to be loved and feel protected. Just because someone is a dad or a mother it does not give them the right to abuse a child. And just because a mother has to protect her child from an abuser who is the child's dad does not mean she is an alienator! Wake up, judges! If this mother were protecting her child from a neighbor who punched the child in the chest or punished them by not feed-ing them, you would mandate that the mother protect her child from the abuse, or you would call her neglectful. But when this ex-act same abuse happens to a child at the hands of the child's own dad, a lot of judges (I know from various experiences) call these mothers who protect the children from the abuse an alienator. A parent has a right—an obligation from God, and the law—to protect their children from abuse. This obligation is in effect no matter who is the source of the abuse. Judges, I implore you to stop punishing women victims of domestic violence for protecting their children from abusive behavior, and stop making excuses for abusers, and giving these general affirmations for a complex issue, like, "Well, he is a father, and he has rights." Consider this example regarding the use of rights, as a justification for evil. Many of these abusive men are also citizens of the United States, and they have the *right* to speak their minds. Ask yourselves this question honestly: With his rights to speak, would you be okay if he called you bitches and whores in your courtroom, like he does his wife inside their bedroom? If the answer is no, the next question is: Why then do you expect the victim of domestic violence to tolerate this evil solely because he is a father with a right? Don't value your life above the lives of us women or these children.

Abusers also use the court system to further abuse women by draining them financially by over litigating a case that the abuser has already made sure the victim cannot afford to fight! People who have been through this hell I am describing are saying in their heart right now, "That's exactly what happens." The problem is, judges are not executing justice, and as evil as the abuser's behavior is, what is more of a tragedy are the judges who are willing to carry out the abuser's evil plans for them with the force of the law.

I was deeply troubled by this injustice, and one day God shed light on why most travesties of justice occur. God told me clearly one day, "An unjust man cannot give justice because he doesn't have it to give." People cannot give what they don't have to give. Unfortunately, some judges know what abuse is, and they still harm the victim for her refusal to just give in to the abuser and make the litigation stop. The judges look at women as if the man's behavior or the breakup of their family is their fault, and judges will feel angry that they have to deal with their case. Judges often pressure the woman to make the litigation go away, as if she can control the case, and when the woman can't do it, the judge abuses her worse than her abuser ever did, because the court has more authority to abuse her than the abuser.

With all the domestic violence I have been exposed to, and all it has cost me spiritually, emotionally, physically, sexually, and financially, the abuse from the judicial system was by far the worst abuse I have ever personally experienced or been made aware of thus far. Systematic abuse is well known for doing far more damage and having more lasting negative effects than all other forms of abuse, which is why abusers seek the authority of courts to try and destroy the victim of domestic violence. If you think, after reading this that I am fighting for the rights of women you discern correctly. But know this: I am not fighting for the rights of women and mothers to the detriment of men or fathers. I am saying that whether you are a man, or a woman, a mother or a father, don't you dare ever abuse children! When I really reflect on my own heart in this, I am actually fighting for the children's sake, more than for any other victims of the domestic violence.

Systematic Violence, Institutionalized Injustice

We, "the people," as the Constitution calls us, must never forget that it was the legal system that made slavery lawful but made it illegal for someone to teach those enslaved how to read a book. It was also the so-called "justice system" that made it lawful for an adult slave owner to rape an African-American child. The legal system made it lawful for African-Americans to be hung from trees in public, and their bodies burned, often times while their spouses and children watched helplessly in horror. It was the law, that allowed the use of concentration camps where Jewish people were shot to death, and their lifeless bodies fell into pre-dug ditches while their family members watched in anguish as their love ones were murdered right in front of them. The people who got caught protecting Jewish people during the Holocaust, by hiding them from those evil executions, were killed because it was the law. The legal system considered these people's helping to prevent murder of Jewish people an injustice, but when they shot a mother in the head while her child watched, it was legal. Now, I don't blame the law per se for this evil, because the law did not create itself. Rather, an unjust lawmaker (i.e., judges and members of Congress) creates unjust laws sometimes. I say that to clarify the problem, because we must do that before we can accurately address a solution by the grace of God. I also want to make clear the fact that although various examples of racism are historical examples I've provided, I am by no means implying that any particular race of people is evil. Every race has had someone do evil, and someone in every race has done well. I just want to clarify that, because racism, like the other evils mentioned above, produces separation, and I want us united because we are stronger together fighting for justice than we are apart.

Also, it was illegal for a woman to even vote because…well, because she was a woman. The truth is that the men who wrote and passed that law were sexist. In our nation it was lawful for a man to beat his wife. The men who passed that law were sexist also. Unfortunately, sexism still exists in our legal system, and there-fore, even when the laws change, the unjust outcomes remain the same, because the hearts of lawmakers and judges still beat with sexism, racism, and the like.

Sexism, hate, murder, false imprisonment, discrimination, rac-ism, and rape, to name a few, have all been lawful in America's legal system, and in other nations around the world. Please don't think I am just speaking of a past problem. Over the course of the last couple of years, we have seen unarmed young African-American men killed by "law enforcement" officers (police). Many have raised their voices in a cry for justice regarding these travesties of justice that have been deeply embedded in America's legal system and laws for hundreds of years. A lot of times those cries have gone unanswered by the legal system on earth, but God has never failed to hear the cry of His people, and God will surely execute justice.

God is a just Judge, and thus, He is always executing justice righteously. God told me during the custody trial I faced, which He allowed me to go through in order for me to have a real heart for justice, that, "an unjust man cannot execute justice." God told me a lot of judges and people in authority, would not correct a man who is abusing his wife, because they too were abusing their own wives. God has let us know, "Freely you have received, freely give" (Matt. 10:8). God told me one day, "Siohvaughn, someone cannot give what they don't have." God explained to me that people often ask wealthy people for million-dollar donations because they know they have it to give. God then asked me rhetorically, "Why don't they ask the homeless man on the streets for the million-dollar donation?" The answer is that he doesn't have it to give. Likewise, God taught me that if a judge is racist or sexist, he or she doesn't have any justice or righteousness to give to someone seeking justice from racism or sexism. They, like the homeless man on the streets, are bankrupt in a sense. This is obviously one of the important reasons God instructs us to "pray for your leaders" (1 Tim. 2:1–3). Judges are lawmakers and thus they are leaders. These examples God used in order to teach me were specific, but the life lesson God was teaching me is a very broad lesson and applicable to any given circumstance.

I have learned from my own personal experience in court that there is no graver injustice than institutionalized injustice. It has the greatest impact on the most people, and the impact is often lasting. And because of this truth, there is no greater passion in me than the pursuit and establishment of justice in our so-called justice system. As I share with you some of the intimate details of what transpired behind the closed doors of the courtroom, during a custody trial I faced, you will better understand systematic injustice and my passion to see it uprooted from our court system for the betterment of us all.

A Perception, or Prejudice?

The law requires that judges be neutral, fair, nonbiased, and not prejudiced toward one party or another in a court case. This is why, when you see the symbol of justice, the lady is wearing a blindfold. The eyes of the law are supposed to be blindfolded to prevent bias and prejudice. But God told me later on that the eyes of justice are not blind, and instead are wide open, because true justice can know everything about you and remain just. And justice comes from God. Human judges, however, are supposed to execute justice as if they were wearing a blindfold, meaning that they should treat the rich the same as the poor, because they cannot see who is rich and who is poor in the case, and likewise, they should treat the black the same as the white, because they are color-blind with the blindfold on. It is not a bad concept, but when it is ignored it can have devastating effects. The law also mandates that when a judge knows they are biased or might show favoritism toward one party over the other, they are to recuse themselves from the case. *Recuse*, in short, means that they fire themselves from working on the case. (How often do you think that happens?) Nevertheless, judges have a duty to follow the law themselves, and they are not exempt from doing so by way of their occupation as judges.

Very early on in the custody trial, I perceived that something was wrong. Before any witnesses were ever called, and long before a single deposition was ever taken, something was clearly wrong. The judge presiding over the case said multiple times that she was a basketball fan and that she loved basketball. I mean, she was smiling from ear to ear. The lawyers began discussing the court schedule for the trial, and when the lawyer began to tell her where my former spouse was in the United States because of his basketball schedule, she interrupted, and said, smiling, "I know where he is." And she did in fact know exactly where he had traveled. She then said, "I told you all, I follow basketball." This all was extremely problematic because my former spouse played professional basketball in the NBA and was seeking custody from a judge who stated how she loved professional basketball. I wanted to have this judge removed from my case. I instructed one of my attorneys to ask the judge to recuse herself for prejudice and bias, but he declined to do so, and thus, she stayed on the case, and this admitted lover of professional basketball made the decision to give the professional basketball player sole custody and to relocate the children over a thousand miles from their mother, their closet emotional tie. By the time this custody trial had concluded, I truly learned the importance of having a zealous advocate representing you.

Trial by Fire

Without any efforts to get this judge to recuse herself, the trial was underway, and this judge presided over the case. The trial itself lasted for several months. Many witnesses were called to testify or otherwise provide evidence for the court. The court also called its own witness to testify and give the judge an opinion as to which parent should have custody of the children. Her name was Dr. Amabile. Dr. Amabile is a medical doctor, a Psychiatrist, as well as a Custody Evaluator, and she has a degree in law. She is a lot of things, but unqualified is certainly not one of them. She has provided numerous custody evaluations wherein she uses her expertise, evaluates evidence, and interviews parents, family, friends, and doctors of the children for whom custody is sought, so that she can provide the court a detailed opinion of which parent should have custody of the minor children, or if both parents should share custody of the children, in order that the children's best interests are served by the custody decision. In all her years as a top custody evaluator in Illinois, no judge had ruled contrary to her recommendation to the court. That makes sense because, otherwise, courts would be ruling against their own witness. It is to be expected that someone would not rule against, or undermine, their own witness. Not so in my custody case, however. The judge presiding over my case made an unprecedented decision and ruled against her own highly qualified witness in order to take Zion and Zaire from me. The Custody Evaluator spent several months to determine who should have custody, and tens of thousands of dollars were spent in order to obtain her professional opinion. She ultimately decided that it was in the best interests of my children that I have sole custody, that the children remain living with me, and that their father have liberal visitation. She went on and explained to the court the detrimental consequences of ordering custody to the contrary. The court didn't listen and take heed to this medical doctor, board-certified psychiatrist, and law-degree holder when she said it was in the best interests of the children that I have custody of them, and that to do otherwise would cause the children to suffer irreparable harm. It's no wonder that this same court didn't listen to me either. I didn't have all the qualifications of this Expert Witness, and as far as this court was concerned, I was likely to them just a housewife, a rich man's wife, and a full-time stay-at-home mom! The court likely figured, "You don't need a degree to do that, and thus your opinion matters not." This Expert's professional opinion, however, of the harm the children would suffer if the court gave their dad custody, instead of me, has proven true. Going from just needing to see a therapist, to being prescribed drugs for mental disorders in just a short time after this judge ruled against her own Expert Witness was evidence of that.

This witness wasn't the only qualified witness who testified in Zion and Zaire's best interests, warranting me to have sole custody of them, and for them to continue living with me. The Administrator of the children's entire school showed up to testify on my behalf, and the Administrative Assistant did also. These academic professionals witnessed my unfailing commitment to and involvement in my children's lives. They were witnesses to the fact that I had not missed a single parent-teacher conference, report-card day, school play, field trip, or bake sale! The Administrative Assistant wept after just once witnessing the reality of the courts and its effect on children. The witnesses didn't stop there, however.

Several doctors and therapists were also a part of this trial. A therapist who treated one of my children gave testimony. She also said that, in her professional opinion, there was abuse, and she reported it. The judge ordered that she be fired! Then a new therapist began treatment. He is a medical doctor, and he gave the same report of abuse that the last therapist did. The judge ordered that he be fired as well.

My lawyer, who personally became a witness regarding the abuse, testified under oath. She explained to the court exactly what she knew about the abuse and how the professional who disclosed it to her recanted ever even speaking to her. She was no longer my lawyer, after she was asked to be fired from working for me.

Again, after an episode of domestic violence, I ended up in the emergency room. The emergency room physician who treated me referred me to a domestic violence shelter in order to specifically see a professional who specializes in the effects of domestic violence. He didn't testify, and that is likely the only reason that he didn't get fired too.

I took his advice, however, and sought help and shelter from the domestic violence. When I did, the domestic-violence-shelter employee said it was domestic violence, and the therapist who specializes in domestic violence and abuse also concluded that it was a case of domestic violence.

Also, I was made to testify for twenty-one days in this custody trial! I had several lawyers come up to me afterward and tell me that in all their experience in decades of practicing law in Illinois, they did not know of a single other instance in which someone had to testify for twenty-one days regarding custody. In other words, it was unprecedented! One lawyer literally told me, "Murder trials end quicker than just your testimony alone, Ms. Wade, during that custody trial!" The court, however, shielded and protected my former spouse from having to testify as much as me. In fact, she said, he only had to testify for four days total! There were three lawyers asking questions, and she basically said that three lawyers would get four days to question him after they had twenty-one days to wear me down!

Now, I know that the American legal system professes that in America, justice is supposed to be blind and thus free from prejudice, but in my case, the judge had taken off her blindfold, and put on 3-D glasses instead. But I thank God for His wisdom and divine protection through it all.

Divine Wisdom Equals Divine Protection

These were very difficult times for me. But God spoke to me and promised me that He was going to give me such a peace that it would seem to others that I didn't care. This was not easy to believe, because I did care, and sometimes I felt sad. Other days I was incredibly frustrated and upset with injustice that had become all the more blatantly obvious. But God did the impossible. He gave me peace during one of the most trying times of my life. I would try to describe to my loved ones the peace I was feeling. It was like God had put me inside of His bubble of protection. When something came against my life, whether judges or media, etc., I could feel that something had hit the bubble, but because I was inside the bubble, it didn't hit me. The protection of God is real! What God said about His peace in me and how it would cause others to think I didn't care, also occurred. And when it happened in court one day, I was amazed. A lawyer who was listening to the custody trial as it went on, afterward was so upset by what the judge was doing that she was crying and visibly upset. She came over to me and told me harshly that I was just calm, as if I didn't care! I was so overwhelmed with the joy of knowing God had spoken to me and surely told me what would happen that I was not at all offended by her going off on me. I was witnessing and experiencing the power of God, and I couldn't help but be glad and excited about it.

Hear No Evil

During the trial, their dad also had witnesses, but they came as adverse witnesses to testify against my interests. God also gave me His wisdom for this. During the custody trial, when a witness came to testify against me, God had me listen to the audible Bible on my headphones. I listened to what Jesus said about me, instead of the lies that were being told about me. I had such a peace and even joy, right in the midst of lies. Another lawyer came up to me after a witness's testimony concluded during the trial and commended me for keeping my cool. He was telling me how it was obvious that the witness was lying about me, and how he would not have been able to remain calm listening to those lies being told if it were him they were lying about. I smiled and told this man, "To God be all the glory for keeping me calm." God indeed kept me calm, and He also kept me wise! God told me one day, "Wisdom wins wars, not brute strength." God had given me wisdom to not do the very thing my enemies wanted me to do, and that was to explode with anger as they provoked me. God is so wise. If you need wisdom for any situation, ask God, because God will give you wisdom freely without finding fault (James 1:5).

Play Dead

I would be angry at times because God had truly made me all right and given me peace, even with the great injustice that had just transpired, but people were treating me like a fragile soon-to-crack glass. They were extra careful around me and would often speak for me, saying, "I know this is extremely difficult for you, and you are depressed because of what happened." That was not true, non-discerning ones! It made me upset, because I was forti-fied by God and more fervent in prayer than ever before. I was

strengthened for the battle by God Himself, strong in my faith in
Almighty God, and I had not grown weary or faint at all! Not even
in the least bit. God, however, gave me wisdom to win the real
war that was going on. The enemy was coming against me fiercely
and without mercy. God told me to look, talk, and act like you are
defeated, dead, in front of the vessels that the devil is using to do
these things against you, Zion, and Zaire. I heeded the wisdom
of God and did just that. I played the part of a defeated woman.
A "woe is me" award should have been given to the Holy Spirit in
me. God told me that my acting defeated was not surrendering
or giving up; it was strategic wisdom from God for the war. God
had me go to court dressed in clothes that looked like I'd slept
three nights in them, without my hair done, and with no makeup.
I only brushed my teeth for my own sake. (It's okay to laugh; I am.)
Seriously, God told me that an enemy won't keep fighting someone he believes is already dead. God reminded me of how I would
watch movies on TV and would think the victim should just play
dead, because then he will leave her alone. This concept isn't just
a way a wise movie producer can fashion the outcome of a film; it
is the wisdom of God. God reminded me that Jesus did this. God
has given Jesus all power, but when Jesus's enemies tried to kill
him sometime prior to His actual crucifixion, Jesus fled to a different town. Jesus even knew when to fold up and run, appearing
defeated! This wasn't a sign of weakness on Jesus's part. God had
given Him all power. But rather it was a sign of wisdom and great
strength in being humble enough to hear from God and follow His
lead. God had given me that same wisdom and told me in so many
words, "Play dead." All of a sudden, the litigation slowed down, the
media shut their mouths, and during this time of calmness, I went
into the presence of God to regain even more strength, rest from
the battle, and gain wisdom for the next moves. I had outwitted
the devil Himself by God's Spirit! The devil thought I was weak,
as evinced by people who spoke to me as if I were taking my dying

breath—which, by the way, used to frustrate me greatly. That is, until God explained to me that they were proof that what God told me to do, as far as playing dead, was working!

I felt from God to share this with you all, because it is a war strategy from God that you can use for both natural and spiritual wars, which often resemble one another. It is strategic warfare to know when to play dead, and it confuses the enemy and causes him to leave you alone as he goes off celebrating a victory entirely too early, a victory he actually never gained! God said it to me, and I found it to be true for myself, "The wisdom of God wins wars!"

Anger Has Roots

There was a time during the custody trial when I was angry about the injustice my children and I had already suffered and about what the court was doing in that moment. I was at times so mad, I told God, "You should have a suggestion box, because if You did, I could suggest some things You should do to every judge who presided over my case!" I was even angry at God. I asked God one day, "Why do You have all power, if You aren't going to use it to stop this madness?" I was a blazing, raging fire, causing third-degree burns at a minimum, and consuming the rest, at the most! Injustice is something that will try to make you come out of character completely. I thought a lot about the Civil Rights Movement, and Martin Luther King Jr., and Malcolm X while suffering one injustice after another in the court system. Prior to this court case, I would barely listen to any teacher trying to educate me about the history of America's so-called justice system and the lives that were lost because of its horrific injustices and uncured corruption. But after the hell manifested on earth through these judges and lawyers in my personal life, I began researching the Civil Rights Movement and those who were a part of it, with no needed motivation from anyone. In other words, nobody had to force me to learn it; I actively sought after it myself after feeling led by God to do so.

God even allowed a law-school professor later on to give me the letter the Holy Spirit of God wrote through Dr. King while he was wrongfully imprisoned in a Birmingham jail. When she gave me the letter, I read it right then and there in class, and I wept uncontrollably, because, for the first time in a long time, I knew I was not alone in these struggles, and what I endured was not an unfavorable outcome of a case; it was actual injustice and corruption in the legal system and those working in it.

That was only the beginning of a glorious turning point God had given me, though. God then led me to the Bible, where He had me study the fact that many times before, the devil would use the law to persecute the children of God. Even Jesus was falsely arrested and sentenced to death for a crime He did not commit. God showed me how the Jewish people were enslaved, beaten, and killed by orders of Egyptian kings for years (Exod. 5:6–15). God told me they called them kings then, but they are the same as judges. God also showed me how Queen Esther and the Jewish people of that time were sentenced to be executed unjustly, because a wicked man befriended the judge (who was called a king back then) in order to convince the judge to use his judicial and law-making authority to carry out the wicked man's plan to kill all those innocent Jews for him. The wicked man lacked the authority to do them harm, so he navigated through the court system to use them to do it for him. God also showed me how, in the book of Daniel, there were wicked men who, because of their jealousy of Daniel, used the judge to enter an evil court order to sentence Daniel to death. God spoke these exact words to me, "I have been dealing with unjust judges for a long time." I felt in my heart that God was also telling me, "Fear not, because I have dealt with this many times before, and I know how to handle this."

When I finally understood and got revelation of what God was showing me, I felt like King David in Psalm 73. Yes, it is true. "My foot almost slipped" too, and I envied the wicked also, because there seemed to be no harm done to them, while I was suffering greatly and being repaid evil for doing what was righteous before God. That was until I entered the presence of God, where He showed me what the end of the wicked was, and His great purpose for allowing me to go through the pain of injustice, and all I had suffered (Ps. 73). My life has never been the same since God did that. I forgave God completely and understood the end of those who had come against God by coming against me. The peace of God that surpasses all understanding had returned to me again, and I was free to serve God without anger, bitterness and lack of forgiveness in my heart toward these people and toward God. And I thank God because He did this work of deliverance in my life quickly.

Wisdom as a Witness

God spoke to me, even before the custody trial commenced, and long before the divorce was filed, and said, "I will hold your hand and help you through this trial step by step." I didn't know why God was saying that when He did. None of these legal matters had come about yet; but before it was all over, I understood God's promise and I witnessed Him fulfill it. God did exactly what He promised directly to me, and in His word to us all, when Jesus said, "I will give you the words to say when you go before the judges and magistrates" (Luke 12:11).

They continuously laid traps for me, while I testified at trial, but God gave me wisdom that kept me from falling into them. When they said Jesus was a weird religion and attempted to take my children from me for me following Christ, I said, "Well, Jesus says don't murder, steal, or lie, if I tell my children otherwise, they would be breaking the law of the land, which just so happens to be the law of God!" Thus, their attempt to take my children from me for my faith in Jesus was failing.

When they called me crazy, God gave me this wisdom. My former spouse admitted that he had not come to see our children for several months straight. I raised my children alone during this time. If I were crazy, as they lied and said I was, what would make their father leave his two children alone, and in the care of a person he knows to be a psychopath? And then give her your blessing when she moves to another state with the children? If they were going to charge me with being crazy, then they would have to also charge him with being neglectful and with child endangerment! The sword was double-edged; it cut both ways!

When the judge noticed that the wisdom of God was in me, and not even these old seasoned lawyers could trap God in me, she literally said, while I was on the witness stand, "I know what the problem is. You all don't know what to do, but I know what to do." And she gave me a look, that if looks could kill, she would have slit my throat right then and there on that witness stand. It seemed more personal than ever after that point. In fact, it was after that when she told my lawyer and me that my former spouse would only have to testify for a total of four days, despite me having to be on the witness stand for twenty-one days. As far as this judge was concerned nobody was going to gather evidence from the celebrity professional athlete beyond four days. This was a blatant violation of my constitutional rights, but this judge wasn't done yet.

Once my former spouse actually took the witness stand, on the third day, she stopped the trial and would not allow my attorney to question him anymore! People, I don't know how much you know about the law, but this was unlawful. She then told us that she wanted us to come into her office, and that I could not bring a court reporter with me. I was obviously not comfortable with this, because these judges had been unjust in times past, and therefore, I wanted a record of what she was about to do behind the closed doors of her office. My attorney reminded her that I have a legal right to have a court reporter present and that I didn't want to proceed unless she would allow the court reporter to make a record. It is so important to have a court reporter, people, especially in cases where injustice is present. If someone loses a case in court, and they want to file an appeal, (the process of having appellate court judges review the case for errors), those appellate-court judges need a record to look at, because they were not present and in person to see and hear whatever wrong the lower-court judge did or did not do. Thus, they need a record of the court proceedings (a transcript from the court reporter). This judge, however, told me that I wasn't allowed to have a court reporter! And she wasn't done yet.

She then dropped the bomb and said that if I did not go into her office without the court reporter, she would go anyway, with my former spouse and his lawyers, and I would be considered un-represented by counsel. Judges are not supposed to have ex-parte conversations with parties or their lawyers. In general, *ex parte* means, without one party to the case. Judges are not supposed to have conversations with or conduct hearings with, just one of the parties from the case present, because the law requires trans-parency with judges and court proceedings, which is why court is open to the public, and you can attend court even when you are not directly involved in the court case yourself. (Hence, the O. J. Simpson murder trial that was watched on television from people's homes all across America.)

Transcripts provide for transparency too. A judge is less likely to do blatant injustice, when a court reporter is writing down every word the judge speaks. They know that the parties to the case can take this transcript and have evidence of their misconduct and lawlessness. This judge denied me the right to both. She told me to my face that she would proceed with my former spouse and his law-yers alone, not having my lawyer or me present, and that I could not have a court reporter present either. I still didn't want to go, but having taken my lawyer's advice, we went behind more closed doors, and without a court reporter!

This is why I am so passionate about helping women in situa-tions like these. We have all heard the saying, "If you don't stand for something, you will fall for anything." I wanted to stand up to that judge's conduct and correct her in love, but instead it was the fall-for-anything advice I ultimately received. My former spouse left that day, and my attorney wasn't allowed to ask him any more questions again. They had a record of me answering questions on the witness stand for twenty-one days, and from him only three days' worth of evidence was obtained, and this was the custody case he filed. The rich and famous don't even have to show up for their own case, according to some unjust judges' new constitutional rules. Indeed, this was a trial by fire, and prejudice was ablaze!

Opening Up: Breaking the Silence

Here I am, faced with one of my worst fears: losing Zion and Zaire. I am being told that I need to open my mouth and speak the truth about what happened behind the closed doors of that four-million-dollar prison that realtors termed a "mansion." I don't care if hell has marble floors, six bedrooms, and a vaulted ceiling—it's still hell. But when I spoke up, all I received from the court was disdain, harsh treatment, and worse abuse than any other I ever experienced.

In sum, the court accused me of parental alienation. I explained to this court how often times my son had been punched in his chest by "Mr. Fist" as a form of discipline if he did something wrong. This is abuse. My son had also been diagnosed with asthma. One Thanksgiving, he was punched in the chest for "crying too much" and because he did not "man up!" like he was told. He had an asthma attack that day. I was the one God used to protect my son that day, even if it meant I would end up being physically abused myself. I did not care. The love I have for my children is the love of God; I was willing to lay down my life for my children. (And that is what God did when He sent Jesus to die for us; Jesus laid down his own life and died, to save ours.) That is the ultimate love. Jesus said, "No greater love than the one who will lay down his life for his friends" (John 15:13). And that is what I did. I laid down my life in that moment and in many others. The judge, however, didn't see it that way. She chose to call protection "parental alienation syndrome," the suicidal man's nonscientific theory, despite the fact that this theory is rejected by the mental health profession at large as well as medical professionals! Whenever someone harms somebody, it is a normal reaction not to want to be around him or her, even if the harmed individual decides to stay with the one who hurt them. Even these judges believe this notion, because when it comes to women who have been abused, many judges ask, "If the woman was abused, why did she stay with the abuser?" This is a good question. The problem is that judges, don't ask this same question or use this same reasoning when a child has been subjected to domestic violence, either directly, or by witnessing their mother being abused. But the same should be true. Judges, ask yourself: if you believe that a woman who has been abused should not want to be around the abuser, why then do you believe that a child who has been subjected to this same domestic violence would want to be around the abuser? Courts have punished the abused woman for not leaving the abusive relationship, and then again punished the abused woman because the child wants to get away from the abuser! This should not be so, judges. It is high time to execute justice!

I was constantly defending myself from the court. I explained to this judge, at length, that for me this custody trial wasn't about who was the better parent. Custody is not a competition. What makes me a good parent is the fact that I have fought for my children's dad to be a better parent, knowing and recognizing that he is a vital part of their lives, and God used both of us to make them. My success as a parent has been reflected in helping him become a better one. And I have never tried to erase him from their lives, but rather I fought tirelessly for him to have a good, healthy role in their lives and to spend quality time with them. I made it clear to the court that I was not fighting for custody of Zaire and Zion because having custody doesn't make someone a parent or a better parent. I was fighting because I am their mother, and I want to be a part of my children's lives. I didn't want her custody decision to destroy my relationship with my children, and my role as their mother. The fight for me was never about custody; it was, and it still is, about my position in my two children's lives. That's all I've been fighting for in these courtrooms—justice for Zion and Zaire, whom I love dearly.

I reminded this judge that long before any custody petition was filed, and long before any judges were involved in our lives, it was me, and only me, who worked with their dad each time he saw his children! No court order was in place to mandate that I do this. The righteousness of God on the inside of me was present and directing me to build and not tear down the relationship my children have with their dad. Countless times, I opened the doors of our home after their dad left it, so that he could spend time with the children. Countless times, I took the children to basketball games to see their dad play and to have five minutes to speak to him after a game. No court ordered me to do that. God ordered my steps then, and God ordered my steps when he said, "Protect your children!" So wake up judges, protection is not parental alienation! I, as well as many other women like me, are not alienators; we are facilitators. Your own ignorance has confused the two. If you are going to remain ignorant or biased against women, then don't remain on the bench! Recuse yourselves for the sake of justice!

I traveled with my children from Miami to Illinois, in order for them to spend time with their dad, so many times. We probably had more frequent flyer miles than the pilot. I did this, and no unjust judge told me to. When we moved to Chicago, I allowed the children's dad into our home countless times to get the children and spend time with them. There was no court order telling me to do that; I just did it because of the righteousness of God on the inside of me.

Another time, my former spouse called me after the separation, and he was sounding very down on the phone. He asked me to please come to where he was playing in Milwaukee, Wisconsin, and bring the boys with me. I asked him immediately, "When?" I never even thought to tell him no. He told me the game was the next day. I went and purchased overpriced airline tickets for Zion, Zaire, and myself and we flew from Miami all the way to Wisconsin so that he could spend time with his children for literally twenty minutes. I laid aside everything I had planned to do that day before he called so that for twenty minutes he would be blessed as a father, and Zion and Zaire would be blessed to have their dad in their lives. I am the furthest person from an alienator. Wake up, judges!

When he was absent from the home, I sent him pictures of me potty training Zion and photos of when Zion dressed himself for the first time, and I invited him to every single birthday party, parent-teacher conference, baseball game, and swim lesson. I did all of this without any court orders or judges, and without their dad ever having to ask me to do so.

Again, the problem is not the woman's reaction to the abuse she and her children suffered from, and it's not the children's re-action for wanting to be away from (alienated from) the person whom the child has witnessed doing the abusing! The problem is bias, prejudice and injustice in the courts. Judges, you have al-lowed whatever bias, prejudice, sexism, or ignorance you have to rule you, and thus when you rule in these courtrooms, it is in an unruly, unjust manner that has hurt these children and women, more than any punch in the chest, bruise, or harsh name has com-bined. Wake up, judges, the worse form of abuse is flowing from you! You have got to change or recuse yourselves.

When I suggested to the court that my former spouse be able to call the children *anytime* he wanted to, the judge literally called me "*controlling.*" Saying someone has the liberty to call when they want, to is not control; it is absolute freedom! Wake up, judges, and put on justice as a garment before you put on your black robes of court apparel. By the way, the court ended up ordering that the only time I can speak to my children is during a two-hour window of time, and if I miss it, then I don't get to speak to my children at all. I suppose the judge didn't call herself controlling when she did this.

One day, one of my children became very ill while at school, and so I picked him up, but ultimately I had to take him to the hospital, and I am glad I did! After the doctors treated him, they began testing for childhood cancers and eventually transported him by ambulance to a hospital that specializes in trauma and childhood illnesses. He ended up being hospitalized there. That same day, before this happened, the children had been scheduled to visit with their dad. But instead of me taking them to see their dad, I took my sick child to the doctor. The judge called me dramatic; "drama trauma" is what she said specifically. The several medical doctors, physician assistants, and nurses who treated my son must have all been "dramatic" as well, because they had my child hospitalized.

I was the only person in the entire case that came up with a schedule for both parents to see the children. But that too was seen as evil in the eyes of the court. All I asked was that the children actually visit with their father. I had spoken to my children on several occasions when they were court-ordered to visit with their dad but were actually with others. Both my children were said to have almost drowned in a single weekend. Another time Zion came home with a back injury and at the time was just a toddler, but he was suffering from back pain just from a simple touching of his back. They too cried for help, but their cry went unheard. For my cry, I was punished.

Women should not be subjected to systematic abuse and injustice for breaking the silence on domestic violence. They should not be punished for telling the truth. From a very early age, children are even taught to tell the truth. There is nothing wrong with the person who speaks the truth. But there is something gravely evil when courts are clothed with corruption, and judges fight to keep the truth concealed and punish women by taking their children from them when they break the silence. In the movie *God's Not Dead 2*, a wise person once said it like this: "Silence is the enemy of the truth."

God on Trial

God said, in His word, "We wrestle not against flesh and blood, but against principalities, against powers, against the rulers of the darkness of this age, against spiritual hosts of wickedness in the heavenly places" (Eph. 6:12). As this trial continued to unfold, and the judge continued in her conduct, this truth became more evident to me.

This trial was never about custody, Zion, Zaire, or me and their dad. This whole case was about something much bigger than us, and it had key players involved other than us. That is exactly what God is speaking of in Ephesians 6:12. The people involved were all like pawns in a chess game, but the real players were God and Satan. The whole trial turned on my relationship with God and His Son, Jesus. I was being questioned extensively about my relationship with God—not my relationship with either of my children, but instead my relationship with Jesus! Literally, this occurred. The adverse lawyer questioning me brought the Bible into court, opened it up, placed it on top of a pulpit-like podium, and began examining me extensively about the Bible! God said it. "We wrestle not against flesh and blood (humans), but against 'rulers of darkness!'" (Eph. 6:12). They didn't ask me if I maintained immunizations for my children's health or if I made sure my children were educated properly. Instead they asked me questions like, did I speak in tongues and if prophets existed today—to all of which,

I said yes! They didn't stop with that though; they went on to specifically ask me if I believed what God said in the Bible, in Genesis 12:3, when God said to Abraham, "I will bless those who bless you, and whoever curses you I will curse." I almost laughed when he asked me, because I was thinking of all the Bible verses he could have read in court, yet he read the one most fitting for himself! I answered him, "Indeed I believe God will curse those who curse me!" I suppose he missed what God was telling him directly in that very moment, but my guess is, before he leaves this earth, the hand of God will be upon him in such a way that He will know that God meant what He said. But nevertheless, they continued questioning me extensively about my faith in Jesus.

God let me know what they doing. They were laying a trap for me to step in, like religious leaders did to Jesus many times before. They would question Jesus about God's Word, "so that they might have something of which to accuse Him of," and this is exactly what they were doing to Jesus in me, that very day (John 8:6). I witnessed the word of God in the Bible, playing out right before my very eyes. Jesus Christ, in me, was attacked with the same persecution He suffered over two thousand years ago. As evil as it was, what they were doing, it was liberating for me. I realized at that moment that this case was not about custody of Zion and Zaire; it was about God. And thus, this battle was not mine! This was good news! It was like a weight lifted off me. The outcome of the case was not mine to make happen. This battle was God's to fight and win!

I was being persecuted for Jesus Christ's sake, and I am so blessed because of it (Matt. 5:10). God told me that the devil wanted me to deny Christ or admit that I love God with all my heart, mind, soul, and strength, because admitting that I love God and believe His word is true, meant that they would say I was crazy because of my faith in God, and they would tell the court, "Take her children away from her." This opposition was really my opportunity to enter into my destiny and begin fulfilling it. This was so amazing to me when God revealed it! The Bible says, "For the message of the cross is foolishness [crazy] to those who are perishing, but to us who are being saved it is the power of God" (1 Cor. 1:18). As it was that day in court, so it is to this day: I would rather have a perishing man call me crazy, than Almighty God call me unsaved and weak!

The choice I was given in effect was quite simple, although a difficult one to make at the time, because I do after all love my children. It came down to this: deny Christ, and possibly keep your children with you, or publicly acknowledge Christ, the Son of God, and they may take your children from you because of it. A holy anger arose within me on that witness stand that day, and I looked at the devil inside of my accuser and told him, in the presence of that natural judge, but more importantly in the presence of the Judge of all judges, "We don't have to go through the Bible question by question anymore. Everything written in the word of God, in my Bible, I believe! If God said it, I believe it!" I made my choice that day, and I have absolutely no regrets about it. The truth is that your children as well as mine are not really our children anyway; they are the children of God. Nothing on this earth belongs to us—not even the air we breathe. Everything belongs to God, and it is God who blesses us to be good stewards over His possessions. We know the reality of this truth all the more whenever God gets ready to take what is His, and there's nothing that mankind can do about it. They can have a title to it, birth certificates with proof of parentage and DNA results backing it all up, but when God takes it away, none of those so-called rights to it can stop Him. God is sovereign, but people don't like to admit it because it scares them that they are not in control. But whether you admit it or not, you are still not in control, and denial won't change that. We don't have to be afraid of God's being in control, because God is love, and when we come to God through Jesus Christ, we come as Jesus is: righteous, holy, just, and blameless before God (1 John 4:17). Because of Jesus sacrificing His life and dying on the cross in our sinful place, we don't have to fear the wrath of God anymore, but those without Jesus should run toward Him quickly, because otherwise, there is the fearful expectation of wrath. This is why I thank God for Jesus, inside and outside of court. God is in control. When people are diagnosed with terminal cancers and outlive the doctor who diagnosed them, this is not luck; this is the power of God! When doctors have told mothers they won't bear children, and six children later, with a set of twins, these parents know the power of God through the cross of Jesus Christ! They know God is in control. The word is true: "The Lord gives, and the Lord takes away, blessed be the name of the Lord" (Job 1:21). Now, I am not saying God took Zion and Zaire away from me. The system failed us, not God. God is to blame for healing us after injustice, and unjust men tried to destroy us. That, God is guilty of.

We as a people have to be free from the fear of losing what really doesn't belong to us anyway. The devil has used this tactic long enough: putting people in hypothetical fear. Hypothetical fear is that fear that says things like: "what *if* their marriage fails, or what *if* they lose their job, and what *if* their children don't graduate, or what *if* people find out what they did when they were younger, and what *if* they get cancer like their family member did?" To hypothetical fear, I say what God taught me: "What if none of that ever happens?" or "What if it does, and God works it together for my good, making me come out better than I was before anyway?" Hell cannot stand this kind of power and sound mind! Those who are battling with fear, make up your mind like I did, and say, "I'm not going to spend my days, or even my minutes, fearing the invisible man of trouble who actually doesn't exist." It is high time to let go of fear, embrace faith in God who never fails and who loves us, and move forward into our destiny. And let's do so regardless of the enemies of God who ask, "What *if* it cost you this or that to serve God?" Tell hell this: doing what God created me to do, will never cost me anything that the blood of Jesus has not paid for already. I'm moving on into my destiny!

It's enough of this hypothetical hamster wheel the devil has had so many people running around on in circles of fret and dread, rather than walking straight into their destiny and trusting that God is in control and God is good! You can likely hear my tone, although you're reading the words in my heart, on these pages. My heart is lifted up in a loud voice, saying, "Enough is enough! Now is the time to be free from all fear, so that we can walk in the love and the peace of God, and fulfill our destinies in Christ with confidence and boldness!"

I remembering during this trial thinking there is nothing wrong with Jesus. Jesus said, "Don't murder; don't steal; don't cheat on your wife, husbands; and wives, you be faithful as well; don't lie; love one another; pay taxes; pay the laborer when he works for you his due wages; honor your mother and father; forgive whenever you need to; rejoice and be glad; fear not; and have peace!" These are all things good parents teach their children and want for themselves. The problem is that some will embrace and use God's teachings, but reject the Teacher, Jesus. So, you see, the problem isn't Jesus.

Even more interesting is the fact that the things Jesus taught over two thousand years ago are either a law in Illinois or public policy of the state today. Also, this nation defines time by the birth and death of Jesus Christ—hence, *B.C.*, meaning "before Christ," and *A.D.*, meaning "*anno Domini* (in the year of our Lord)." In every courtroom I have ever been inside, it says "In God we trust" somewhere, and on every dollar we spend, it is printed the same: "In God we trust." But despite these truths, when I said I believed it, and that I teach my children the same, they started persecuting me all the more and saying that my Christian faith was some alternative religion. There were more lies in that courtroom than birds in the sky. I let it be known quickly that I don't have an alternative religion—or any other religion. I believe in Jesus Christ. It was religious leaders who crucified Jesus because He refused to keep up with their rule-keeping religious ways. I have a relationship with God not a religion. Religion keeps rules and condemns the minute one is broken. I know I am not perfect, so I allowed Jesus to save me by grace, not by my rule-keeping ability! That truth about Jesus and the new covenant He established when He died on the cross is an enemy of religion. Religion wants to control people, but Jesus came to make us free—and free indeed (John 8:36). You cannot reconcile religion and Jesus. You just cannot. The law calls God religious. God never called Himself that. God said, "I am the way, the truth, and the light" (John 14:6). He never mentioned He was religious. Unjust judges are calling Christ religious when He doesn't call Himself that. That is their problem, not God's—or mine! They are the ones filled with religion, thinking if a person believes certain things, they are a part of some religion. Ah, the ignorance this breeds, and the harm it causes, thus giving me all the more reason to hate religion!

I allow God in me to correct this nation, because I love it. My love for this nation is another reason I hate religion. Religion is responsible for the attacks on 9/11 in America. Religion is without a relationship with God, and void of revelation of the love of Jesus. Thus, religion produces hate. We should never confuse the strikingly different two! Religion caused the deaths on 9/11 in America—not God. Jesus is the reason those families have been healed from that loss. Again, you cannot reconcile religion with the Messiah and His love for us. Thus, if people want to blame God for something, blame Him for all the blessings in your life. He is certainly responsible for all of mine.

By the end of this trial, it was blatantly obvious that God was on trial, not me. And in any respect that I was on trial, it was because they were trying my faith in Jesus. And when I refused to deny Jesus Christ, the devil turned up the fire! But "let it burn" was the resolution in my heart. God has given me wisdom to know, "There is nobody who has left house or father or mother or brother that will not receive a reward in this life, and salvation in the next" (Mark 10:29). I wasn't losing; I was winning in this life and in the next.

On the same day this happened to me in court, I was informed that President Obama was questioned about his faith in Jesus too. I was in court on the witness stand, so I didn't get a chance to hear his answer, but I was told that President Obama didn't deny Jesus Christ or his faith in Him, on the same day that I wouldn't either. God really blessed me when He allowed me to hear that news. For this reason, I really honor President Obama, his wife, Michelle Obama and his family. Both the president and Only Lady Michelle Obama have done great things, but this one thing I honor them for above all others: not denying Christ. I remember this labor of love from them above all the rest. You've likely noticed that I called this woman of worth "Only Lady Michelle Obama," rather than "First Lady Michelle Obama" like many others refer to her. That is intentional. "First lady" implies that there is more than one lady, and to that evil, we say, "Hell no, and no to hell!" All the married women are either saying or thinking, "Amen!" And I am laughing right now, but I am so serious at the same time!

They Meant It for Evil, But God Meant It for Good!

March 11, 2011. The day began like any other day, but before it ended, my life and the lives of my children changed forever. I woke up that morning and prepared breakfast for Zion and Zaire and got them ready for school, just like any other morning. We got in the car, and like we did every morning on the way to school, we prayed together, each taking turns to pray for the others. We arrived at school, and I gave them both really big hugs and several kisses, because they were scheduled to be with their dad for that weekend. When I dropped the children off at school, however, Zion said something that seemed incredibly strange to me at the time, and he looked very sad. He said, with tears in his eyes, "Mama, my tee-tee is going to pick me up today, and I won't be back to see you, but you all can pray." I didn't know what, or why, Zion was speaking that way, so I promised Zion that I would see him on Sunday after he spent time with his dad that weekend. (I don't make promises anymore after that day.) Also, Zaire's teacher contacted me and told me that, while in Chapel that day at school, Zaire had begun weeping and saying, "only God can help us." She said he just kept crying uncontrollably and repeating, "only God can help us." Zaire would not tell her any more than that. Although at the time I did not understand why Zion and Zaire were behaving the way they were that day, or why they had said what they'd said, I would soon know.

That same evening, I received a phone call from my lawyer. He literally sounded saddened, and I knew at that moment, given his tone, that something was very wrong. He eventually told me, "Siohvaughn, she gave him custody." I remember standing at that moment with the phone in my hand, in nothing but the pure strength of God Almighty. After I got off the phone with my lawyer, I very calmly told my mother, who was with me, what the lawyer said, and I went upstairs into my bedroom and began to talk to God about what I had just been told. God spoke to me, and I heard God say, "Have you considered My servant, Siohvaughn?" At that moment, God reminded me of where I heard God speak those words before. It was in Job 1:8. Then, I understood. Surely the devil had come against me like he did Job, *but* God is in control, like He was with Job! And before it was over, God restored all of Job's losses, and before it's over, God will restore me completely too! God is the same yesterday, today, and forevermore (Heb. 13:8).

I then heard God ask me, "Do you trust Me?" I responded, "The Lord giveth, and the Lord taketh away. Blessed be the name of the Lord!" I didn't even know, at the time when I said those words, that they are in the Bible too, and they are from the book of Job! I know it was not me in that moment still standing after hell itself attacked me and my boys, and I know I was not still standing at that moment in my life because of my own strength. I was truly standing in the strength of God. God promises us in His word, "When you are weak, My strength is made perfect" (2 Cor. 13:8). My love, I have been in the perfect strength of God and for me, this is not just a Bible verse to quote. I have lived the power and truth of God's Word, which I know, can keep me. God's word has literally saved and sustained my very life. Every loving parent reading this knows and understands that to take someone's children from them, hurting their children is worse than anything you can ever do to the parent directly. God feels the same way. God loves us so much that while we were guilty of sin before God, He sent Jesus to die in our place on the cross. Romans says, "God demonstrates His love toward us that while we were still in sin, Christ died for us" (Rom. 5:8). I answered God's question that day, and better than that, I showed God that I trusted Him. I left my bedroom and told my mom and my friend who was visiting, "I'm ready to go to the show." We had already planned on going to the movies that day, and so we did as planned. We went and saw the movie, *Unknown*, starring Liam Neeson. I was not depressed or suicidal, but rather, I was convinced: God is in control! I had the peace of God that surpasses all understanding. Jesus promised to give this peace in His word, and He gave it. This faith in God saved me from what very well could have killed me. Jesus said it then, and it is true today: "Your faith has saved you, go in peace" (Luke 7:50).

The lawyer went on to explain to me that ultimately, the court gave my former spouse custody of the boys, because she *predicted* that he would do a better job of facilitating my parenting time and my relationship with the children and me. This, however, was problematic in and of itself, because he had never had our children full-time or even part-time, warranting for her to say she can predict the way he will behave. In other words, she gambled with the lives of my children, and my relationship with them, and she crapped out, as you will clearly see in the next chapter of my life.

Trial is the most appropriate word that I can use to describe what occurred during that court case. Not a trial in a legal sense, for that was a small matter compared to what was really happening in that place and in the spirit realm. For me, I mean a trial as in "I was tried by the fire of injustice, evil, temptation, and suffering." I was tested greatly, but in the end, I was God-approved! Man shunned me, but God celebrated me, and I celebrated God! Many people heard of what the media said I lost, but a select few, until now, heard about what I gained. Yes, they said they took Zion and Zaire, but they did not take Jesus from His position as Lord over all the earth and its fullness, and because the earth and everything in it, including Zion and Zaire, belong to God, they had not taken Zion and Zaire, either. I had never had custody of Zion and Zaire, and neither had their dad, but God alone owns Zion and Zaire and is in control of their lives and the very air they breathe! God called me to be a mother. Before the unjust custody decision, and even after the hell they undeservedly afflicted me with, I am still Zion and Zaire's mother, and there is nothing the devil or any unjust man or woman can ever do to change that. It is true that the enemies of God have labored in vain once again. It's okay to laugh out loud at hell for being the best at being the worst! All thanks be to Jesus Christ, the Messiah! They meant it for evil, but my God meant it for good!

For those who are thinking, "Siohvaughn, you are indeed a woman of faith, and I can hear it in the words I am reading, but you are going to have to explain to me better how you can reconcile the court giving your former spouse custody with you not losing." I am glad you thought it! (For those who didn't think it bear with us a moment, because this will surely bless you as well.) I want to share with you the experiences I had that help explain this truth, and a principle God taught me that applies to any of our lives, especially if we are facing trials and difficulties.

Before the custody decision, my mind was consumed with not losing God's sons Zion and Zaire. When the judge made the custody decision and took Zion and Zaire from me, I finally had time and a clear mind for the first time in years. It was similar to an experience that King David in the Bible had when his newborn son had become very ill. King David went off alone, prayed, and fasted earnestly for his child not to die. David was weeping, not eating, and in turmoil, but when the child died, the Bible says that King David got up, began eating, stopped weeping, and he lived again (2 Sam. 12:17–23). For some, this may not make sense at first glance, but I pray God will give understanding according to His will, in Jesus name. I had been holding my breath in pure agony going through that trial at times, but when the war ceased, I was able to exhale and breathe again. The war ending with me still standing, when I had numerous reasons to give up and die, was indeed the power of God and great victory.

Also, as you read earlier on, I struggled with idolatry of my family, including my children. My obsession with taking care of them and always putting them first seemed like love, but God told me it was fear. Where there is love, fear is cast out. I did love my children back then too, but the love wasn't perfect love, because perfect love casts out fear (1 John 4:18). The Bible says, "Where there is fear, love has not been made perfect" (1 John 4:18). When I didn't have any more idols to hold on to and use as an excuse not to fulfill my destiny and purpose in life, then I finally got up and lived for real. Prior to that I lived in limbo as I waited for injustice to make a decision concerning the lives of two children who I loved more than myself, and I was paralyzed by fear. But when God allowed me to face my greatest fear, and overcome it then I knew that God is able to keep me in perfect peace and give me joy no matter what adversity. I have a sound mind, can laugh, can love, and can live—all of which are a blessing for my children and me. Indeed, God gave me victory! Always remaining in a safe haven, never confronted by trouble, does not give evidence at all of someone's strength, but being tried by fire, and knowing Jesus will get in the fire with you, not always delivering you from the flame right away, but showing you that if Jesus is for you, not even a consuming fire can consume you! My God! People, this is the power of God! This is victory! This is strength, and this is faith in Almighty God and His all-powerful, sufficient Son, Jesus, the Christ! I used to think, back then, that when I had some money, I had power, but when my life was set ablaze by the fiery trials of injustice, the money was the first thing to burn, and I knew who had real power then! It was the God who kept me when everything around seemed to be burning down fast. All power belongs to God, and this I know for myself now.

Attack vs. Assignment

Now, I want to share with you the principle God gave me that anyone can use when facing difficulties. It also will explain to you why I have such tenacious faith in God and know that God did give me victory, regardless of the unjust decision made by feeble mankind. God promises believers in Jesus Christ that "No weapon formed against you shall prosper, and every tongue that rises against you in judgment, you shall condemn" (Isa. 54:17). One day I was spending time alone with God, and this promise of God about no weapon forming against me will prosper, with the custody trial order, was hard to reconcile. God answered me. God, through His Holy Spirit, began explaining to me that there is a difference between an attack and an assignment that is formed against people's lives. What God promises will not prosper is the assignment, not the attack. Let me share with you specifically what God means by this. It will bless you.

I learned that in this trial I was not being tried as a mother, and the purpose of the enemy was not to separate me from Zion and

Zaire. For everyone admitted I was a good mother, and separation is inevitable anyway, either through death someday, or they will grow up and have their own families with whom they live, God willing. God revealed to me what was really happening with this custody trial, and how the whole thing was never about custody or the children, but it was about the enemy trying to end my life, in an effort to try and stop me from fulfilling my destiny and the purpose for which I was created, including writing this book. With this revelation, I learned something profound that has helped me as well as countless others facing very serious problems—and even those facing troubles not as severe. God let me know clearly that the enemy didn't want Zion or Zaire; he wanted my life. God let me know that the devil himself thought that if he could separate me from those children whom I love deeply, then he figured suicide would follow. You see, custody, and the children being separated from me physically, were just the natural manifestations of a very real spiritual attack. God explained to me that this is a tactic the enemy often uses in people's lives, not just mine. God explained to me that when you pray because something is attacking your life—whether the attack be sickness, injustice, divorce, or betrayal—pray against that attack, and also pray against the assignment behind it. God told me to pray against the assignment behind it as well, because the attack—whether it be sickness, fear, depression, divorce—may not be the actual result the enemy is trying to bring about. The attack is the means, and the intended result is—or what the enemy actually desires to do against you is—the assignment. Usually the means/attack will manifest as some natural event such as a custody trial, divorce, loss of job, financial crisis, etc. The enemy's desired end is usually something way more significant resulting in a spiritual loss, such as a loss of hope, loss of life, and turning away from God, etc.

For illustrative purposes, and because God desires those reading to understand for their good, God gave me an example to share with you: When the devil tries to attack someone's finances, this financial attack is the means. It may have been a job loss, or foreclosure, or even both. The person whose finances have been attacked can see that they are suffering financially, and so they are praying against bankruptcy and financial loss. However, what they cannot see is far more significant and is the real reason Satan attacked them in the first place. God told me, in this example, that the devil could care less if this person files bankruptcy or lost a job. What the devil really is after is their life, their faith, their hope, and their relationship with God, who is the source of all things. The devil really desires that they commit suicide because of the financial loss they suffered. The suicide is the end result that the devil wants, not bankruptcy. Bankruptcy and financial loss are merely a temporary means to try to bring about a permanent and destructive end: suicide. So God told me that, in this example, both bankruptcy and suicide should be prayed against, but suicide even more, because that is what the enemy really wants; that's the real assignment behind the attack. People recover from bankruptcy all the time; suicide, however, is a different story.

God is so good and faithful to turn what was meant for evil into good. You may be asking yourself how you will know the assignment behind it. That's a good question, and God is willing to answer it, so please take time to pray and ask God, in Jesus name, to reveal to you the assignment behind the attack. The Bible says the Holy Spirit helps us in our weaknesses, "for we do not know how to pray as we ought, but the Holy Spirit makes intercession for us with groaning's which cannot be uttered. Now He who searches the hearts knows what the mind of the Spirit is, because He makes intercession for the saints according to the will of God" (Rom. 8:26–27). You can also pray the way the Holy Spirit of God taught me: "Heavenly Father, in Jesus's name, I cancel every assignment behind this attack of the enemy." It may not be God's will for someone to understand or know everything about what they are going through, but it is God's will for His children to prevail and enjoy the victory Jesus Christ died for us to have, and His promises to those who are the children of God.

It is also wise to pray against the assignment behind the attacks of people doing evil, because everything evil that happens is not the devil. The devil cannot be in more than one place at a time. That defeated foe is not omnipresent. In other words, he is not God! I have seen evil manifest, and it was not the devil but an evil decision a human being made in their flesh. In fact, God asked me one day, "Did I notice how, in the Bible, Jesus said that "the thief (the devil) comes, to kill, steal, and to destroy, but I have come that they may have life, and have it to the full" (John 10:10). This scripture teaches us the three things the devil attempts to do, and thanks be to God, it also tells us what Jesus has done already, which cannot be undone. However, when God speaks about the flesh of a human being, that evil carnal nature of man, God says, in the flesh dwells no good thing, and "the works of the flesh are evident, adultery, fornication, uncleanness, lewdness, idolatry, sorcery, hatred, contentions, jealousies, outbursts of wrath, selfish ambitions, dissensions, heresies, envy, murders, drunkenness, revelries, and the like, of which I tell you beforehand, just as I told you in time past, that those who practice such things will not inherit the kingdom of God" (Rom. 7:18; Gal. 5:19–21).

Notice how three things are mentioned when discussing the devil, but a list nearly as long as a human leg is given when discussing the evil deeds of mankind. This is why we need a Savior, because we all have something we need to be saved from: mostly the devil and evil men of the last days (2 Tim. 3). Don't fret if you believe you have sinned in the flesh, because we all have, and that's the reason we all need a Savior: to save us from our sinful nature, and much more. Thanks be unto God for our Lord and Savior Jesus Christ who forgives us, cleanses us from sin, and makes us righteous before God, transforming us into His likeness and character. So if you have done any of these things mentioned above, receive Jesus as your Lord and Savior. The Bible says, "If you confess with your mouth the Lord Jesus, and believe in your heart that God raised Jesus from the dead on the third day, you shall be saved" (Rom. 10:9). Through Jesus, your sins are all forgiven—past, present, and future—and you are made righteous before God by faith. This is good news! I hope you were blessed by that wisdom, and knowing the difference between an attack versus an assignment of evil, because it certainly has blessed my life.

The devil meant the custody trial for evil, wanting me to just give up and kill myself. However, God meant it all for good, desiring that I live the abundant life He promised. Within a couple of months of this trial by fire, God told me to enroll in law school. I applied and was accepted into the John Marshall Law School in Chicago, for the glory of God. And as you will see in the chapters to come, this was indeed a date with destiny.

If the devil would have known that Jesus would come out of that custody trial preaching the Gospel of Jesus Christ through me with a passion for the purpose of God for my life and the lives of many others, he would have personally gone and picked up Zion and Zaire and brought them back to me! God is victorious, and all His enemies are defeated foes! My beating heart, filled with passion and purpose, along with my joyful steps into my destiny, are living proof of that truth!

"But as for you, you meant evil against me; but God meant it for good, in order to bring about as it is this day, to save many people alive" (Gen. 50:20).

THE AFTERMATH

*The Lord is near to those who have a broken heart
and saves such as have a contrite spirit.*

—Psalm 34:18

The fires of the custody trial itself had ceased, but there was an aftermath that proved to be more difficult than the trial. The pain of Zion, Zaire, and me being separated from one another seemed at times to be almost unbearable. But quickly, after this manifest injustice of the custody judgment, things worsened, because even for the small number of times the judge allowed me to spend time with my children, I was prevented from being with them during those times also, and the pain penetrated more deeply. As you recall, the judge presiding over the custody trial predicted that if she took Zion and Zaire away from their mom, their dad would facilitate visitation between the children and I, and also facilitate a close and loving relationship with the children and me. Like I said, this judge gambled with the lives of two innocent children, and she crapped out. And the dire, unjust decision she made was the worst one made during the entire duration of the case, because her decision had the most detrimental effect on Zion and Zaire. Knowing they suffered at the magnitude they did was not easy to endure, but with God it was possible. The judge had done the greatest evil to Zion, Zaire, and myself ever done, but I witnessed God do even greater, good by providing us with healing, hope, restoration, and deliverance for our lives.

The Aftermath

Despite the judge having been warned of the serious and irreparable harm that would result if she took my children from me, and despite that warning coming from one of the top Medical Doctors and mental health professionals in the entire Midwestern region of the United States, the judge did it anyway. But this judge wasn't done yet. She went beyond just taking the children from me, disregarding the professional opinions of several witnesses and ruling against her own witness, who testified that I should have sole custody of both my children, and she did the unspeakable. This judge ordered that Zion and Zaire were not to be able to see me, hug me, give me a kiss on the cheek, or cry on my shoulder, for thirty days consecutively right after she made the custody decision! She is quoted as stating, "Once the thirty-day transition period has terminated, a regular parenting schedule can be implemented." The effect her manifest injustice had on Zion and Zaire was everything from unceasing crying for lengths of time, to bed-wetting and nightmares, and all the way to psychiatric drugs—and beyond. This judge didn't do what was in the best interest of Zion and Zaire, and the effects her decision caused clearly show that. What she did was seek a way to punish me, because she didn't like me; in fact, I believe she hated me. This was by far one of the hardest things I ever had to endure in my life—having Zion and Zaire cry out to me for help, and I felt there was nothing I could do to help them. I had to trust God with my children at that point, or I wasn't going to survive it in order to be there for them.

Sometime after this thirty-day-punishment period, I was scheduled to have the first court-ordered visitation with my children. My children and I had not seen one another in over a month (the longest time we had been a part in their entire lives). Instead of my being able to see them, however, I was forced to go into court because of a motion that was filed in court. The motion asked the court to prevent me from being able to see my children. The motion was filled with allegations, saying things like the children didn't want to see me, and they believed I thought they were demons. (These are actual allegations that were used by the way!) Remarkably, in just a few weeks after the judge's decision to give my former spouse sole custody of our children, they alleged that the children didn't want to see me! As you recall, this judge who gave him custody said that if she gave him custody, he would facilitate a close relationship with the children and me. Again, she rolled the dice, and she crapped out, and my two small children suffered greatly because of it. Unfortunately <u>for her</u>, this was just the beginning of my children and me being torn apart from each other. The determination to totally remove me from the lives of my two children was just really getting started at that point. Very quickly, the interference with my court-ordered visitation with my children, and continuous refusal to allow me see them at all, grew as time went on, and it got increasingly worse. Here's some of what I mean:

In April of 2011, even though the court ordered that my children be able to come home for a short weekend, I was told that if I wanted to see my children, I would have to drive several miles away from home, close to midnight, instead. The judge, however, did nothing to rectify this interference.

In May of 2011, the first Mother's Day after the madness, I had court-ordered visitation with my children for Mother's Day; however, my children were brought to me late and then taken away again in just a couple of hours—and on Mother's Day! Again, the court did nothing to correct this interference, either.

Countless times, I called my children, and I was not able to speak to them for days and weeks consecutively. The court, again, did nothing to intervene and correct this.

The rest of 2011 carried on this way, and 2012 was worse. In the beginning of the year, I finally got an opportunity to see my children, but the children were taken from me an entire day early, cutting my time with them short. The court remained silent and refused to correct this also.

May was Zion's birthday, and his dad threw him a birthday party that even the media managed to attend, but I was not invited at all. I was not even given the opportunity to say, Happy Birthday to Zion, in fact. The court did not intervene then, either.

In June, the judge's failure to see the future correctly continued to hurt my children and me, and the effects of her unjust decision became increasingly troublesome as time went on. In the early summer of 2012, I was supposed to be with my children for a court-ordered visitation in Illinois. Although the court order required the children be brought to me on a Friday, my children were not brought to me until the next day. Despite this deviation from the court's order, there were no consequences for the celebrity dad. A short time later, however, they accused me of being just a *few hours* late for the dad's time-sharing with the children, and they had me arrested for kidnapping! People, if kidnapping is the same as being a few hours late, then parents all over the world kidnap their own children several times a week!

In order to constitute Kidnapping in Illinois, the law requires that the abducted child be taken out of the jurisdiction. I was in my backyard with my children; playing and swimming when they said the children were kidnapped by me. I had not taken them out of the state, city, or county. I had not even taken them out of the yard! But some of the corrupted police of Illinois arrested me right out of my pool, in my own backyard, while I was still in my bathing suit. Corruption is not just a crime; it has a name and a face. My God, I saw it that day up close and personal, like never before. I saw unjust judges breaking the law, but it went to another level when I saw the police acting in corruption as well. By the way, police need warrants in order to come onto people's property for things like this most of the time. The police officer who arrested me said he had a warrant. When I asked him if I could please see it, he took a blank sheet of paper out of his pocket, opened it, shut it immediately, and shoved it back in his pocket. I said, "There is nothing on that paper. It's blank!" I was crying, "Why are you doing this?" The officer then placed me inside of a police car, and nobody could hear my cry from there. I looked outside of the police-car window, and I saw my ex-husband's bodyguard—who was the former Chief of Police for Oak Lawn, Illinois—with the police officer who arrested me and nearly broke my arm, and they were in the same unmarked car together. I literally had an asthma attack and fainted. I don't know how long I was out, but when I came to, I was being put into an ambulance. Again, corruption is a crime with a name and a face, and the same is true of domestic violence and abuse.

After I was falsely arrested and falsely imprisoned, I had to go back to the judge in family court. Now, although the judge in the criminal court seemed to be infuriated by my false arrest and imprisonment, the judge from family court, in Cook County, Illinois, had nothing to say to those who orchestrated my arrest. Instead, she told me that if I opened my mouth and told my children that their dad had me arrested, she would make sure that I never saw my children again! The pains of injustice. Time and time again, these judges wanted me to keep silent. It is true what was said: "Silence is an enemy of the truth."

Later on in the criminal case, the trial began regarding the kidnapping charges, and the others they tacked on as another means of malicious prosecution. When we got to trial, after the criminal judge (not the judges from family court) heard the first few witnesses testify against me, the judge went off on them. Almost every witness who testified against me in that criminal case was impeached (found to have lied on the witness stand). The judge found me not guilty of every charge against me and reprimanded those who testified against me. God was with me, delivering me from being put in prison for years for crimes I never committed.

Now, although I was not guilty of the crime they charged and tried me for, the devastating effects of being arrested and put in prison for a crime I didn't commit were still afflicting me—and my children. I had physical injuries; the officer who arrested me almost broke my right arm, and I had to go to the hospital, doctor, and physical therapy for several months before my arm functioned properly again. But the physical scars were healing. The emotional scars, however, had the more lasting and traumatic effects. The police arrested me without cause for a crime I never did, and they held me in a filthy prison against my will, refusing to allow me to make even a single phone call the entire time I was in jail. I wasn't permitted to speak to my lawyer or anyone else. The police are the ones who kidnapped me!

Just a few weeks later, I was supposed to have visitation with my children, but instead, I was not allowed to see them, speak to them, or even know where they were. I was calling and e-mailing, but to no avail. The court again refused to intervene and correct this grave pattern that had clearly been formed. This was a monster the court created, and while the court used its power to do evil, it refused to use that same power to correct.

In July and in August, I was supposed to have court-ordered visitation with my children, but instead my children were not given to me, and I was not allowed to know where they were for weeks. I also was not allowed to talk to my children over the telephone during this time. The court again did nothing to help correct this lawlessness.

In the same summer, I later found out that my children were in the same state as me, only ten miles away, approximately, but nobody told me. My son was crying because he thought I knew they were in Chicago close by me, but that I didn't want to see them. That was a devastating blow, to say the least!

Again in that same year, another motion was filed, asking that I not see my children. This time they told the court they wanted to take the children to the Olympic games and promised that, once the games were over, they would bring the children to me. The Olympic games ceased, and my children were nowhere to be found. I wasn't even told where they were, let alone allowed to see them as promised. The media, however, circulated photos of my children with their dad in another country during this time. Remember, when I was accused of being a few hours late, they had me arrested and charged with kidnapping, and the judge promised me that if I told my children their dad had me arrested, she would make sure I never saw them again. When my children were kept from me, however, for several days, and even taken out of the country, the judges all remained silent, and did absolutely nothing to correct it!

Then again, around Christmas time, I was supposed to be with my children for part of Christmas break, but the children were not brought to me until a day later, even though the children's school informed me they were absent from school that entire day. The court continued to keep silent and do nothing.

Then came time for Zaire's birthday, and I wasn't invited to his birthday party either. Another devastating blow, to say the least! And the only thing more devastating is the same court that crucified me for being late for taking my child to the emergency room—where the doctors ended up having to admit him because he was so sick—these same judges sat back, closed their mouths, and crossed their arms, refusing to execute justice when, time and time again, I was prevented from seeing my children, pursuant to their own court order. These judges had such disdain for me, and such reluctance to uphold the law when the deeds done were from the rich and famous, that they refused to enforce their own court orders. Everything done to me that kept me from seeing, or being able to even speak on the phone with, my children or to know where they were for days and weeks at a time, was not a violation of my order. I didn't have a court order; the court did. All of these things were a violation of the court's own court order, and when I asked them to uphold their own court order, the judges refused.

In March I was entitled to have visitation with my children; I was denied it. The court again did nothing to execute justice for myself or for Zion and Zaire.

Again in April, I was entitled to have visitation with my children for a certain period; I was denied that full time also. The court did nothing yet again.

In May, I was entitled to court-ordered visitation for Mother's Day, but like the previous year, all I got was interference instead. This time a motion was filed, alleging to the court that the children were "anxious" about spending time with me and did not want to visit with me. This time, however, they went on to ask the court for me not to see my children *period*! The court again did nothing to rectify this continual pattern of behavior that caused the same result: the children and I are kept from seeing one another.

By this time the court case had been transferred to Florida, and unfortunately, the same unjust spirit that reigned in Illinois Family Courts was present inside that court in Florida too, and the separation from my children continued and even worsened.

In May, I was not allowed to see my children pursuant to the court's order again! This court did nothing to enforce its own court order either.

In the early summer of that same year, I was denied the ability to even speak to my children on the telephone, and I was also not given the opportunity to see them.

In July of that same year, I was supposed to see my children, and again I was not allowed to. The court again remained silent.

The same took place in August. Then, in September, I traveled over a thousand miles to see my children, and I spent money I had to borrow to get to Florida to see them when I was supposed to. When I was in Florida, I wanted to go visit my children's school and be able to speak with their teachers face-to-face, like parents do. However, I was threatened and told that if I went to the children's school, there would be "legal consequences" to suffer.

At this point I realized I was not going to be a part of my children's lives no matter how hard I tried, how much money I spent, or how many miles I traveled. I realized only God could fix it.

In October, I wasn't allowed to see my children, from October 25th-27th as I was supposed to, and again I wasn't allowed to speak to them on the phone either.

Many other instances like those detailed above continued to happen whenever I was supposed to spend time with my children. I went days again where I could not get in contact with or speak to my children, more birthdays I wasn't invited to or allowed to even speak to my children over the phone just to say, "I love you and happy birthday," even up until this very week that I write this. If I were to state every time this occurred, it would surely be a book in and of itself. It suffices to say that the unjust decision that judge made, gambling with the lives of two children, was a gamble she most certainly lost.

Unfortunately, the few-and-far-between times when we did finally get a chance to actually be together, that proved difficult too. Every time Zion and Zaire would leave, it was like I would die all over again, and I watched them die with me. They sometimes stood at the threshold of the front door to the house, crying, with their arms wrapped around me, saying, "Mommy, I don't want to go." And each time they did, it was like losing them all over again. Every time I embraced them, I knew it meant there was a time when we would be separated from one another again, and because of this judge's erroneous decision, it could be several months before we saw one another again.

During this time, I remember praying a lot for women whose children had passed away in death. I recall wondering why God had me praying for women whose children had died. I was thinking, "Zion and Zaire are still alive, so why do I feel overwhelming compassion to this degree for women who lost their children that way?" I was literally thinking, "Shouldn't I be praying for other mothers and fathers who lost their children unjustly to corrupt custody decisions?" And then God gave me understanding. He explained to me that even mothers whose children are not alive on the earth certainly live. We pass from death to life (John 5:24). The problem, and the pain that these mothers have suffered, was not because of death; it was the pain of the separation that seemed unbearable for them. And both the mothers whose children were no longer living here on the earth, and thus they were separated from their children, and the mothers like myself, whose children were living on earth, but they were kept from their mother—we all felt the pain of being separated from our children. God told me Zion and Zaire didn't have to die for me to feel the pain of separation. God showed to me that my pain even extended beyond the level of expected grief and mourning, because of my purpose in my children's lives. This may bother a fairly decent mother whose children are taken from her, but for a Godly mother it comes to kill, because this type of mother understands her place and purpose in her children's lives. She knows that her purpose in her children's lives is so much greater and extends well beyond the day-to-day parenting. A Godly mother's role in her children's lives extends well into the destiny of her children—and even her children's children. A Godly mother, by the grace of God, plants generational seeds of greatness in her children that spring up and bear fruit that lasts for many generations. Separation is serious for a mother who understands her God-given purpose in the lives of her children, which caused this separation to be all the more painful for me. But thanks be to God because God has indeed turned the pain of it all into my purpose, as you will soon learn in the coming chapters.

So there I was in the aftermath, still standing, having survived the devastation of divorce, children unjustly taken away, reputation assassinated worldwide (media's latest kill), lied about, falsely arrested, falsely imprisoned, given a sexually transmitted disease, so-called friends all gone, broke financially, and soon to face foreclosure on my house! It was enough to make even the strongest of them, from Samson to Geronimo, give up and die. But because of, and *only* because of, the grace and power of God in my life, I not only survived it, but I thrived in it. God empowered me, and in the midst of the madness, God made me stronger, wiser, and more humble and loving than ever before. God said it, and it is true: "God's grace is sufficient, and His strength is made perfect in our weakness" (2 Cor. 12:9). This, my friends, is clearly the truth! God also said, "I chose the weak things of this world to confound the strong" (1 Cor. 1:27). Surely, according to my enemies, and even to myself then, I was the weak thing. But as certain as Jesus is Lord, by the grace and power of God, I confounded the strong!

This I also found to be true, and I know it for myself: if God is for you, nobody can be against you! Not even you! I am a living, breathing witness of this. I wanted to give up many times and throw in the towel, but God refused to let me cave in. This rough road I was on with my children led to somewhere great, and God was not about to let adversity or my hate for it take me off the path to destiny!

Now, some of you may have heard or read about me likely before ever opening this book, and watched my name be dragged through the depths of slanderous mud, but to be clear, God meant this too for good! God used the media and all those who lied about me to get your attention. God did not do this so that you could look at me, but beyond me. And then you would see the Christ that clearly has saved me, kept me through that hell on earth, and completely healed my heart and restored my life! And God is not finished yet!

What can I tell you to sum up all that hell meant against me? Namely this: the devil is an idiot. He was an idiot concerning Jesus's life too, and he was a mere pawn in the game of life then as well. God told me that looking at life is like looking at checkers game. Somebody has to be the black piece on the board and someone else the red. In the "game" of life, somebody has to be a vessel of honor and somebody else a vessel of dishonor (Rom. 9:21). God showed me that the Messiah had to be Jesus, and the fool who betrayed him had to be Judas! The devil surely thought that killing Jesus would stop Jesus from saving us, healing all manner of diseases, teaching us the truth, preaching the good news of the Gospel of grace to us, delivering us from evil, giving us hope, and so much more, but it was the very death of Jesus that was needed to ensure that Jesus provided these blessings to us, and so much more! *Hallelujah!* Likewise, because the devil is still an idiot, he was sure that if he caused that divorce and corrupt custody decision, he would make me kill myself and die.

Well, I did die. I died to all the old ungodly beliefs of worthlessness and despair I had, as well as to some behaviors and habits that needed to go. I died so that Jesus Christ could live in me, and through me, and thus I can be an effective blessing in the hand of God for my own life, family, and you as well (Gal. 2:20). And amazingly, after that death, now I am living for the first time in my life! I am living on purpose, with a purpose, and this, my love, is the perfect will of God for us all! So, I want to take this time to *thank God, Jesus, and the Holy Spirit,* and all my true friends and family members who helped me along the way. I also want to thank all those who came against me! It's not a typo. I thank every unjust judge, every lawyer who stole from me, all the lovers of money involved—and a special thanks to the media. You have all been instrumental in the Glory of God in my life, but only because of God using even your behavior for my good, and the good of the people of God! For God is the One who caused all these things you meant for evil to be for His glory and my good!

God has indeed proven Himself faithful again. God allowed all the pain injustice caused my children and me, and He used it to ignite a passion in me for justice more than I ever dreamed of. It was the custody trial by fire and its aftermath that God used to blaze a trail for my path into my destiny. God was doing again what He has always been faithful to do; God took what was meant for harm and worked it together for my good (Gen. 50:20). And if God did it for me, God will do it for you. Always, know and believe, that God is not a respecter of persons (Acts 10:34).

"All things work together for the good of them that love God and are the called according to His purpose" (Rom. 8:28).

FROM PAIN, TO PASSION,
TO PURPOSE!

To everything there is a season,
and a time for every purpose under heaven

—Ecclesiastes 3:1

Labor Pains Producing Passion

Well before the divorce, the custody trial, its aftermath, and all the lies told by the media, God had begun revealing to me my purpose in life. God showed me that what I had been going through was akin to being in labor. Being in labor is something I can relate to, so I was excited about this understanding God was giving me. God reminded me how, in the Bible, Jesus said, "A woman when she is in labor has birth pangs, but as soon as that child is born she forgets the pain, for the joy that a child has been born" (John 16:21). God then began showing me that all the pains I had endured from all that I had suffered were labor pains. And rather than allowing the pain to break me, God used it to help make me better in every way. God then showed me that it was the pain He allowed me to feel that produced in me a passion for God, for people, and for purpose. But for the pains of injustice, I would not have been ready to lay down my life for justice. God told me that He could have let me go straight to purpose, bypassing pain, but if He would have, I would not have the passion. Many people have a purpose, but they lack passion, and thus are not nearly as effective as God intends for them to be.

Jesus knew that He was born to be crucified for our sins. That's His purpose—and much more. When Jesus was in the Garden of Gethsemane and was in such distress that His tears became drops of blood, He needed more than knowledge of His purpose to not run away, and instead to stay and allow Himself to be betrayed, falsely accused, arrested, publicly humiliated, beaten beyond recognition, and then crucified. To walk toward that, when you possess the power to walk away from it all, takes passion. Jesus had passion for our Father in Heaven. He had passion for people, and Jesus had passion for purpose. And like God did with Jesus and all that He suffered, God took *everything* that was meant for my harm, and God used it for good (Gen. 50:20).

During those trying times, God showed me that He was also using the different things I was going through—especially my journey through the court system—to train and equip me, as well as to place inside me compassion, love, and a willing heart to seek after God with everything in me and to truly advocate for people, giving them what legal professionals refused to give me. I'm not upset with them, either. Those lawyers were trying to fulfill a high calling, a purpose, devoid of the passion it takes to actually make a righteous difference. God told me clearly that for me, law is not a career; it is a calling. Now, I understand and realize that even the pain had a purpose in my life and produced in me a passion necessary to be an effective instrument in the hands of Almighty God, in order to fulfill my destiny. So all that I had suffered and seemed to have lost, and the pain I felt through natural circumstances, was the birth pangs from my giving birth to my destiny.

Before I gave birth, however, I had to endure labor. I never thought I would say this, because what I suffered in this labor was extremely painful, but I am glad I went through it for the benefit of my family, those reading this and myself. God gave me insight and understanding about being in spiritual labor, and I believe it will bless many people. God does not want for His people to be in labor spiritually and not even realize it, thus miscarrying their purpose and aborting their destiny without ever knowing they did. God doesn't want that to happen anymore. And God said, "My people are destroyed for lack of knowledge" (Hosea 4:6). Thus, God wants to share with you what He taught me about giving birth spiritually. In fact, God always intended this lesson to be for many, and not just for myself.

Labor Can Be Lonely

When God was teaching me, He used the natural labor environment to show me what happens in spiritual labor. God explained to me that when a woman is in labor naturally for her safety, as well as the safety of the child, not many people are permitted in the labor-and-delivery room. The doctor who helps the woman deliver the child is wise for permitting a labor-and-birthing environment like this. It is wise. God, likewise, for our sakes as well as the sake of the purpose God put inside of us to give birth to, only permits a very small number of people to be around during these times. It is important to know that God is not punishing the woman in labor; He is protecting her and her destiny that she is pregnant with. It's important to remember during spiritual labor and to be conscious of the fact that God is always with us, and we are never alone. Loneliness doesn't become a real problem until it convinces someone they are alone. Then the person feels unprotected by God, and fear will try to come in. We need to pray before this happens, and read and meditate on the word of God and be conscious of the fact that God is with us.

God also showed me that He will call us to be alone with Him during times of birthing because, once you give birth to your destiny, it is like flying. When you walk into and are fulfilling your destiny, you are soaring with God spiritually. Flying spiritually is like flying naturally. Some of the best planes are those private planes. Private planes are just that: private. Not everyone gets on the private plane, because not everyone fits on the private plane. And although these luxury planes are among the best of planes, they cannot have a lot of baggage or people on them, or they will crash. Our destiny planes are the same. They are God's best on this side of Heaven, but they are not built to hold too many people or too much baggage—spiritual baggage, that is, like jealousy, lack of forgiveness, and the like. These things—and some people, even relatives—God will have to remove, because they cannot go with you where God is taking you. Do not fear this or people's reaction to it; it is for your good. God knows better than you do who would, or what would, take your plane right out of the sky, and thus, for your sake as well as theirs, God is saying that: During these times, be with Me (God), and maybe a very select few. God means this for good too.

Hurting People Sometimes Hurt People

If you have ever been in labor or witnessed a woman in labor, you know that sometimes she gets angry. Labor hurts, and God told me that sometimes hurting people hurt people. Naturally speaking, when a woman is in labor, she may very become angry with, often yell at, and even physically grab tight the hands of those around her, because the pain is excruciating. Now the person who gave her their hand to hold did so to help her, but because of her pain, she is bearing down on them and hurting them. Have mercy on those in labor, because this bearing down, and the pain it may cause, is not intentional. I am speaking from experience.

It can also be frustrating for a woman in labor to be in what seems like unbearable pain, to the point of literal bloodshed, while everyone else in the room is calm, smiling, and pain-free. That alone can hurt. Their relaxed, pain-free state can appear to a hurting, laboring woman as "they don't care what I am going through, or they don't understand what I am suffering." Either way, this misconception can lead to mishap. This woman in labor can begin to become frustrated with the very ones who are there to help her give birth. I have experienced this myself while in labor, both naturally and spiritually.

I remember sometimes it hurt so bad in spiritual labor that I didn't want anyone to help me. I just wanted them all to get away from me and let me give up and die. God, of course, refused to allow this to happen, but I was still frustrated at times. Those couple of people that God allowed near me—their persistence—became an annoyance. I didn't want to hear any encouraging words, because to be encouraged meant to get back up and go another round. And to go another round meant to feel another blow of pain from what was transpiring during those difficult times. It was akin to having contractions. Contractions cause pain in labor. They don't happen all the time during labor, but when they come, sometimes it hurts so much that it seems better to stop the labor altogether. And contractions—the natural pain in labor—like the spiritual pain in labor, has a purpose. It is the contractions that make room for a woman to give birth to her child. It's the contractions of spiritual labor that produce passion and character and make room for our destinies. Thus, there is a beneficial reason for labor pains. At the time I was in labor, however, I just wanted the pain to stop. Therefore, I didn't want to hear "you can make it *through* it." I just wanted to be delivered *from* it.

I remember that, at one point, I didn't even want to hear from God. I literally told God, "Don't talk to me anymore." That was the devil himself, that pushed me to that point. The devil knows the Word of God is extremely powerful, and it is life! And because that defeated foe could not kill me himself, he was working overtime to get *me* to do the job for him. I'm glad God did not take heed to what I was saying and instead had already forgiven me when Jesus died on that cross for my harsh and rash words. God also healed me from that deep pain, and I learned that God's love truly endures all things. God let me know He had already forgiven me, and as far as what I said, "It was just the labor pains talking!" To this day that makes me smile. God truly is love. It was after this that God told me hurting people hurt people. And I thank God for His love for me, because God saw past my faults and had compassion.

Be Encouraged

Some labors are more painful than others. Naturally speaking, for example, when I had my first son, I gained a lot of weight, my labor pains were fierce, and the labor was long. I thank God past experiences don't define or shape my future, and instead God does. When I had my second son, by the grace of God, I did not gain any excess weight, and my labor was much easier. I was even laughing at times while in labor. In fact, the labor and delivery were so easy that the nurse was telling me to hold the baby in and not to push! She wanted to call for the doctor in order for him to hurry and get inside the room, because Zion was just sliding out. I wasn't pushing, but he was still coming, without effort, sweat, pain, or tears like in the past. God used this to teach me a powerful truth that has brought me a lot of peace and hope: the same affliction will not arise twice in our lives (Nahum 1:9). Thus, we don't have to fear giving birth to our destiny because of any past experiences. Be encouraged because yesterday does not define or shape your today; God does. Only give God that power. Don't give it to your-selves, to past circumstances, and certainly not to another!

Time's Not Wasted

Naturally speaking, before giving birth, a woman is pregnant for a period of time and goes into labor. Spiritually speaking, before a man or a woman gives birth—men give birth spiritually too— there is normally a preparation period in which you are equipped by God, trained, taught, and given wisdom, revelation, and in-sight about what you are called to do. And often, God will give you rest. (There must be some break in between contractions, or labor might actually become unbearable, rather than just feeling that way.)

In other words, God is teaching us that there is a preparation period before giving birth to destiny. During the preparation pe-riod, it is important to remember that preparation is as important and necessary as what you are preparing for, if not more important. I often felt idle, like time was being wasted during these moments (for a lot of them, I was still and not being busy). These times are not wasted or idle; they are vital. God showed me that it is like the time a baby spends inside of the womb of her mother. That time is critical for the development of the child. It is dangerous, or some-times deadly, for the child to be born prematurely. It can harm not only the child but the mother as well. So I encourage any of you in labor not to fret about the time it takes to get you prepared.

Your preparation is also an indication of your destination. God told me that a woman who has twins or triplets is in labor longer and may experience much more pain than those who give birth to one child. Likewise, spiritually speaking, there are people whose labor has been more difficult and lasted much longer than others in labor, and sometimes it is because they are giving birth to some-thing even greater. They are literally giving birth to double and triple and multiple things!

Always remember that your time is not wasted, and God is able to redeem the time. God said, "I will restore to you the years the locust has eaten" (Joel 2:25). God already has provision for you if you believe your time was eaten up. Fear not, and be encouraged, because God is willing and able to pay you back in time that seemed to be lost, proving to you that with God, your time is never lost!

Giving Birth to Destiny

Well, you've now been able to hear me share about my labor pains in the previous chapters, and you understand how God developed passion from the pain of labor, but I also want to share with you the purpose as well as some of the many joys God has brought about in blessing me to give birth to my destiny.

It was during the early parts of the divorce case that God led me to finish college, because I had put my life on hold to be a wife and stay-at-home mother back then. Shortly thereafter, God blessed me to earn my Bachelor's degree in Psychology. I was glad about that, and I felt quite content with the accomplishment, but God wanted to bless me all the more for my destiny. God then had me apply to graduate school, where He blessed me to receive my graduate certification in Professional Counseling.

Not too long after that, God led me right into my purpose all the more while I was driving downtown in Chicago and at that time, thought I was lost. I soon discovered I wasn't lost at all. I ended up pulling over in front of a building near State Street so that I could use my phone to get directions for where I was headed. I looked up from my phone, and to my right was the John Marshall Law School. As soon as I saw the law school, I immediately felt overwhelming joy, and I knew that it was God telling me to go to law school. I forgot all about getting those directions. I put my double blinkers on, left the car, and went inside the law school. I went to the registrar's office and asked one of the staff members to tell me how to apply for law school. God had spoken to me, even when I was a little girl, about being a lawyer, but it had gotten buried underneath everything I had been through. But that day, in that moment, God seemed to knock any remaining dirt off my destiny, and He pulled my purpose out! I took home an admissions packet that day and began the process of applying to law school. God blessed me to be accepted, and He has continued to bless me from that day forward and has proven to me that He leads and guides me.

During my first year of law school, God blessed me to make the academic dean's list, and I was in the top 25 percent of my class. As much of an honor as this was, God wasn't done yet. After only taking a few courses at the law school—I was a part-time student—God told me to sign up for the Moot Court Competition, in which I would be competing against numerous law students who had taken twice as many law courses as I had. I was nervous at first, and I entered into the competition just thinking I could gain some experience from it, but I had no expectation of winning the competition. For those who don't know, moot-court competitions are huge for law students. They are important both for excelling in law school as well as for practicing law, because often the winners are looked upon very favorably by lawyers and judges. Generally, in most moot-court competitions, as it was with the one in which I participated, law students take on the role of a lawyer, are given an actual case, conduct real legal research, and then present their case to actual judges and lawyers, against opposing counsel, to win.

Regarding the moot-court competition I was in, we first were presented with a legal issue, which came from an actual case. Then we had to conduct real legal research. Next, we prepared both legal and public-policy arguments for our client's case, in order to present them inside of a federal courtroom downtown in Chicago, where we argued our client's position against opposing counsel. Afterward, all of us students were judged, and only one team would be chosen as the winner to advance to the next round.

When it reached the final round, one law-student team was chosen as the winner of the entire competition. My team consisted of Jesus, of course, one other law student, and me. God gave me wisdom while preparing for the competition. God told me that although we could bring in, and rely on, notes while in court presenting our cases to the judges, He wanted me to memorize my client's facts, the law, as well as the public policy in support of her position, and the legal arguments God helped me develop for her. All of this wisdom God gave me proved to be wisdom indeed.

My teammate and I were blessed to advance all the way to the final round and win the entire competition. That was a miracle I had not expected from God, but He did it anyway! Oftentimes, because of God's goodness, He will bless us with miracles that we didn't even pray for or expect. For me, this was one of those times. More to my surprise was the fact that God wasn't done yet. At the end of the competition, I was the last acting attorney to speak for our client, and God blessed me to advocate for this woman the way I had prayed to God that a lawyer would have advocated for my children and me. The client I was representing had been discriminated against, and God had given me such passion to fight for her. I mean, I literally gave it everything I had, and when I did, I realized that's all I know how to do. This passion God gave me is not something I *do*; it is a part of me. God gave me the exact words He wanted me to finish my fight for justice with: "An injustice anywhere is a threat to justice everywhere." The judges were literally in tears at the end of the argument.

When God gives you passion, it even ignites a passion in others. There was an actual judge sitting on the bench, judging the competition that day, who offered me a job right then and there. God also blessed me to win the award for Best Oralist in the entire Moot-Court Competition. And for it all, to You God, be all the Glory! After finishing my the argument that God gave me, one of the judges cried and told me, "Many students do well in school, and they learn from a classroom, but what you have is from above!" This judge knew God was with me, and it was God who was giving me the ability to advocate passionately for people. Out of all the honors and awards God bestowed upon me that day, hearing that truth from her was by far the greatest honor of them all.

God continued to show me favor and bless me in education, as He moved me forward in my purpose. He blessed me to be at the top of my class again, and to be awarded multiple academic law school scholarships. God also blessed me to receive the CALI Excellence for the Future Award, for receiving the highest grades in my entire class. God has proven to me that He indeed made me a woman of worth (hence, the Foundation God birthed through me: A Woman's Worth Foundation, Inc.). God said that although many daughters have done well, a woman of worth excels them all. (Proverbs Prov. 31). To God be the glory, because that is exactly what God was doing. God was blessing others, but He was surpassing them all through me for this divine purpose He has given me.

When God bestowed these prestigious academic honors upon me, I was considered "the least of them" among my classmates. Again, I was just in my second year of law school, and the other students were in their final semester, ready to graduate in a couple of weeks. These were the most difficult classes in law school, which is why graduating students in their final semester of law school were in them. Although I was only in my second year, God allowed me to be enrolled with the graduating students, and God caused me to surpass them all for His glory. I learned that with the purpose of God for your life, there will always be the provision and blessings of God, to see that God's purpose and destiny for your life is fulfilled for the glory of God!

And although God had blessed me beyond measure, He still wanted to bless me more. God also blessed me to be extended an invitation to be on the Law Review Journal, the most prestigious academic endeavors a law student can be accepted into. Not only was I accepted, they invited me. God is really "good people," and when God blesses you, it is always far beyond what you ever thought, imagined, or prayed for. God is a big God, and whatever He does, He does it big! In fact, God has blessed me to the point where I can practice law in the state of Georgia right now, while I am still a law student. That's right, you read it correctly. I have been admitted and given certification by the Georgia Supreme Court to practice law in the state of Georgia, while still going to law school and without having taken the bar exam yet. With God, when He causes it to rain, it pours! God had not forgotten that He created me on purpose—for a purpose—even when I had. God is faithful.

God also blessed me to give birth to a new vision for His ministry: A Woman's Worth Foundation, Inc. God changed the vision for A Woman's Worth Foundation, and has given me the ability, coupled with His passion, to help women who are hurting and broken like I was—especially the burdened housewife. God has blessed me and led me to devote time and resources to helping women survivors of domestic violence and their children, and He has shown me clearly that He will help them through me with their legal issues, especially child custody and divorce. With this purpose, God has given the provision.

In addition to law school and the ability to practice law now in Georgia, God blessed me to obtain a certificate in order to provide Professional Domestic Violence Counseling, as well as to obtain a degree in theology. God allowed me to open several shelters for survivors of domestic violence as well. God has also used me to counsel numerous women who have been victims of domestic violence, and I have been able to witness God taking some of these women from homeless to homeowner. I told you, God is not a respecter of persons! God promised me, "A ministry of restoration will rest upon you." God made me an instrument of healing, restoration, and hope in His very own hand. Oh, God is so good!

I also am watching God restore me in the area of finances as well. Many years prior to the pain I suffered within the realm of the court system, God had promised me that I would own my own real-estate business. Time went by, and I hadn't given it much thought, but God always remembers to do what He promises He will do. God has blessed me to open my own real-estate-investment company. God has taken me from homeless to homeowner of multiple properties and land. God told me I will use you and this business to restore lives, by restoring living to certain people! Indeed, God has done this numerous times. Many women's lives have been completely restored for the glory of God. God has blessed me to deal in land and homes—from leasing to vacation rentals and more. My God is faithful to do what He promises!

The power of God is at work in my life, restoring me completely, from the inside out. God is doing everything He promised me He would, and He isn't finished blessing and restoring yet! He, who began a good work in me, is faithful to finish (Phil. 1:6). I believe, and I declare, that the best is yet to come. I wasn't always this filled with faith, though. There were indeed times when I didn't think God would do what He promised. Nearly everyone else who had promised me anything had lied. But as it is written in the Word of God, let every man be a liar, but not God! (Rom. 3:4). God had me to write down every prayer I remembered I made to Him, and He told me to put a checkmark beside every prayer He had answered already. One day, I picked up that list, and I saw substantially more checkmarks than I saw prayers I am waiting on answers to. I knew it was time to stop doubting God. God is the One who had to come and deliver me from fear, doubt, and unbelief. So be encouraged if you are struggling to believe God for something. God's strength is made perfect in our weaknesses (2 Cor. 12:9). My love, the Word of God is true, and God has shown me this, time after time, by allowing me to witness the veracity of His Word in my own life.

So stay encouraged, even if you have been waiting years for God to answer your prayers. There was a time in my past that I thought God had forgotten about me, because many years passed by, and it seemed to only be getting worse. No matter how much time passes, know this: God is faithful to do what He promised. There is so much more to this specific revelation and teaching that God told me to write an entirely different book about it, and that too is worth the wait.

My life is living, proof of the power of God to heal and restore, no matter how evil or dark it becomes in life. Every one of you reading this knows that I should have been dead. It is the power of God that has kept me alive and sustained me, and now it is the love and power of God that is restoring my life completely. Yes, my God is faithful! You can trust Him, and if He promised you *anything*, He is absolutely faithful to do everything He promised you. God cannot lie (Titus 1:2). Notice that the word of God doesn't say, "He chooses not to lie." It says, "God cannot lie." You can trust this level of holiness, people. I did, and God is blessing me, raining down His faithfulness, promises, hope, joy, peace, provision, restoration, and a clear vision of my purpose in life—and even in my children's lives. God is good! I am glad I gave my life to Jesus Christ. Jesus has never failed me, disappointed me, or lied to me. He has been faithful to provide for me, protect me, and continuously give me the hope and faith I need. My God is good. And He is not just good only because of who He is or what He did for me; my God is also good because He is not a respecter of persons (Acts 10:34). If God did it for me, He is able and willing to do it for you too!

The Best Is Yet to Come
God has promised me many things, and I believe He will do them all. After I witnessed God taking the depths of that pain and turning it into passion to bring forth my purpose, I cannot help but believe God, and that, with Him all things are possible. After all

I have endured, I don't just pray to God for a miracle anymore. I realize, I *am* the miracle, and that is how I know God is able no matter what. God has done many great things for me, but the best is yet to come. And you know what Jesus always says, when someone has faith in God: "Be it unto you according to your faith" (Matt. 8:13; & Matt. 9:29). Therefore, declare this truth with me, in faith in Jesus over your own life and the life of your family, because God is not a respecter of persons. Let us say with great boldness and confidence, "The best is yet to come!" Amen!

"Your latter shall be greater than your former" (Job 42:12).

CHAPTER 42: A MINISTRY
OF RESTORATION

The Lord restored Job's losses when he prayed for
his friends. Indeed the Lord gave Job twice as
much as he had before.

—Job 42:10

This chapter has intentionally been titled "Chapter 42," because of the restoration God has surely begun in my life. In the Bible, the number forty-two represents rest after trials. For example, the children of Israel went to forty-two stations before they entered the promise land where they had rest. In the book of Revelation, there is the mention of the three and one-half years (forty-two months) before Jesus's rest comes. And, it's the forty-second chapter of the book of Job where God restores all of Job's losses after an extremely dire trial. I'm in the forty-second chapter of my life, so to speak, because God has begun restoring me after my trials. The Bible speaks of giving by grace what you have received by grace. I have received restoration from God and thus can give it. My hope is that after you have read this book, as well as this chapter, God's restoration for you will have begun or will even be completed. And although God has used my life and my testimony as an instrument of restoration, God is the Restorer. And when you look at my life, and all that you now know about me, I have no doubt that restoration will take place in your life, because my life is about so much more than me. I realized this is true for my life as well as for others God has chosen—and it is this truth that God used to lead me to write this final chapter of this book this way.

This chapter has been written especially for those who have similar needs that I once had and have encountered similar challenges in order to help them receive the restoration, hope, and wisdom I did, by sharing with them some of the things God ministered to me on my journey.

It's All About God, and That's All Good!

After the custody trial, I read again about the life of Job in the bible, and I realized that God wants to teach us about Himself, not about the people we read about in the Bible. These people have been used by God in order for us to learn about God, not them. In other words, God is the moral of the story, not any one of them. The same is true today. The same applies to me. My life story really isn't about me. It's about God. And telling my story has the purpose of allowing people to get to know who God is. When God blessed me with that truth, it transformed me, because I knew that if it is about God and not me, there is no limit to how God will bless those He chose to read this book! I had even more hope than ever before for the readers of this book, and for my own life.

I say that because if the book of Job was just about Job, all we would be reading is this awesome testimony of how this specific man's life was restored by God. However, because of what

God said (reading about our lives isn't about us, it is about God), that means the book of Job isn't about Job getting restored; it is about God, the Restorer. God showed me this means that what God did in the forty-second chapter of Job, God can and is willing to do for God's glory in our lives as well! I am a witness of the love of God and the fact that God is no respecter of persons, which is why the same God who restored Job is restoring me right now, even as I write. And the good news for you is that God will do it for you too.

Special Dedication to the WOW Women

God led me to dedicate this chapter especially to all the WOW women—that is, those who are women of worth, women of wisdom, and women of wealth.

God spoke to me very clearly one day while I was still going through the fire, and He told me, "Many woman will be healed and restored by your testimony." All I could do was weep. I did not weep because I was feeling sorry for myself, and I did not have any regrets about what God was saying. I wept instead because all I could think in my mind and say in my heart was, "God, they are worth it." God had shown me His heart for you all, and God gave me His heart for you as well. I wept for quite some time in the presence of God that day, and I just kept saying to Him, "God, they are worth it." And indeed, all you WOW women who have read my life story and been blessed by it, you are worth it. All you women who have read these pages and said in your hearts, "God, thank you, I needed that," you are indeed worth it. Every woman who learned what to do from God through me, you are worth it, and all the women who learned from God through my story what not to do; you all are worth it too. To every woman, and even every man, whose lives have been transformed and made better by my life story, you are worth it. To all the woman who have been healed, restored, and given the hope, wisdom, and faith they needed as they journeyed with me through my life on these pages, you are worth it.

WOW women, you must always remember, and never allow anyone or anything to make you forget, that your worth is determined by God alone. You don't determine it, your spouse doesn't determine it, and neither do your family, finances, and material things determine your worth. To the famous WOW women, the public does not determine your worth, and neither does the media.

Nobody determines your worth but God alone, because it is God alone who created you! When Dodge manufactures a car, nobody else tells them what it is worth. The manufacturer, the creator, makes that determination alone! God created you, and God, the manufacturer of your very wonderful being and destiny, is the only One who determines your worth. Never look to any man, woman, child, or to the opinions of friends or foes, or your physical appearance, careers, degrees, money, or any other created thing, to ever determine your worth again! Be free from all wrongful determinations of your worth, now, in Jesus name.

You are and always will be exactly who God says you are! "You are nothing less than My best," says God. You are the masterwork of God's hands, you are fearfully and wonderfully made in God's own image and likeness, you are the righteousness of God in Christ Jesus, you are God's beloved, you are a Royal priesthood, you are the head and not the tail, you are above only and not beneath, you are a joint heir with Christ Jesus, you are victorious, you are an overcomer, you are the apple of God's eye, you are the bride of Jesus Christ, you are a daughter of God, and much more greatness lies in your identity. And because of it, you are blessed and not cursed, and you can do all things through Christ who strengthens you (Phil. 4:13). If anyone is thinking, "Well, they just don't think that's who they are," have no worries; it's still true even if you don't have the faith yet to believe it. Jesus is Lord, whether people believe it or not, and this is true because the Lord is who God predestined

Jesus to be. The same virtues hold true for you as well, whether believed or not, because, like Jesus, you are predestined by God. But I pray that faith will bear fruit in you, and God will cause you to believe in Him and in who He created you to be. Our spiritual growth comes in phases like our natural and physical growth does. We grow and understand at different paces, but we are all growing in understanding. And likewise, we don't always believe the truth or understand it at certain phases of our lives, but nevertheless, the truth remains true. For example, when you were a baby, your mother and father knew you were a girl. Although you lacked the understanding at that phase in your life to know and understand that truth, it didn't stop it from being the truth about you. Likewise, when you are a newborn in Christ Jesus, you don't understand a lot of things yet. But even if understanding is lacking, the truth isn't; it remains. And I believe Jesus will give to each of us the growth we need to take us where He wants us to be in Him. Jesus is the author and the finisher of your faith, and God who began a good work in you, is faithful to finish it (Heb. 12:2; Phil. 1:6). God is maturing us all, taking us from babes in Christ to full-grown in order for us to give birth to our destinies (Heb. 5:13–14).

So know the truth is this: you are exactly who God says you are, and nothing can change that! You are indeed fearfully and wonderfully made, both today and forevermore. I feel from God that you can read this over and over again every day, and the same will be true for each new day. This word is neither past nor future tense. I hear God saying, "It is present and eternal," because He is His word, and His word is ever present and everlasting (Isa. 40:8). God determines your worth, and God has determined that you are worth dying for!

Don't Be Afraid to Fly!

WOW women, God has given you wings to fly and a destiny to fulfill. Allow God to show you, and accomplish through you, the purpose for which you were created. Now is your set time for favor if you are reading this, in Jesus name. Surely God has led you to do so, and His leading is intentional. God wants you to be free from fear and to no longer allow it or anything else to hold you back from being the woman God created you to be. You are filled with incredible gifts and innumerable talents—and for a reason. God has already equipped you and called you according to His purpose if you are reading this. The Bible says, when you hear God's voice, harden not your hearts (Rom. 8:28), and God told me to tell you, on May 6, 2016, while writing this, "Don't be afraid to fly!" That word came from God especially for WOW Women! God has not given you a spirit of fear, but God has given you power, love, and a sound mind (2 Tim. 1:7).

So don't be afraid to fly, and don't make excuses for not fulfilling your destiny. I did this for too long, and I risked not being able to write this book by God's Spirit and to bless your life the way God called me to. I was acting as if I were too busy to do what God called me to do, but the truth is that I was busy doing nothing. I am mature enough to admit the truth. I don't want you to fall into the trap I was in for years. And if you do get caught in it, I don't want you to be discouraged. Instead, let God deliver you out of it, so you can fly!

Fear used to have me believing that the reason I wasn't doing anything with my dreams, talents, and desires was because I was busy taking care of my family. I would tell myself, "My family needs me," and, "I need to be a good wife, and support my [then] husband." That was all fear talking and trying to reason me out of fulfilling the very purpose for which I was created. What I was doing for years looked like love and devotion, but deep down, it was fear. Fear was holding me back from accomplishing my dreams and fulfilling my destiny. You see, even though I was married, God created me as an individual woman, and God gave me my own individual gifts, talents, dreams, and desires to accomplish. God created me for His purpose—not mine, not a spouse or children or anyone else's, but His! Indeed, God blessed me with the gift of family, including my children, but He never intended that I would relinquish the purpose of God for my life because of the gifts of God in it.

So WOW Women, don't hide behind your spouse or your children, saying, "I need to help them," and, "I must be there for them," as an excuse for not fulfilling your own destiny. Fly! You can fly while having a husband and children, and God will keep them. They belong to God anyway. Don't make excuses not to fly anymore. Fly! "Now, is your time to fly," says God. So fear not, because God doesn't give you something to the detriment of something else, but God will do things in order. If you read Genesis you will see that when God was creating the world, one of the first things He did was bring order (Gen. 1). God's purpose for your life is of top priority to God. And when you seek first God, His Kingdom, and His righteousness, all the things you have need of, and your family has need of, are added to you. This is the order of God.

WOW women, God has a great purpose for your life. I pray you fulfill it, and I believe that with God, you will indeed fulfill it. You are well able. Whoever God calls, He equips. And every WOW woman reading this, is called by God. I'm excited to see you fulfill your destiny. So, WOW women, rise and shine, let God shake the past off you, and fly! Fly, WOW Women, fly!

God told me, right after I finished writing by God's Spirit, the preceding paragraphs regarding flying, that one of the purposes of every believer is to, "set the captives free" (Isa. 61:1). God then showed me that the words He has spoken to you through me on these pages have a purpose from God: to unlock the prison doors of fear you have been bound in, allowing you go free out of that prison. God told me, not just walking out slowly, or trembling in fear, but God has called you to come out of the prison of fear, and Fly! I am excited, because whatever God does, it is so great!

WOW women, you have a very great calling, and the purpose of God for your life is great! Always remember, "Many daughters have done well, but you surpass them all" (Prov. 31:29). So fly, WOW women, Fly!

God's Not Guilty

I want to encourage people who are facing dire difficulties. During the most awful times in my life, I found myself angry with God because of what was happening. God didn't allow me to feel condemned about the anger I felt, but He did allow me to realize that it was counterproductive. It was also a way for the devil himself to try to keep me from seeking God at the very moments I needed Him the most. I understand what it is like to go through extremely difficult trials, and I have learned, after being delivered from them, *don't be mad at God.* And if you are someone who is angry with God, don't stay angry, because God is not guilty of the persecution you face.

When people go through difficult things in life, they often ask God, "Why did this happen?" One day in May, I was spending time in God's presence, and God gave me a revelation about evil things happening to righteous people. God showed me that it is like in war. In times of war, there are solders, those who choose to be a part of the battle, and there are civilians, those who are innocent. They coexist in the world, regardless of their roles or intentions, and the mere existence of a war affects them both, regardless of their position on or off the battlefield. (Please note that God is not calling soldiers evil. This is being used for illustrative purposes only.) Sometimes acts of war have harmed and even killed civilians who are not a part of that war. Likewise, God showed me that in the world there is sin, with sinners existing in it simultaneously with the righteous. They coexist, regardless of their roles or intentions also. God explained to me that, although the righteous may not be committing acts of war (willfully sinning), they may still be affected by it because they coexist in the same world with the soldiers and the war.

This coexistence is the reason many times that bad things happen to righteous and even innocent people. This is not God's act of war against His own beloved. God has sent Jesus to die for you to be saved. God would not take such drastic measures as the sacrifice of the life of His Son to save you, just to turn around and destroy you. So you don't need to blame God for another act of war or allow the enemy to deceive you into faulting God for the faults of others. Likewise, don't blame yourself either for the behavior of others, because there is nothing you did to cause it and nothing you could have done to stop it.

Jesus said, "Then you will know the truth, and the truth shall make you free" (John 8:32). Jesus is the truth, and when you know Jesus and the unconditional and unfailing love He has for you, it makes you free—free from blaming God, and free from blaming yourself. And it even makes you free from blaming the one who actually caused the harm. You are free to truly move on with joy and peace in your life, thanking God because even when people or the devil means something for our harm, God means it for our good!

Introduction: The Importance of Thoughts

When I was faced with divorce and then my children were taken from me, I learned just how vital our own thoughts are. I believe God wants me to share with you what He blessed me to learn about the importance of thoughts, especially during difficult times.

God showed me how many people have been misled to believe that how they feel is beyond their control, but this is not so. You can control your emotions and how you feel by thinking the right thoughts. And God wants us to learn how to effectively do this, because what we think about and meditate on directly affects our emotions and triggers our words, and that produces our actions. In other words, every thought has the potential to give birth to words and emotional feelings and eventually produce behaviors. Thoughts are fruit bearing seeds planted by someone. This means thoughts will produce something, whether it is fruit of faith and joy because they are thoughts of what God says, or depressing and negative fruit because they are thoughts about something the devil or an unruly coworker, critical family member, or even your own self says. Thus, the thoughts we think and meditate on are important.

When God was explaining the importance of thoughts and their power to produce words and actions, He explained to me that thoughts are like parents. Parents, like thoughts, produce offspring. Thoughts produce words and emotions, which is like parents who produce children. Naturally speaking, children often share the same DNA, the genetic makeup, of their parents, and thus children resemble their parents. Children will look like their parents, share the same beliefs as them, share the same interests, and even talk like them. Likewise, words and emotions, the children of thoughts, will often resemble their parents (the thoughts). Words and emotions will have the same beliefs as them, talk like them, etc. This is serious, because God tells us that we have the power of life and death in our tongues (Prov. 18:21). Thus, we want our thoughts to be godly thoughts that produce godliness, peace, and joyful words, which in turn produce the same in our lives. The power of thoughts to produce words and emotions makes them of extreme importance.

We can see the importance of thoughts by looking at all of creation. Before God created the world, He had the thought to do so. After God thought it, He spoke the words to create it; hence, "Let there be light, and there was light" (Gen. 1:3). Words are powerful—and not just for God but for us too. We are made in God's image and likeness. When God wants to get something done, He speaks. We should be wise and follow the lead of the Creator when we need to get something done. We need to open our mouths and speak. But we must first think righteous thoughts, and thus we will speak righteously, and that produces peaceful and joyful righteous living.

Guarding Your Thoughts

When it comes to thoughts, we must also be wise to guard our minds against evil and negative thoughts. The enemy does sends negative thoughts of despair and defeat. This does not mean to be afraid, because God has not given us a spirit of fear but of power, love, and a sound mind (2 Tim. 1:7). It just means we need to be aware of this tactic and guard against it with the wisdom and the Word of God.

One very powerful and effective way we do this is through prayer. In the Bible, God tells us to put on armor (this is spiritual armor), which protects us from the attacks of the enemy (the evil thoughts he sends) (Eph. 6:10–18). God showed me how in that passage of scripture He gives us double protection for our minds with His armor: the helmet of salvation as well as the shield of faith. God began to minister to me and told me that the importance of guarding our mind (thoughts) is why He specifically says to "take up" the shield of faith. Once the shield of faith is lifted up, it covers the head (the mind and thoughts). God's instruction for us to protect our minds twice as much as anything else, even our hearts, is because God knows that the mind is the place where the enemy attacks the most.

This is why doctors will often say about a person who committed suicide that before they took their own life, they *contemplated* suicide. Contemplating is thinking in meditation form. Before anyone ever becomes depressed, they have negative, death-producing thoughts. That is why God is saying thoughts are vital, not idle. They will produce something. We can't control that part, but we can control what we think about. God tells us to think on things that are lovely, just, pure, holy, of good report (Phil. 4:8).

God would not tell us to do something we were incapable of doing. In fact, God showed me how to do this—how to control our thoughts—which I will explain in just a bit.

In addition to controlling our thoughts, we must remember to pray. Some things just seem stronger than us, and that is okay, because whatever or whoever it is, it is not stronger than Jesus. So don't forsake prayer. Remember, God said, "If you call upon me in the day of trouble, I will deliver you and you shall glorify Me" (Ps. 50:15). Notice that God did not say He *might* deliver you, or He *probably* will deliver you, or *it all depends on your good works* whether He will deliver or not. God says none of that. He simply says to call on Him, and He *will* deliver you, and you shall glorify Him. So let us remember the benefits and power of prayer, as we protect and guard against negative and evil thoughts.

Training Our Thoughts to Control Our Thoughts

God told me that when we train our minds, we subdue our emotions that dictate our actions. God then told me that we can train our minds by making a <u>conscious effort daily</u> to think the right thoughts. He told me this is mental exercise, and it can and should be done every day of our lives. This is wise to do, even if you have not struggled much with attacks on the mind such as depression or suicide. Because whatever struggle you had or whatever sin you were in it all began with an evil thought (James 1:13–15). That is the Word of God, so it is without question the absolute truth!

This mental exercise is done akin to the way we would train our body, God told me. The two are similar, which makes sense because the mind is a part of the body and is housed there. When training the body, people make a conscious decision to exercise, and they purposely do push-up, sit-ups, running, walking, stair climbing, weight lifting, swimming, etc., to intentionally train their bodies. The physical movement is the exercise we have consciously decided to do. When we train the mind, we intentionally think thoughts.

And like exercise, the more of it you get, the stronger and healthier you become. With thought training, however, the more thoughts you have that are filled with God's Word, the healthier you become in every area of your life. You become stronger and healthier mentally, emotionally, physically, spiritually, financially, and in your relationships with God and others. Thoughts have a powerful effect on our entire lives. So let's start training our thoughts.

God also gave me this wisdom for thought training. If you have been attacked in a particular area, such as finances, health, or relationships, you can find Bible verses specific to that area you have felt attacked in, write them down, and read and meditate on them daily. God gave me this wisdom when I was struggling with fear. I mean, I was terrified when my spouse and I first separated. Every morning when I first woke up, it was as if the devil himself were sitting at the end of my bed waiting to remind me: "Your husband left you." Then right after that evil thought came a flood of more, followed by feelings of sadness and hopelessness. Eventually fear took deep root in me. Because I had been attacked so severely, God led me to read Bible verses about the sovereignty and power of God daily, and as often as I needed during the day. Once you have your Bible verses, make a conscious effort throughout the day to meditate on these verses and any Words of promise that God has spoken directly into your life. Fill your mind with right thinking, and leave no room for negative, evil thoughts.

Also, intentionally think the thoughts that God says and thinks about you. Think to yourself, "I am healed," "I am forgiven by God," "I am a Royal priesthood," "I am a joyful," "I have so much peace," "I am wise," "Everything will work together for my good," "I will fulfill my destiny, and on time, in Jesus name," etc.

And more importantly, think to yourself about who God is. This can be done in your thoughts and with your words. Meditate and declare: "God is faithful," "God always keeps His promises," "God will deliver me," "God means this for good," "God hears and answers my prayers," "God loves me enough to have Jesus die for me, so God loves me enough that through Jesus, He will answer all my prayers," "Jesus cares for me deeply," etc. Do this regardless of whatever laundry list of problems the devil has tried to send your way.

God says, "Submit unto God, resist the devil, and he must flee!" (James 4:7). Resist the enemy sending thoughts your way, trying to tell you how you feel or what is going on in your life or how something will turn out, regardless of what you see happening around you. This is not denial; this is faith. The devil doesn't know how anything will turn out, which is why fear is always in a hypothetical form like, "*what if* something bad happens?" It's just Satan's fear tactics, these hypothetical scenarios he comes up with. They are not even real, but he wants us to think on them anyway, just long enough to then begin speaking the negative thoughts, because our words have the power to produce what we say. All the devil can do is *try* to get someone to use their own power against themselves, because he has no power at all against the believer himself, and Jesus made sure of that (Hebrews 2:14). So resist the temptation of thinking and meditating on negative and evil thoughts. God showed me that actively training our thoughts—getting mental exercise—is a way to resist evil thoughts, actively produce Godly thoughts producing powerful changes in every area of our lives.

My Divine Purpose In Having a Burden, for the Burdened Housewife

So, needless to say, there is a burden in my heart for the burdened housewife. And contrary to what I found to be a misguided popular belief, the rich man's wife tends to have even more of a burden on her than other wives. Thus, my burden for her is all the more. There is love in my heart for the broken-hearted, and a deep desire to see them delivered, healed, and restored completely. This takes God. So I really want the women, especially the burdened housewife, to hear my heart: I love you, and I have prayed for you more than you know. I want God to restore you and heal you greater than He did for me, in Jesus name. Please be strong and faint not. God will heal you. God hears your cry, and He cares. I know this is true because I have lived the burden, and the weight of it nearly killed me...but God! Thus, I know and can testify to the power of God to remove every heavy weight, as He heals you and gives you laughter and joy about the very things and people that once broke you. So hold on, and be strong. God is with you and for you.

Have No Regrets

WOW women, you are indeed royalty, and if you haven't behaved like the royalty you are, repent (change your mind about that behavior and get in agreement with God about it), and have no regrets! That is the will of God. God told me this concerning the mistakes I had made: "I don't want you to be proud of what you did, but I don't want you to be ashamed, either." Ever since God spoke these words to me, I have been free! And "whoever the Son of God sets free is free indeed" (John 8:36). So let God set you free from your past to walk as the royal woman of worth that you are, leaving regret where it belongs: behind you!

You are royalty, and that won't change. Other things in life change, but that will remain. A lot had changed for me financially. Money did what God said it does, it got wings and took flight (Prov. 23:5). But I am the richest I have ever been, because I am God's royalty. You see, now I know that I am royalty. I was royalty when I was in rags, and I was royalty when God restored riches unto me. I learned that the tax bracket you fall into doesn't make you royalty. This means that even if my income changes, my status as royalty won't change with it. Royalty isn't about monetary wealth or ambitious gain. Royalty is about the One who created both you and all riches! Royalty is God, and it comes only from above. It comes from above your salary, above your education, and above your experience or your natural bloodline or whose family you may have married into. Royalty comes from the King of Kings, the real royal family; it comes from God! (1 Pet. 2:9). The good news is that I didn't get this royalty from any man, so no man can take it. No man gave me my crown, and therefore, no man can dethrone me from royalty. This royalty cannot be repossessed! There is no debt I could ever owe to relinquish the right to this royalty. Jesus paid my debts in full (Rom. 3:24). I am and always will be a part of God's royal family! That is what it means to be wealthy, to be rich, to be royal. I am the royalty of God, because God said so, and when He did, that settled it! The same is true for you. Whatever God does cannot be undone (Eccles. 3:14).

Domestic Violence: A Form of Modern-Day Slavery

Before closing, I want to share with readers, especially the judges reading this, something very profound that God showed me about domestic violence, because I believe it will be of great help to judges as well as those who have been affected by domestic violence in some way.

Throughout my journey, God began to enlighten my understanding about domestic violence. God did this knowing it would even facilitate my healing process, as well as heal many others that God counseled through me. This, however, was only part of the reason God gave me such understanding.

In my experience in courts of law, especially family courts, I witnessed time and time again something common among many judges. They were harsh and showed great disdain toward victims of domestic violence. Judges seemed not to believe a woman had been abused, because the woman didn't "just leave" the abusive man or that environment. This needs to be addressed and corrected. Correction often comes in the form of education, and thus it is appropriate to educate judges who preside over cases involving domestic violence and abuse, so that they will begin to execute justice for those victims affected by it.

The way God enlightened me about the reasons a victim of domestic violence doesn't "just leave" was profound, and it made perfect sense to me when God revealed it to me. Hopefully, it will enlighten judges and all readers, once explained, and we can work together to end domestic violence rather than perpetuate it.

God showed me, in many important ways, that domestic violence is like a modern-day form of slavery. In the Bible, God calls sin slavery, and those who are bound by it "slaves of sin" (John 8:34). That is because sin is binding. It is a sin to fear man. I believe that God tells us 365 times in the Bible, albeit in various ways, to "fear not." And God tells us why. "Fear of man is a snare" (Prov. 29:25). A snare is a trap, something very difficult or impossible to get out of. I believe every victim of domestic violence has been bound by fear—fear of the abuser, fear of losing custody of the children, fear of no longer being financially stable, fear of humiliation, and so on—and thus the victim ends up bound. And whenever someone is bound, it is difficult and seemingly impossible to "just leave," and thus some victims stay in the violent environment, and many have lost their lives because of it. Looking at physical slavery, which took place in this nation, is how God gave me understanding regarding domestic-violence victims and the bondage they are in.

Those who were slaves were victims of abuse as well. They were physically beaten, emotionally abused, raped, and often killed. And albeit this was a terribly abusive environment for them to be in, many—the majority, of them—didn't "just leave." And God showed me that they didn't "just leave" largely for the same reason that those enslaved mentally, emotionally, and spiritually by domestic violence don't "just leave."

Slave owners and abusers utilize the same abusive strategy and behaviors to control their victims. Slave masters in physical slavery first bound their slaves mentally, emotionally, spiritually, and financial, and most often they did so through the use of fear. The same happens to victims of domestic violence. The abuser's control over them (enslavement) begins in their mind, emotions, and spirit. That is why victims of domestic violence will often tell you that the mental and emotional abuse they suffered was far worse than any other type of abuse. For slavery it was the same, which is why, even after the Emancipation Proclamation that legally set the slaves free, they were still not free.

All abusers, whether slave owners or abusive spouses, attack the mind and emotions first, and strongly, because they want to control the victim with fear. Slave owners would often rape or otherwise abuse the wives of men on the slave plantations in front of them, as a means to break them down mentally and emotionally. It also put fear in them of leaving, or even attempting to leave, the abusive environment. Abusers do awful things to women or in front of them, such as harming the children, to try to break the woman mentally and emotionally in order to gain control of her through fear.

This mental and emotional enslavement was so effective that slave owners did not have to keep slaves in chains or shackles, because the slaves were too afraid to leave. The same is true for victims of domestic violence. The abuser doesn't have to physically restrain the woman from leaving or even use physical abuse; the other forms of abuse have made her feel very afraid to leave. But like the slave, just because you don't see any chains on her doesn't mean she is just free to go. If someone could look over at a slave plantation and see slaves walking around, not bound in chains and shackles, that did not mean they were free to "just leave" their very abusive environment. The slave, like the victim of domestic violence, knows there will likely be severe if not deadly consequences for leaving the controlling abuser behind.

And slaves, like victims of domestic violence, have no financial freedom to "just leave," either. Some questions for many bound by controlling abusers are these: If I leave, where am I going to go? and How will I support myself and my children? These are understandable questions. The abuser, like the slave owner, controls the finances, so if the victim of domestic violence leaves, like the slave who flees, they don't have any money to take with them. That is the reason God showed me that some slaves who were set free often returned to their slave master. Victims of domestic violence leave on average approximately seven times before they finally never go back (and that is those who don't die from domestic violence first).

No judge would expect a slave to "just leave," and likewise, they should not expect for victims of domestic violence to "just leave," either. Their sufferings are a lot alike in very important respects, and thus their behaviors model one another. Domestic violence is a modern-day form of slavery, and unfortunately, the way judges enforced slavery in this nation's past, they enforce it now, by allowing abusers to use judges as a means to further abuse the victim. I implore the judges reading this: please don't treat victims of domestic violence with any more harshness and disdain, for they are doing the best they can with the worst situation they probably have ever been in. Instead, use your God-given authority to help them by executing justice.

Injustice: A Double-Edged Sword

Please understand that my use of domestic violence victims as a prime example of injustice that has plagued the American court system is by no means exhaustive of the types of injustices people face. There are many other types of injustice that people face in the American court system. Regardless of the specific type of injustice or the specific party to the case, injustice affects us all, including those who make unjust decisions. It is important for us to know, and for judges to remember, that injustice is a double-edged sword, cutting both ways. Indeed, it can harm those against whom the sword of injustice is wielded, but it will also deeply cut the one wielding the sword (i.e., judges and those in authority). Thus, this invaluable lesson is worth diving more deeply into.

One day while I was reading my Bible, God showed me that the concept of precedent is not new to the American legal system; it's in the Bible also. In John 8:10, there was a woman who was caught by the religious leaders of that day in the act of committing adultery. They dragged her out in a public place where Jesus was teaching. They brought her to Jesus for Him to judge her. (They also wanted to catch Jesus saying the wrong thing, so they would have something to accuse Him of and could put Him to death too—again, injustice wanting to cut both ways.) These men began citing the law to Jesus and telling Him that the consequences for anyone caught in adultery was to be stoned to death. Jesus is a wise King, however, and He was able to discern the evil and injustice in the hearts of the woman's accusers. Thus, Jesus responded to them by saying, "Whoever among you is without sin, let him cast the first stone at her" (John 8:7). Every one of the woman's accusers left without stoning her to death, because each of them had sinned. Jesus then asked the woman, "Woman, where are those accusers of yours? Has no one condemned you?" She responded, "No one, Lord." And Jesus said to her, "Neither do I condemn you; go and sin no more" (John 8:1–12).

Now, at first glance, it seems obvious that Jesus saved this woman from death, but when you understand the concept of precedent, Jesus saved them all, including her accusers. You see, Jesus knew every one of those people had sinned. The Bible clearly states, "If anyone says he is without sin, he is a liar" (1 John 1:18). Jesus also knew that God calls every sin adultery, the thing they accused her of. For God, sleeping with someone who is not your spouse is surely adultery, but for God, so is every other sin, including the desire to do it. Thus, if the punishment for committing adultery is to be killed by stoning, and everyone in that crowd that day had sinned against God in some form or another, which for God (the Judge), is adultery, then everyone, including all those accusers, would have been killed too for committing the crime of adultery—except Jesus, of course, who is without sin. Jesus was the only one there who had never sinned, but even Jesus chose not to stone her, because Jesus, in all His wisdom, knew that would have set the precedent, and everyone else would have to be put to death also. Thus, Jesus was not only just saving this woman from being killed, He was saving everyone else too, including her accusers—and including all of us too. The very law these accusers sought to enforce would have become the very precedent demanding their own death. But Jesus, being a righteous, merciful, and wise Judge, knew the effect of establishing such a precedent, and He chose rather to execute justice in righteousness, love, and mercy. And—let's be honest—we all need God's mercy because we are all human, and thus we all make mistakes.

Jesus is doing the same thing today as He did back then, and there is invaluable wisdom and insight to gain from His actions and reasoning, especially for judges. Judges, please remember that whenever you are judging, you are setting a precedent, and the decisions that you make are not just about the fate of those who stand before you in the courtroom. It becomes your own fate, as well as the fates of those you love and care about, because you are not just issuing an opinion; you are creating laws that can affect us all. This is a very high calling, and to whomever much is given, much is required (Luke 12:48). Also, judges, it is wise to remember that with the same measure you judge, you will be judged (Matt. 7:2). Thus, judge justly—or recuse yourself if you know that you won't. As we can all see, Jesus knows a lot about judging and even making difficult decisions, but He also knows the deadly effects that making an unjust decision can have on everyone, even on those asking the judge to execute the injustice.

Lastly, the law is meant to serve the ends of justice. That is the purpose for which it was created. Thus, justice is the master, and the law is the servant, and, "no servant is greater than his master" (John 13:16). Whenever the law does not serve the ends of justice, it needs to be stricken down, because it no longer serves the purpose for which it was created, and in turn it becomes a viral infestation of injustice, affecting many. Thus, we would be wise to take heed to this truth and remember it whenever judging: "injustice anywhere is a threat to justice everywhere."

To all the WOW women around the world, if you have been healed and restored by the end of this story, that is of no surprise to me, because by the end of it, I was healed and restored too. And while I am not surprised by your healing, I am honored and elated for your sake and my own. I say this because God tells us to give freely by grace what we have received freely by grace (Matt. 10:8). God has given me healing and restoration, and now that I have received restoration from God, I am able to give it to you, which is exactly what God did when He wrote this book through me. This is a part of my purpose.

So, WOW women, thank you for helping me fulfill my purpose by receiving the restoration that rests heavily on the pages of this book, from its beginning until it's ending. If you are reading this book, you have truly been set up by God for a blessing of restoration. For God spoke to me and promised me, "A ministry of restoration shall rest upon you." In allowing God to write this book through me, I gave you by grace what I received from God by grace. So now let the restoration of God rest upon you, in Jesus name. God and you, and all God will do for you through this life of mine, has made my life worth living and my story worth telling. So until we come together again, know that I love you, and God loves you deeply. May God bless you and keep you and cause His face to shine upon you, and restore and heal you, showing you favor to fulfill your destiny, in Jesus name I pray.

"For those God foreknew, He also predestined to be conformed to the image of His Son, so that He would be the firstborn among many brothers. And those He predestined He also called, those He called He also justified, those He justified He also glorified..." (Rom. 8:29–30).

PRAYER OF SALVATION

If there is anyone who hasn't given their life to Jesus and received Him as their Lord and Savior, now is the time. God loves you, and His love for you is the reason He sent Jesus to die in your place on the cross. God has no desire to send you to hell. He loves you. Just simply pray this prayer and be saved. "Heavenly Father, I believe that you love me, and I thank you for loving me and sending Jesus to die in my place on the cross and Him shedding His blood for all of my sins, past, present and future. I confess and believe Jesus is Lord and that You raised Jesus from the dead and have forgiven all of my sins in Jesus name."

NOTES

1. South Suburban Family Shelter, 2010, http://www.ssfs1.org
2. DomesticViolence.org, 2016, http://www.domesticviolence.org
3. American Bar Association, 2016, www.americanbar.org
4. Domestic Violence and the Law: Theory and Practice E, Schneider, C. Hanna, J. Greenberg & C. Dalton (Second Edition)
5. Social Work Today, 2016, www.socialworktoday.com
6. Information on Domestic Violence, http://www.domesticabuseshelter.org/infodomesticviolence.htm 2016, www.nytimes.com
7. Code of Conduct for United States Judges, last revised 2014, http://www.uscourts.gov/judges-judgeships/code-conduct-united-states-judges
8. "Letter from Birmingham Jail," Dr. Martin Luther King Jr., April 16, 1963, https://kinginstitute.stanford.edu/king-papers/documents/letter-birmingham-jail
9. "The Making of a Slave," Willie Lynch (2009)
10. God's Not Dead 2
11. Black's Law Dictionary, Ninth Edition, 2012

12. National Domestic Violence Hotline, 2016, http://www .thehotline.org/2013/06/50-obstacles-to-leaving-1-10/

13. Domestic Violence, Abuse, and Child Custody: Legal Strategies and Policy Issues. Edited by Mo Therese Hannah and Barry Goldstein. (2010).

Made in the USA
San Bernardino, CA
28 June 2016